DeepL: The Complete Guide

Professional Translation, Writing, and Real-Time Voice — the Multilingual Workplace

Ken Tannenbaum

2026

Finnoybu Press

DeepL: The Complete Guide

2026 Edition

Professional Translation, Writing, and Real-Time Voice — the Multilingual Workplace

---

Published by Finnoybu Press

For permissions and inquiries: press@finnoybu.org

First Edition: 2026

About the Author

Ken Tannenbaum is a technologist, entrepreneur, and AI governance researcher. He is the founder of Finnoybu Press and the founder/steward of the AEGIS Initiative, an open framework for AI safety and accountability. Learn more at aegis-initiative.com.

When he's not building governance standards for artificial intelligence, he's helping everyday people understand and use it.

Dedication

For the people doing real work in more than one language, who needed the translation to sound like a person wrote it.

The AI for Everyone Series

This book is part of the **AI for Everyone** series by Finnoybu Press, designed to help real people use AI tools effectively. Visit **press.finnoybu.org** for the latest titles and updates.

Collection One: Product Deep Dives

- *ChatGPT: The Definitive Guide (2026 Edition)*
- *ChatGPT: The Power User Guide (2026 Edition)*
- *Claude: The Definitive Guide (2026 Edition)*
- *Claude Code: The Power User Guide (2026 Edition)*
- *Gemini: The Complete Guide (2026 Edition)*
- *Gemini: The Advanced Guide (2026 Edition)*
- *Copilot: The Workplace AI Guide (2026 Edition)*
- *Copilot: The Advanced Workplace Guide (2026 Edition)*
- *Perplexity: The Research Playbook (2026 Edition)*
- *Perplexity: The Advanced Research Playbook (2026 Edition)*

Collection Two: Product Guides

- *NotebookLM: From Sources to Audio Overviews (2026 Edition)*
- *DeepSeek: Code, Math, and Reasoning (2026 Edition)*
- *Cursor: The AI Code Editor (2026 Edition)*
- *OpenClaw: Agentic AI for Everyday Work (2026 Edition)*

Collection Three: Cross-Platform Skills

- *AI Systems Playbook (2026 Edition)*
- *AI Prompt Engineering (2026 Edition)*
- *AI for Developers (2026 Edition)*
- *AI for Business (2026 Edition)*
- *AI for Students (2026 Edition)*
- *AI Governance for Practitioners (2026 Edition)*
- *Securing Agentic AI (2026 Edition)*

The Extended Series — Product Guides, Volume II

- *Codex: The Cloud Coding Agent (2026 Edition)*
- *Grok: Real-Time AI from xAI (2026 Edition)*
- *Mistral: Vibe and the Open European AI (2026 Edition)*
- *DeepL: Translation, Writing, and Voice (2026 Edition)*

The Extended Series — The Capability Set

- *Automate Your Work with AI (2026 Edition)*
- *Build Apps Without Code (2026 Edition)*
- *AI Literacy for the Workplace (2026 Edition)*

Table of Contents

Introduction

I wrote this book because there is a difference between a translation that is correct and one that is good, and DeepL is the tool built entirely around that difference — a difference most people never notice until they see it.

For years, machine translation taught us to lower our expectations. The free translators were genuinely useful and unmistakably robotic: they got the words right and the music wrong, producing output that no native speaker would have written and everyone learned to accept as the cost of instant, free translation. We used it to get the gist, and we quietly rewrote anything that mattered. Then DeepL showed up and translated the same text into prose that simply read like a person wrote it — right register, right idiom, natural rhythm — and the gap between the two was not about accuracy. It was about *quality*, the thing that turns a translation from a rough draft you have to fix into output you can actually use.

That difference is DeepL's whole reason for being, and it has grown into more than translation. The same language intelligence that made DeepL's translations sound human now also improves your *own* writing, and translates *speech* in real time. DeepL today is a specialist platform for working across languages — and a quietly powerful one, because in a world of sprawling do-everything AI, doing one thing exceptionally well is its own kind of advantage.

I want to be precise about why that advantage is real and not just marketing, because it is the premise the whole book rests on. The general-purpose assistants that dominate the AI conversation are extraordinary generalists, and a generalist can translate — ask one to render a paragraph into Spanish and it will do a creditable job. But a generalist is optimizing for breadth: it is also writing your code, answering your questions, and summarizing your documents, and its translation is one capability among hundreds, tuned to be good-enough across an impossibly wide surface. DeepL optimizes for one axis only. Every increment of engineering effort, every model improvement, every interface decision points at the same target: language that crosses a barrier and still sounds like a person produced it. When the job in front of you is genuinely *about* language — moving it between tongues, polishing it, carrying it across a spoken gap — the specialist that has spent its entire existence on that single problem tends to win, and to keep winning at the margins that matter, which are tone, idiom, register, and the thousand small decisions that separate output you can send from output you have to fix. That is not a knock on the generalists; the rest of this series is largely about how good they are at what *they* do. It is a statement about fit. The cleanest test, which I will return to throughout, is to ask whether your task is about language itself or about content and reasoning. The first is DeepL's department. The second belongs to the assistants elsewhere on the shelf.

What This Book Covers, Briefly

DeepL is a German specialist AI language company whose product has grown into three connected lines: **DeepL Translate**, for translating text and documents at a quality professionals trust; **DeepL Write**, for improving and rephrasing your own writing, including in a second language; and **DeepL Voice**, for real-time spoken translation in meetings and conversations. The thread through all three is the thing DeepL has always been about — language that sounds like a person produced it.

This book covers all of it: getting started and choosing a plan; translation done well, including documents, glossaries, formality controls, and the quirks of different languages; DeepL Write for your own prose; DeepL Voice for live speech; using DeepL at work for localization, regulated content, multilingual teams, and the privacy that sensitive material demands; building on the API and integrations; and — as this series always does — an honest account of where DeepL gets things wrong and when a human still belongs in the loop.

If you want the quick map before the full one, here is the shape of the three product lines and how they relate. **Translate** is the original and the largest: paste text or hand it a document, pick a target language, and get back a translation that preserves both meaning and — this is the part that distinguishes it — the way a native writer would actually phrase it. Around that core sit the controls that turn a good translation into a precise one: glossaries that lock your preferred terms in place so a product name or a defined contract phrase comes out identically every time, and formality settings that let you choose whether the output addresses the reader as a stranger or a colleague. **Write** takes the same language intelligence and turns it inward. Instead of converting someone else's words, it improves your own — grammar, clarity, phrasing, tone — and it is quietly remarkable at the specific problem of writing fluently in a language you can read better than you can compose. **Voice** extends the whole thing into live speech, so a conversation between two people who share no language can actually happen out loud, with captions and a searchable transcript left behind when it ends. The thread is constant across all three. Whether DeepL is translating a contract, smoothing your email, or carrying a supplier call, it is chasing the same standard: output a person would accept as natural.

One practical note belongs up front, because it will save you confusion the first time you read a price or a quota. DeepL meters usage by *characters*, not by the *tokens* you may know from other AI tools. A token is roughly a word-fragment, the unit large language models think in; a character is exactly what it sounds like, a single letter or symbol. If you have spent time around the general assistants in this series, you have trained yourself to estimate cost and limits in tokens, and that instinct will mislead you here. Throughout the book, when I talk about how much you can translate or what a plan includes, the unit is characters. It is a small thing, but it is the kind of small thing that produces a surprised face when a quota runs out faster or slower than expected, so I am flagging it now and will flag it again where it matters.

Who This Book Is For

- **Anyone working across languages** who wants the result to sound right, not approximately right.
- **Businesses and teams operating multilingually** – localizing content, supporting customers in many languages, handling material they cannot afford to leak or to render machine-made.
- **Developers and language professionals** who wire DeepL into their own software and translation tools, for whom it is infrastructure rather than a website.

You do not need to be technical for most of this book. The API and integration material in Part VI is signposted so you can navigate around it; everything else assumes only that you sometimes need to work in more than one language.

A few concrete portraits, because the three groups above are abstractions and the people inside them are not. There is the **occasional crosser** – someone whose first language carries most of their life, who hits a language barrier a few times a week and wants the result to read well: the partner email to a German client, the apartment listing in another country, the message to a relative abroad they want to get exactly right rather than approximately. For this reader the free tier and the basics of text and document translation may be most of what they ever need, and that is a perfectly good place to stop. Then there is the **professional who lives in two languages** — the translator, the localizer, the support agent, the marketer at a company that ships across borders. For them DeepL is not a website they visit but a tool that runs through the whole working day, inside a translation environment or a content pipeline, and the chapters on glossaries, formality, localization, and integrations are written squarely for them. And there is the **builder** — the developer wiring DeepL's API into a product so that translation happens automatically and invisibly, the moment a new help-center article is written or a new user message arrives. For this reader DeepL is infrastructure, and Part VI is the part of the book that matters most. Most real users do not sit in one portrait forever; they drift between them as their needs grow, which is why the book is built to be read whole even if you enter through a single door.

It is worth being honest about who this book is *not* for, too, because that clarity will save you time. If you are looking for a general AI assistant to answer questions, write code, brainstorm, or do research, DeepL is the wrong tool and this is the wrong book to open first — the rest of this series covers those assistants in depth. If you need *some* rendering of a language DeepL does not support, you will be better served by one of the broad general translators, and I say so plainly in Chapter 2. And if your translation needs are a sentence a month, almost any free tool will do; the case this book makes is for people who do enough cross-language work to feel the difference between output they can use and output they have to fix. DeepL rewards the people who lean on it. This book is written for them.

How to Read This Book

The book is in seven parts, plus reference.

Part I: Meet DeepL is orientation — what DeepL is, why its quality genuinely leads (and where it doesn't), and how the three products fit together.

Part II: Translation is the original core — text and document translation, glossaries, formality and tone controls, and the quirks of different languages.

Part III: DeepL Write turns the quality on your own prose — fixing, rephrasing, workplace tone, and writing fluently in a second language.

Part IV: DeepL Voice covers real-time spoken translation — live translation, voice-to-voice and meetings, and transcription.

Part V: DeepL at Work is the professional core — localization workflows, legal and medical and regulated content, multilingual teams and support, and the privacy and security that make DeepL trustworthy with sensitive text.

Part VI: Building on DeepL is for builders — the API, the CAT-tool and browser and app integrations, and managing cost and quota.

Part VII: Judgment and Limits is the honest close — what DeepL gets wrong and when to use a human, and responsible use.

Reference wraps with a language and feature matrix, an API quickstart, a glossary, and resources for staying current.

Read straight through or jump around. New to DeepL: Parts I and II. Here for Write or Voice: jump to Part III or IV. Evaluating it for serious work: Part V, then Part VII. Building on it: Part VI.

To make those routes concrete, here are the paths I would actually recommend for the most common reasons people pick up this book. If you have **never used DeepL and want to start translating well today**, read Chapter 1 to fix the mental model, skim Chapter 2 for the quality argument, then go straight to Part II — Chapters 4 through 6 will have you translating text and documents competently within an hour, and Chapters 7 and 8 (glossaries and formality) are the upgrades that separate casual use from professional use. If you are a **non-native writer who wants help composing in another language**, the center of gravity is Part III; Chapter 13 in particular is written for you, and you can read it almost in isolation. If you are **evaluating DeepL for a team or an organization**, the chapters that will answer your real questions are Chapter 17 on localization workflows, Chapter 19 on multilingual teams and support, and above all Chapter 20 on privacy, security, and compliance — and then Part VII, which is where the book is most candid about the limits you will need to plan around. If you are a **developer integrating DeepL**, Part VI is your home: Chapter 21 on the API, Chapter 22 on integrations, and Chapter 23 on managing cost and quota, with Appendix B as a quickstart you can keep open beside your editor. And if you handle **legal, medical, or otherwise regulated material**, do not skip Chapter 18; it is the chapter that draws the line between where DeepL is a genuine asset and where unreviewed machine output becomes a liability you own.

A word on how the parts build, for those who plan to skip. The parts are written to stand reasonably on their own, but a few dependencies are worth knowing. Part I is genuinely foundational — even if you came for Voice or the API, the quality argument in Chapter 2 and the product map in Chapter 3 frame everything after them, and they take only a few minutes. Within Part II the chapters compound: glossaries (Chapter 7) and formality controls (Chapter 8) assume you have met the basics of text and document translation first. The professional material in Part V leans on the privacy groundwork it shares with Chapter 20, and the judgment chapters in Part VII are the ones I would ask everyone to read regardless of why they came, because they are where the book is most honest about the tool's limits. If you read nothing else cover to cover, read Part I and Part VII; the middle you can enter through whichever door is yours.

A Note About Accuracy

This corner of the software market moves quickly. Plans, prices, supported languages, feature availability, and interface details will have drifted by the time you read this. This book is accurate as of mid-2026.

The durable parts — what translation quality means, when to trust the output and when to verify it, when a human belongs in the loop, how to think about privacy and cost — will hold. The price points and the exact language list will not. Where a detail changes fast, I flag it and point you at DeepL's current documentation rather than pretending it is permanent.

Let me name the specific categories most likely to have drifted by the time this is in your hands, so you know exactly what to re-verify rather than distrusting the whole book. **Plan names and prices** change as the market moves; treat any figure I quote as a snapshot to confirm on DeepL's pricing page. **Supported languages** expand steadily, and — a subtlety that catches people — support is not uniform across features: a language may be available for text translation but not yet for spoken output in Voice, or available as a transcription source but not a synthesized target. So "does DeepL support Norwegian?" is almost never the right question; "does DeepL support the specific thing I need, for my exact language pair, right now?" is. **Voice features** are the fastest-moving of all, because that product line is young: dates I give for when a capability launched or is expected are explicitly perishable, and I mark them as such in the text. **Regulatory specifics** are their own category — the privacy and compliance landscape that surrounds professional translation is genuinely in motion, and where I touch on it I describe the durable shape rather than asserting a fixed legal state, because the details belong to current terms and your own counsel, not to a book. When you see a flagged date or a "verify the current docs" pointer, take it literally; it is there because that exact fact has a short shelf life.

There is also a class of claim I have deliberately *not* made, and the absence is intentional. I do not quote invented statistics, made-up studies, or URLs I cannot stand behind, because a book that pretends to a precision it does not have is worse than one that admits where the ground is soft. Where I describe how quickly a post-editor moves through machine output, or how much localization costs against the traditional approach, I describe the *shape* of the gain — large, real, repeatedly observed — rather than a fabricated number dressed up as research. Trust the direction of those claims; verify any specific figure against your own work.

A Note About Quality and Trust

DeepL's defining strength — output that reads naturally — is also the source of its most important caution, so I raise it here and return to it in Part VII. Because DeepL's translations are so fluent, its occasional errors are fluent too, and a beautiful wrong translation is far easier to trust than a clumsy one. The whole book is written in that double light: DeepL is genuinely excellent and genuinely worth your trust for an enormous range of work, *and* the better the prose, the more it rewards verifying the meaning rather than admiring the polish.

It is worth understanding *why* this is the deeper trap, because once you see the mechanism you will catch yourself falling into it. With the old, clumsy free translators, the mediocre prose did you an accidental favor: it kept you on guard. You read output that obviously came from a machine, you stayed skeptical, and you reread anything that mattered because the surface itself warned you not to trust it. DeepL removes the warning. The output reads like a competent colleague wrote it, and competence invites trust — so when the rare error arrives, it arrives wearing the same natural, confident prose as everything correct around it. A dropped negation, a flipped number, a defined term rendered as the ordinary word that sounds like it: none of these announce themselves, because they are not awkward, they are *fluent*. The very quality that makes the tool worth paying for is the quality that lets its mistakes slide past a reader who is admiring the writing instead of checking the meaning. The discipline this book asks of you is therefore simple and specific: verify *meaning*, not style, on anything where being wrong has a cost — and verify it harder, not softer, precisely because the prose is good. This is not a reason to distrust DeepL. It is the single most important habit for using a genuinely excellent translator well.

Let's Get Started

DeepL is not a general assistant, and this book will not pretend it is. What it is — more completely than any rival — is the specialist that makes the language sound human, whether it is translating someone else's words, polishing your own, or carrying a live conversation across a barrier that used to stop it cold. For the enormous and growing amount of work that crosses languages, that quality is not a nicety. It is the difference between output you can use and output you have to fix.

Turn the page. Let's start with what DeepL is.

Part I: Meet DeepL

Audience: everyone.

"In language, correct and good are not the same thing. The whole of DeepL is built around the difference."

— A working principle

Chapter 1: What DeepL Is

The first time I understood what made DeepL different, I was comparing two translations of the same German business email side by side. One was technically correct and unmistakably machine-made — the words were right, the grammar held, and no native speaker would have believed a person wrote it. It had that flat, slightly off quality we had all learned to accept as the price of free translation, the tone of a tool rather than a colleague. The other read like a person. The register was right, the idioms landed, the sentence rhythm was natural; if you had told me a bilingual coworker had written it, I would have believed you. The second one was DeepL, and the gap between the two was not a gap in accuracy. It was a gap in *quality* — the difference between a translation that is correct and one that is good.

That gap is the whole reason DeepL exists and the reason it earned a devoted following in a category everyone assumed was already solved. This chapter is about what DeepL is, what it isn't, and why a company whose defining trait is *the quality of the language it produces* grew from a translator into a full platform for working across languages — and now across the spoken word too.

The One-Sentence Definition

DeepL is a specialist AI language company — German, built around translation — whose product has grown into three connected lines: **DeepL Translate**, for translating text and documents at a quality professionals trust; **DeepL Write**, for improving and rephrasing your own writing, including in a second language; and **DeepL Voice**, for real-time spoken translation in meetings and conversations. The thread running through all three is the thing DeepL has always been about: language that sounds like a person produced it.

A few words in that sentence carry the weight.

"A specialist" — this is the first thing to understand, and it sets DeepL apart from the general-purpose assistants the rest of this series covers. DeepL does not try to do everything. It is not a chatbot, not a coding agent, not a research tool. It does language — translation first, and now the writing and speaking around it — and it does that narrow thing exceptionally well. In an era of sprawling do-everything AI, DeepL's focus is a feature, not a limitation. When the job is moving meaning cleanly between languages, a specialist beats a generalist more often than not.

"Built around translation" — DeepL made its name on machine translation that was simply better than what came before, especially for European languages, and especially on the quality dimension that the big general translators tended to miss: not just *what* the words mean but *how* they should sound in the target language. That reputation for quality is the foundation everything else is built on. Chapter 2 takes the quality question head-on, because it is the heart of why anyone chooses DeepL.

"Three connected lines" — DeepL is no longer only a translator, and this is the part even longtime users sometimes miss. **Translate** is the original and still the core. **Write** turns the same language intelligence inward, helping you improve your *own* writing rather than convert someone else's. **Voice** extends the whole thing into real-time speech, so a conversation across a language barrier can happen live. Chapter 3 maps the three and how they fit together; for now, hold that DeepL is a product family, not a single tool.

"Language that sounds like a person produced it" — the through-line, and the thing the side-by-side emails made vivid. DeepL's bet, across all three products, is that fluency and naturalness are not a nice-to-have on top of correctness — they *are* the product. A translation that is accurate but robotic fails at the actual job, which is communication between people. DeepL optimizes for the version a human would actually write or say, and that is the quality its users pay for.

To make that abstract, take a single line and watch the two priorities diverge. The French sentence *Je vous serais reconnaissant de bien vouloir me faire parvenir le document* is a routine, slightly formal business request. A literal engine might give you "I would be grateful to you to kindly make reach me the document" — every word accounted for, the meaning recoverable, and no English speaker on earth who would write it. The version that sounds human is "I would be grateful if you could send me the document." Nothing was lost in meaning; everything was gained in usability. The first is something you fix before sending; the second is something you send. Multiply that one decision across every clause of every document you handle, and you have the entire difference DeepL is built to deliver.

What DeepL Is Not

Five clarifications up front, because each is a misconception I have watched lead people astray.

DeepL is not a general-purpose AI assistant. If you want something to answer questions, write code, brainstorm, or research, DeepL is the wrong tool, and this is the wrong book to reach for first — the rest of this series covers those assistants. DeepL is for language work: translating, improving writing, and now translating speech. Judge it on that, not on whether it can do the things it never set out to do.

DeepL is not "just Google Translate with a different logo." This is the assumption that costs people the most, because it leads them to skip a tool that would genuinely serve them better. DeepL and the big general translators overlap in function but differ in priority: DeepL has historically led on translation *quality* for the languages it supports, particularly European ones, while the broadest general translators lead on sheer *language coverage*. Chapter 2 makes that comparison honestly, including where DeepL does not win. But "they're all the same" is simply false, and believing it means leaving quality on the table.

DeepL is not only a translator anymore. The name says "translation," but the product has outgrown it. If your picture of DeepL is a box where you paste text and get a translation, you are missing Write (improving your own prose) and Voice (live spoken translation), which turn a single-purpose translator into a platform for multilingual work. A large part of this book is about the two-thirds of DeepL that is not the thing it is famous for.

DeepL is not a substitute for a professional human translator on the highest-stakes work. DeepL is excellent, and for an enormous range of real work it is more than good enough on its own. But for the content where a subtle error carries real legal, medical, or reputational consequence, the right model is DeepL-plus-a-human, not DeepL alone — the machine doing the heavy lifting and a qualified person reviewing what matters. Chapter 24 is honest about exactly where that line falls, because knowing it is part of using the tool well.

DeepL is not careless with your text. Because translation often involves sensitive material — contracts, internal documents, personal data — DeepL has built privacy and security into its professional offering as a genuine selling point, with strong data-handling commitments and European data protection at its core (Chapter 20). For regulated and privacy-conscious users, that posture is not incidental; it is a reason to choose DeepL over a free tool whose data terms are an afterthought.

Each of those five clarifications has a cost attached when someone ignores it. I have watched a small agency lose a week because they assumed DeepL could research and draft marketing copy from a brief — it cannot; it translates and refines language, it does not invent it. I have watched a freelancer paste a client's confidential merger document into a free consumer translator without checking the data terms, then spend an anxious afternoon wondering what had been retained. And I have watched the opposite mistake too: a perfectly competent team paying for a separate "premium translation service" while DeepL sat unused on their desktops, because someone senior had decided years earlier that "machine translation isn't good enough" and never revisited the claim. The misconceptions are not academic. Each one quietly steers someone toward the wrong tool, the wrong workflow, or the wrong amount of trust.

The pattern under all three failures is the same: someone formed a mental model of DeepL — too broad, too unguarded, or too dismissive — and then acted on the model instead of the reality. The agency's model was "DeepL is an AI, and AI writes things," which is true of the chatbots in the rest of this series and false of DeepL. The freelancer's model was "translators are interchangeable, so the free one is fine," which ignores that what you can safely paste depends entirely on a tool's data terms, not on whether it translates well. The dismissive team's model was a snapshot from years earlier, frozen while the technology moved on underneath it. Getting the model right — specialist, privacy-serious on its paid tiers, genuinely excellent but not a content generator — is most of what it takes to avoid all three. That is why a chapter that seems to be merely defining the tool is actually doing load-bearing work: the definition *is* the guardrail.

Why Quality Is the Whole Game

It is tempting to evaluate a translator by how many languages it speaks or how fast it returns a result. DeepL's real advantage is harder to count and more decisive in practice: the output is *usable as written*, far more often, with far less fixing.

A translation that is merely correct still fails if it sounds wrong — if the tone is off, the idiom is clumsy, the register is too stiff or too casual for the context. You can tell it was machine-made, and so can your reader, and that costs you something every time, whether it is a customer who trusts the email less or a document you have to rewrite before you can send it. The hidden cost of a mediocre translator is all the human cleanup it demands afterward. DeepL's quality is, in practical terms, *the cleanup it saves you*. When the output reads naturally on the first pass, you can actually use it — paste it, send it, publish it — instead of treating it as a rough draft you still have to fix.

That is the whole game, and it scales. For one email it is a small convenience; across the volume of cross-language work a real organization does, it compounds into hours, money, and trust, in ways Chapter 2 makes the full case for. It is why people who care about the output, and do enough of this work to feel the difference, tend to become loyal to DeepL specifically — and why this book treats quality not as one feature among many but as the organizing idea behind all three products.

There is a subtler edge to the quality story that is worth naming early, because it threads through the whole book. The very fluency that makes DeepL's output usable also makes its occasional errors *harder to catch*. A clumsy translation announces its own unreliability — you read it, wince, and stay on guard. A beautiful translation invites trust, and when a beautiful translation is wrong, it is wrong in a confident, natural-sounding voice that slides past your defenses. This is not a reason to distrust DeepL; it is a reason to verify *meaning* on anything that matters rather than admiring the polish and assuming the polish guarantees accuracy. The better the prose, the more the rare error rewards a second look. Chapter 24 returns to this in detail; for now, hold it as the flip side of the quality coin. The thing that makes DeepL worth using is also the thing that makes its mistakes worth watching for.

What DeepL Actually Does

Set the philosophy aside and look at the capabilities. Across its three lines, DeepL gives you:

High-quality text translation between a large set of languages, with the naturalness that built its reputation (Chapter 5), plus controls most translators lack — glossaries to lock in your preferred terms (Chapter 7), and formality and tone settings to fit the context (Chapter 8).

Document translation that preserves formatting — hand it a Word file, a presentation, or a PDF and get back the same document in another language, layout intact, rather than a wall of stripped text (Chapter 6).

Writing improvement through DeepL Write — grammar, phrasing, clarity, and tone for your own prose, including help writing fluently in a language that is not your first (Part III).

Real-time voice translation through DeepL Voice — spoken translation for live meetings and conversations, including voice-to-voice, so people who do not share a language can still talk (Part IV).

A developer API and deep integrations — so all of this can live inside your own software, your translation tools, your browser, and your workflow rather than only on DeepL's website (Part VI).

What ties these together is the single standard the company is built on: in every one of them, the goal is output a person would actually accept as natural. That is the constant beneath the growing product surface.

It is worth pausing on what that list does *not* include, because the absences are as defining as the features. DeepL does not answer questions, summarize documents into bullet points, draft an essay from a prompt, write or debug code, search the web, or hold an open-ended conversation about whatever is on your mind. Every one of those is something the general assistants elsewhere in this series do, and DeepL declines all of them on purpose. The product surface grows along one axis only — more ways to work with language as language — and never sprawls into the general-assistant territory next door. When you size up whether DeepL fits a job, the cleanest test is to ask whether the job is fundamentally *about language itself* — moving it between tongues, polishing it, carrying it across a spoken barrier — or about *content and reasoning*, which is someone else's department. Translation, refinement, live interpretation: yes. Thinking, researching, creating from nothing: no. The boundary is sharp, and DeepL stays on its side of it deliberately.

Who's Using DeepL

Roughly three overlapping groups, in my experience.

Individuals working across languages — anyone who writes, reads, or communicates in a language that is not their first, and wants the result to sound right: the email to a foreign client, the document in another language, the message they want to get exactly right rather than approximately.

Businesses and teams operating multilingually — companies localizing content, support teams serving customers in many languages, and any organization whose work crosses borders and cannot afford to sound machine-made or to leak sensitive text. For them DeepL's quality and privacy together are the draw, and Part V is written with them in mind.

Developers and language professionals — translators and localizers who use DeepL inside their professional tools to work faster (Chapter 22), and builders who wire its API into their own products (Part VI). For this group DeepL is infrastructure, not a website.

This book serves all three, and the parts are arranged so you can read the one that is yours and skim the rest.

The three groups are not walled off from one another; most real users drift between them. Consider a marketing manager at a mid-sized European software company. She starts as an *individual* — translating the occasional partner email so it reads naturally in German. Then her company decides to localize the whole product site into six languages, and overnight she is a *business* user, worrying about glossaries so the product name and feature names come out consistently, about whether the translated text will leak before launch, about how to keep tone uniform across thousands of strings. A year later, when the localization volume justifies automating it, she brings in a developer who wires DeepL's API straight into the content management system, so new pages get draft translations the moment they are written — and now the company is a *developer* user too, with DeepL running as quiet infrastructure behind the scenes. One person, one company, all three groups in turn. The categories describe needs, not fixed identities, and the same reader often grows through several of them. That is part of why DeepL is worth understanding whole rather than only through the one door you happened to enter by.

The Through-Line

If there is a single idea to carry out of this chapter, it is the one the two German emails made concrete: in language, *correct* and *good* are not the same thing, and DeepL is built around the difference. Everything distinctive about it — the translation quality that made its name, the Write product that turns that quality on your own prose, the Voice product that brings it to live speech, the privacy posture that lets you trust it with real material — flows from that one commitment to language that sounds like a person produced it.

The rest of Part I fills in the picture — why the quality is genuinely better and where it isn't, and how the three products fit together into a single platform for multilingual work. For now, the one-sentence version is enough to build on: DeepL is the specialist that makes the language sound human, and using it well starts with knowing which of its three tools the job in front of you actually needs.

Chapter 2: Why DeepL, and the Quality Question

A colleague of mine once shipped a product page in five languages using a free translator, felt good about the hour it saved, and then spent the next three days fielding confused emails from the German and French markets. The translations were not *wrong*, exactly. The grammar held. The facts survived. But the copy read like a form letter translated by a machine — stiff in the wrong places, oddly formal in others, with the kind of word choices that make a native speaker's eye snag every other sentence. The page worked the way a tourist's phrasebook works: it got the meaning across and announced, at every turn, that no one fluent had been involved. He had not saved an hour. He had borrowed three days at a bad interest rate.

That story is the entire case for DeepL in miniature, and it turns on a word that sounds soft until you have been burned by its absence: *quality*. This chapter is about what quality actually means in translation, why DeepL leads on it for the languages it serves, where the big general translators legitimately beat it, and why getting the quality right the first time is not a luxury but the thing that saves you money. I am going to make DeepL's case here, because the case is real — but a guide that pretended DeepL won every comparison would be doing you the same disservice as the marketing it replaces.

What "Quality" Actually Means

Most people, asked whether a translation is good, check whether it is *correct* — whether the words mean what the original meant. That is the floor, not the ceiling, and modern machine translation cleared the floor years ago. Almost every serious translator on the market today will get the literal meaning right for a straightforward sentence. If correctness were the whole job, the category would be solved and this book would be very short.

The job is not correctness. The job is producing language a native speaker would actually accept as natural. That is a much taller order, and it lives in the parts of language that a word-for-word swap cannot reach.

Register — whether the translation sits at the right level of formality. German alone has the *du/Sie* distinction that can make the difference between sounding like a friend and sounding like a stranger; Japanese has whole grammatical systems of politeness. A translation that is correct but pitched at the wrong register is the linguistic equivalent of wearing a swimsuit to a funeral. Everything is technically present; nothing is right.

Idiom — whether the phrasing is the way a native speaker would actually say it, rather than a literal rendering that is grammatical but alien. "It's raining cats and dogs" translated literally into most languages produces a sentence that parses and baffles. Good translation reaches for the equivalent expression, not the equivalent words.

Flow — whether the sentences have the rhythm of the target language. Different languages distribute information differently: where one front-loads, another saves the verb for the end; where one prefers short declaratives, another builds long subordinate clauses. A translation that preserves the *source* language's rhythm reads, in the target, like a person speaking with a heavy accent on the page.

Consistency of voice — whether a document sounds like one author throughout, in the right tone for its purpose, rather than lurching between formal and casual or technical and breezy.

These are the dimensions where translations are won and lost, and they are exactly the dimensions a literal engine misses. DeepL's reputation was built on getting them right — on producing, far more often than its rivals, the version a bilingual human would have actually written. That is what people mean when they say DeepL's translations sound natural. They are not being vague. They are pointing at register, idiom, flow, and voice, all landing at once.

There is a fifth dimension worth naming, because it is the one that fails most invisibly: **what the sentence is actually trying to do.** Language carries intent that the surface words underspecify. A line that reads, in the original, as a gentle nudge — "it might be worth revisiting the budget" — can come out, in a literal rendering, as a flat directive, because the target language marks tentativeness differently and the engine reached for the plainest form. Nothing is mistranslated; the *speech act* is. The reader receives an instruction where the writer offered a suggestion, and the relationship shifts by a degree without either party knowing why. Good translation preserves the move behind the words — the request that is really a request, the hedge that is really a hedge — and that, too, is something a word-for-word engine is structurally blind to.

To make the four dimensions concrete, take one short German sentence a customer-support agent might write: *Könnten Sie uns bitte die Rechnungsnummer mitteilen?* The literal scaffolding is "Could you us please the invoice-number communicate?" A weak engine, preserving German word order and reaching for the dictionary's first English word, produces something like "Could you please communicate to us the invoice number?" — grammatical, recoverable, and faintly robotic. *Communicate* is the tell; no support agent writing in English says it. The natural version is "Could you please send us the invoice number?" The register is right (polite but not stiff), the idiom is right (*send*, not *communicate*), the flow is right (English subject-verb-object instead of German verb-final), and the intent is right (a courteous request, not a demand). One sentence, four dimensions, and the difference between an answer a customer reads without noticing and one that quietly signals "you are talking to a machine." Now imagine that decision repeated across every line of a hundred support replies a day. That is the scale at which quality stops being an aesthetic preference and becomes an operational fact.

Why DeepL Leads on European Pairs

DeepL came out of Germany — Cologne, specifically — and it built its early reputation on European language pairs: German, French, Spanish, Italian, Dutch, Polish, and their neighbors, translated to and from English and one another. This is not an accident of geography but a matter of focus. A company that concentrates its attention on a particular family of languages, with the linguistic expertise and the training emphasis to match, tends to produce output that handles those languages' specific quirks — their formality systems, their idioms, their grammatical machinery — better than a translator spread thin across hundreds of tongues at once.

Independent evaluations have borne this out repeatedly. In professional comparisons, where fluent reviewers judge translations the way a real reader would, DeepL has consistently come out ahead of the big general translators on these European pairs — fewer errors, fewer awkward passages, fewer of the small wrongnesses that mark text as machine-made. I am deliberately not quoting you a specific “X percent fewer errors” figure, because the exact numbers move with every model release on every side and any single benchmark I anchored to would be stale within a quarter. The durable finding is the pattern, and the pattern has held for years: for the languages DeepL prioritizes, and especially for European ones, it tends to produce the more natural, more usable translation. That is the perishable detail giving way to the durable one.

It is worth being clear about *how* those evaluations are run, because the method explains why DeepL’s lead is real and not a marketing artifact. The serious comparisons do not score translations by counting matching words against a reference — that approach, the old automatic-metric style, rewards literalness and would actually penalize the very naturalness DeepL is good at. They use **blind human judgment**: fluent reviewers are shown translations of the same source text with the system names stripped off, and asked which they would rather have received, or asked to rank them, or asked to count and rate the errors they find. Because the reviewers do not know which engine produced which output, brand loyalty cannot tilt the result. When DeepL wins those, it wins because native speakers, not knowing what they are looking at, kept preferring its sentences. That is a far stronger claim than topping a number-matching benchmark, and it is the kind of evidence the durable finding rests on.

A second reason the lead holds is less about benchmarks than about feedback loops. DeepL’s user base is heavily concentrated in exactly the languages it is best at — European professionals translating European pairs all day — and that concentration becomes a flywheel. The work the company sees most, the corrections its professional users make, the contexts it is asked to handle, all skew toward the pairs it already leads on, which sharpens those pairs further. A translator spread across two hundred languages cannot focus that way; its attention is divided by the breadth it is proud of. Depth compounds on depth. None of this means DeepL is permanently ahead — model releases on every side reshuffle the standings — but it explains why the *pattern* has been stable for years even as the specific numbers churn.

The Honest Comparison: Quality Versus Coverage

Now the part the marketing leaves out.

DeepL supports somewhat more than a hundred languages. The broadest general translator — Google’s — supports well over two hundred, and that gap is not trivial. If your work touches Swahili, Zulu, Telugu, Khmer, or any of a hundred other languages that DeepL does not yet cover or covers less deeply, DeepL simply is not an option for that pair, and the question of who translates them *better* never comes up. Coverage is a real axis of quality in its own right, and on raw breadth the general translators win, clearly and uncontroversially. For a humanitarian organization working across dozens of low-resource languages, or anyone whose needs are defined by reach rather than polish, the broadest translator is the right tool, and I would tell them so.

So the honest frame is two-sided, and it is worth stating plainly because almost no one selling you anything will: **DeepL wins on quality for the languages it supports, especially European pairs. The general translators win on coverage — on sheer number of languages and on the long tail of niche and low-resource ones.** Those are different questions, and the right answer depends on which one you are actually asking. If you need French that a Parisian would accept, reach for DeepL. If you need *some* usable rendering of a language DeepL has never trained on, reach for the translator that covers it. Neither choice is a compromise; they are answers to different problems.

There is a quieter point underneath this. "Quality" and "coverage" pull against each other by their nature — concentrated excellence versus broad reach is a genuine trade-off, not a temporary state of the market. A company can lead on one or chase the other, and DeepL has consistently chosen depth. That choice is the reason it is better where it is better and absent where it is absent. Understanding the trade-off is most of understanding the tool.

The Resource Curve Most People Don't Know to Ask About

There is a refinement of the coverage question that matters enormously in practice and almost never comes up until someone is burned by it: *coverage is not binary, and quality is not uniform across the languages a tool claims to support.* A translator that "supports" two hundred languages does not support them all equally. The languages with mountains of training data on the open internet — the major European ones, the major East Asian ones — get excellent treatment everywhere, including from the general translators. The so-called low-resource languages, the ones with comparatively little digitized text to learn from, get visibly thinner treatment from *everyone*, DeepL and general translators alike.

A line in the supported-languages list tells you the pair will run; it does not promise the output will be good.

This has two practical consequences. First, when you are choosing between DeepL and a general translator for a pair DeepL does cover, the right test is never the marketing list — it is a short, honest trial on *your own* text in *that specific direction*. Take a paragraph you understand well, translate it both ways, and read both outputs as a native reader would. The gap is usually obvious within a paragraph, and it is the only evidence that actually concerns you, because it is your content and your pair. Benchmarks are about the average case; you live in a specific one.

Second, translation quality is rarely symmetric. A pair may be strong in one direction and weaker in the reverse, because the model has seen more text flowing one way, or because the target language is grammatically harder to generate well. English-to-German and German-to-English are not guaranteed to be equally good, and for less common pairs the asymmetry can be pronounced. When the *direction* of your work matters — say you mostly translate *into* a language rather than out of it — test that exact direction rather than assuming a strong pair is strong both ways. The most common version of this trap is testing the easy direction (into your own native language, where you can't fully judge the awkwardness) and trusting it for the hard one (into a language you don't speak well enough to catch the errors).

Why Quality Is Worth Paying For

Here is the objection I hear most: the free translators are *good enough*, and good enough is free, so why pay? The answer is the three days my colleague borrowed.

A translation that is merely correct but not natural is not a finished product. It is a draft — a draft someone fluent now has to read, catch the awkward passages in, and rewrite before it can go out. That human cleanup is the real cost of a mediocre translation, and it is invisible until you are paying it. It does not show up on the translator's price tag; it shows up in your colleague's afternoon, your reviewer's billable hours, your own evening spent fixing copy you thought was done. The free translation was free the way a free puppy is free.

Put plainly, the value of DeepL's quality is the work it *removes* — the rewriting a clumsier translation would have forced on you after the fact. When the output reads naturally on the first pass, you can use it as written — send the email, publish the page, ship the document — rather than treating it as a rough draft you still owe time to. For one sentence, that difference is a shrug. For a support team answering customers in a dozen languages all day, a company localizing thousands of pages, or a professional whose reputation rides on how their words land abroad, it compounds into real hours, real money, and real trust. The math that looks like "free versus paid" at the level of a single translation is actually "free plus cleanup versus paid minus cleanup" at the level of the work, and at volume the second column wins more often than the first.

This is also why the people who become genuinely loyal to DeepL tend to be the ones who do *enough* translation to feel the difference. If you translate a sentence a month, any decent tool will do and the quality gap is a curiosity. If translation is woven through your work, the gap is the difference between output you trust and output you have to babysit, and that is worth paying for the way a good knife is worth paying for if you cook every day.

Putting a Number on the Cleanup You're Avoiding

If you want to make the case to yourself — or to a manager who controls the budget — the argument becomes concrete when you estimate the cleanup cost directly rather than waving at it. The mediocre-translation tax is not mysterious; it is reviewer time, and reviewer time has a rate.

Work it through with a realistic case. Suppose your team localizes a steady stream of content — product copy, help articles, customer emails — and a fluent reviewer currently goes over every machine translation before it ships. With a weaker engine, that reviewer is doing real rewriting: fixing the stiff phrasings, catching the wrong-register lines, smoothing the flow. Call it, conservatively, several minutes of genuine editing per short piece. With a translator that lands naturally on the first pass, the same reviewer is doing something much lighter — a sanity read to confirm the meaning is intact, not a rewrite — and that might take a fraction of the time. The difference between "rewrite each one" and "verify each one" is the entire value proposition, and across hundreds of pieces a week at a professional's hourly rate, it is not a rounding error. It is frequently larger than the entire subscription cost, by an order of magnitude, which is why the "free versus paid" framing collapses the moment you account for the labor on both sides.

Two honest caveats keep this from being a sales pitch. First, you should *still* verify — quality reduces cleanup, it does not eliminate review, and Chapter 24 is emphatic that the most dangerous errors are the fluent ones that a hurried reviewer waves through precisely because the prose reads so well. The win is that review gets faster and lighter, not that it disappears. Second, the math only favors paying when your volume is real. For genuinely light use the cleanup tax is small in absolute terms and the free tier is the rational choice, which is exactly the recommendation Chapter 4 lands on. The point is not "always pay." It is "count the cleanup, because it is invisible and it is usually the biggest number in the comparison."

A Common Mistake: Judging Quality on the Wrong Sentence

One trap deserves a flag because it leads careful people to the wrong conclusion. When evaluating any translator, the instinct is to test it on a hard, interesting sentence — a pun, a proverb, a line of poetry — and judge the tool by how it handles the showpiece. This is the wrong test for most real work. The showpiece is the rare case; nearly all professional translation is ordinary prose — emails, documentation, product descriptions, support replies — and what you actually want to know is whether the tool handles *that* gracefully, at volume, without supervision.

A translator can stumble on a clever idiom and still be the right choice if it renders the thousand ordinary sentences around it beautifully, because the ordinary sentences are the job. Conversely, a tool that nails the one proverb you tested but produces faintly stiff prose on everything else will cost you on every line that matters. Test on representative text, not on the trick question. And when you do hit a genuinely hard line — the pun, the legal term of art, the culturally loaded phrase — that is precisely the spot to slow down and bring human judgment in, which is the subject the back of the book returns to. Use the machine for the ninety-five percent it does superbly; reserve your attention for the five percent where the stakes or the subtlety actually warrant it.

The Quality Question, Answered

So: why DeepL? Because in translation, *correct* and *good* are different achievements, and for the languages DeepL supports — European ones above all

— it reaches *good* more reliably than anything else, producing the natural, register-right, idiom-aware version you can actually use without a fluent human cleaning up behind it. And why not DeepL, sometimes? Because it cannot translate what it does not cover, and the broadest general translators reach languages DeepL has never touched. Hold both halves and you will choose well: DeepL when quality on a supported pair is the point, the broad translator when coverage is.

That settles the *why*. The rest of Part I turns to the *what* — because the company that earned its name on translation quietly became three products, and knowing which of them a given job needs is the next thing worth getting right.

Chapter 3: The DeepL Product Family: Translate, Write, and Voice

Most people who use DeepL are using a third of it. They translate constantly — French and German, perhaps — and consider themselves power users, never suspecting that the same company also polishes your *own* writing before it goes to a client, and translates a live call with a supplier in Madrid with the words flowing back and forth in near-real time. They think DeepL is a box you paste text into. It is three tools wearing one name, and most of us have only ever opened one door.

That is the most common misunderstanding about DeepL, and this chapter exists to clear it up. The name says "translation," and translation is where DeepL started and still its center of gravity — but the product has grown into three connected lines, and a great deal of what makes DeepL useful now lives in the two-thirds most people never notice. This chapter maps all three: what each is for, how they connect, and how to know which one the job in front of you actually needs. Think of it as the floor plan for Parts II through IV, each of which takes one product and goes deep.

One Intelligence, Three Directions

The cleanest way to hold the three products in your head is to notice that they are not three separate technologies but one capability — DeepL's language intelligence — pointed in three different directions.

Translate points it at someone else's words, converting text written in one language into another. This is the original, the famous one, the thing the company is named for.

Write points it at your own words, improving and rephrasing prose you have already written rather than converting anyone else's.

Voice points it at speech, translating the spoken word in real time so a conversation can cross a language barrier as it happens.

Convert others' words, improve your own, translate speech as it is spoken — three directions, one underlying competence. The naturalness DeepL is known for shows up in all three, because all three rest on the same thing: a model with a real feel for how language is supposed to *sound*. Once you see the three as facets of one capability rather than three unrelated apps, choosing between them stops being a guessing game.

It helps to notice *why* one capability splits into three products rather than living as a single tool with three buttons. The underlying skill — judging what natural language looks like in a given language and producing it — is shared, but the *input* differs in each case, and the input is what defines the product. Translate takes text in language A and a target of language B; the source and target are different languages. Write takes text in language A and, in effect, targets a better version of language A; the source and target are the same language. Voice takes a stream of audio rather than a block of text, which means it has to solve problems the other two never face — recognizing speech in real time, coping with accents and crosstalk and false starts, and producing output fast enough that a conversation does not stall. Same competence, three genuinely different jobs, which is why each gets its own product, its own interface, and its own part of this book rather than being folded into one screen.

DeepL Translate: Converting Others' Words

Translate is the core, and for most people it is the reason they are here. You give it text or a document in one language; it gives you back the same meaning in another, with the quality that built DeepL's reputation. That much is the picture everyone already has.

What that picture usually leaves out is how much *control* Translate offers beyond the basic paste-and-go. It translates not just loose text but whole documents — Word files, presentations, PDFs — and hands them back with the formatting intact, so a translated contract still looks like a contract rather than a wall of stripped text. It lets you build glossaries that lock in your preferred translation of specific terms, so your product names and house vocabulary come out the way you want every time instead of however the model guesses. It gives you formality and tone controls, so the output can be deliberately formal or casual to suit the context. These are the features that separate a translator you *use* from one you merely *try*, and they are why Part II — Chapters 4 through 9 — is the longest in the book. Translate is deep enough to deserve it.

Reach for Translate when the words you are working with are not yours and need to exist in another language: the email from a foreign client you need to read, the document you need to send abroad, the page you are localizing for a new market. If the task is *moving meaning between languages*, Translate is the tool, and Part II is your territory.

It is worth seeing how those controls actually change the output, because the difference between paste-and-go and Translate-used-well is large. Picture a small company localizing its website into German. With raw paste-and-go, the product name might be translated literally in one place and left in English in another, the formality might wobble between the friendly *du* and the formal *Sie* from page to page, and a key technical term might come out three different ways across the site. Now add the controls: a **glossary** pins the product name and the house terms so they render identically everywhere; the **formality setting** locks the whole site to *Sie* so the brand voice is consistent; and because Translate preserves **document formatting**, the team can hand it the marketing one-pager as a Word file and get back something that still looks like the one-pager, not a stripped block of text they have to re-lay-out. None of that is exotic. It is the ordinary difference between a translation that needs cleanup and one that is ready to publish — and it is exactly why Part II spends six chapters on a product most people assume they already understand.

DeepL Write: Improving Your Own Words

Write is the product longtime users most often miss, and it is the one that surprises people most when they finally meet it, because it inverts the whole premise. Translate works on someone else's language. Write works on *yours*. You give it text you have written, and it gives you back a better version of the same text — cleaner grammar, sharper phrasing, improved clarity, and a tone you can steer. It is not translating anything. It is helping you say what you were already trying to say, better.

There are two distinct reasons people use it, and they are worth separating.

The first is improving writing in your own native language. Even fluent writers produce first drafts that are wordy, stiff, or unclear, and Write is a tireless editor for tightening them — fixing the grammar, smoothing the phrasing, adjusting the register from blunt to diplomatic or casual to professional. For anyone who writes for work and wants it to land right, this is a genuine everyday tool, and Chapters 10 through 12 cover it in full.

The second is writing in a language that is not your first, and this is where Write quietly becomes something special. If you can compose serviceable-but-imperfect French or German — the kind that gets the meaning across but reveals at every turn that you are not native — Write can lift it toward something a native speaker would accept, correcting the errors and smoothing the non-native phrasing while keeping it *your* sentence rather than a translation of one. For the millions of people who work in a second language every day, that is a different and more dignified kind of help than translation: not "write it in your language and I'll convert it" but "write it in theirs, imperfectly, and I'll help you get it right." Chapter 13 is devoted to exactly this.

There is a subtle distinction inside Write that trips people up, and it is worth getting straight now because it shapes when the tool helps and when it quietly works against you. Write is not the same as translation-then-editing, and it is not a thesaurus. It works on the text you give it, in the language you give it, and its job is to make *that* text read more like a native, fluent version of itself. That means it is at its best when you have genuinely tried to say the thing and want it improved — not when you have nothing and want it written. Write will not invent content you did not supply, will not research, and will not turn a one-line note into a finished memo. If you hand it almost nothing, it will polish almost nothing. The reason this matters: people sometimes expect Write to do the heavy lifting of composition, get a disappointing result, and conclude the tool is weak, when in fact they asked the wrong tool the wrong question. Write improves prose that exists. The thinking and the substance are still yours.

Reach for Write when the words *are* yours and you want them better — clearer, more correct, better-toned — whether you wrote them in your first language or your fourth. If the task is *improving your own prose* rather than translating anyone's, Write is the tool, and Part III is where you'll want to be.

DeepL Voice: Translating Speech

Voice is the newest line and the one that most visibly extends DeepL beyond its origins, because it leaves the written page entirely. Translate and Write both work on text. Voice works on *speech*, translating the spoken word in real time so people who do not share a language can still talk to each other live.

The capability that makes this vivid is voice-to-voice translation, which DeepL brought to market in April 2026 — I flag the date because it is recent and the feature set around live voice is exactly the kind of thing that will keep evolving, so treat specifics here as a snapshot rather than a permanent state. The premise is straightforward and a little remarkable to use: you speak in your language, the other person hears it in theirs, they reply in theirs, and you hear it back in yours, with the lag low enough that an actual conversation can happen rather than a stilted exchange of pasted sentences. For a meeting with an overseas supplier, a conversation with a patient or customer who does not share your language, or any live human exchange across a language barrier, Voice turns translation from something you do *to text afterward* into something that happens *to speech as it occurs*.

It is worth being clear-eyed about what real-time voice translation can and cannot do, because the demo always looks more frictionless than the daily reality, and a chapter that only sold the magic would be setting you up to be disappointed. The honest version: Voice is genuinely useful and genuinely imperfect. There is latency — small, but present — so a Voice-mediated conversation has a rhythm closer to a phone call with a slight delay than to two native speakers talking over coffee. It depends on clean audio; a noisy café, several people talking at once, or a bad connection degrades it the way they degrade any speech system. And it is translating speech *as it is produced*, which means it cannot wait for the end of a rambling sentence to figure out where it was going, the way a human interpreter can. For a focused two-person conversation — a call with a supplier, a consultation with a customer or patient who does not share your language — it works well and changes what is possible. For a chaotic eight-person meeting with crosstalk, expect more friction. Knowing the envelope is part of using it well, and Part IV is honest about exactly where the edges are.

Reach for Voice when the language barrier is in a live conversation rather than on a page — a meeting, a call, a face-to-face exchange that needs to happen now, in both directions, out loud. If the task is *talking across languages in real time*, Voice is the tool, and Part IV — Chapters 14 through 16 — covers it, including the transcription that naturally falls out of a system built to understand speech.

How to Know Which One You Need

If you take one decision rule out of this chapter, make it this, because it resolves nearly every case: **ask whose words they are, and whether they are written or spoken.**

If the words are *someone else's* and you need them *in another language* — Translate. If the words are *yours* and you want them *better*, in any language — Write. If the words are *spoken*, live, and need to cross a language barrier as they happen — Voice. Other people's text, your own text, anyone's speech: three questions, three doors, and the answer is rarely ambiguous once you ask them in that order.

The one case that genuinely confuses people sits at the seam between Translate and Write, and it is worth resolving because choosing wrong produces subtly worse results. Suppose you need to send an email in German, and German is not your first language. There are two routes, and they are not equivalent. Route one: write the email in your native English and run it through **Translate** to get German. Route two: write the email in your own imperfect German and run it through **Write** to fix and smooth it. Which is right depends on a question about *you*: how good is your German? If your German is weak — you would struggle to produce even a rough version — Translate is the honest choice; you are converting from the language you actually command. But if your German is decent-but-not-native, Route two through Write often produces something better and more genuinely *yours*, because you are correcting your own phrasing rather than receiving a translation of an English sentence that may carry English habits of thought into German. The deciding question is not "which tool is better" but "in which language did I actually do the thinking?" Translate when the thinking happened in another language; Write when the thinking happened in the target language and only the execution needs help.

A second seam, less common but worth a flag: when the words are spoken but you do not need them live. If a colleague sends you a voice message in Italian and you want to know what it says, that is not really a Voice job in the real-time sense — Voice is built for *live* conversation. For after-the-fact understanding of recorded speech you are closer to the transcription territory Part IV also covers, where speech becomes text you can then read or translate. The "is it live?" half of the question matters as much as the "is it spoken?" half. Voice earns its name on the *real-time* part; drop the real-time requirement and the right tool may be a different one.

The products also combine more often than you might expect, and the combinations are where fluent users live. You might translate a document with Translate, then run your own cover note through Write to make sure your second-language email landing on top of it is as polished as the translation underneath. You might take a Voice meeting with a supplier and later translate the written follow-up with Translate. They are designed to sit beside each other in a single workflow, not to be chosen between once and for all, and most serious users end up reaching for two or three of them across a single project without thinking about it.

Two worked examples make the hand-offs concrete. Imagine you are negotiating a partnership with a company in Italy and you do not speak Italian well. The kickoff is a video call: you run it through **Voice**, speaking English and hearing Italian come back, so the live conversation actually happens. Afterward there is a contract draft in Italian: you run it through **Translate** to read and understand it in English, formatting intact, with a glossary keeping the legal terms consistent. Then you write your reply — partly in careful Italian to show goodwill — and run that through **Write** to lift your imperfect Italian toward something a native speaker would accept before it goes out. Three products, one negotiation, each doing the part it is built for.

Now the smaller, more everyday version: you are a non-native English speaker drafting an important email to an English-speaking client. You write it yourself, in English, then run it through **Write** to fix the small non-native tells and tune the tone to "professional but warm." No translation happens at all — the words were yours, in the target language, and you only wanted them better. The lesson in both examples is the same: don't think of yourself as picking one DeepL product. Think of the three as a single multilingual toolkit, and reach for whichever one matches the words in front of you right now — others' or yours, written or spoken.

The Floor Plan

So this is the shape of the thing the rest of the book explores. DeepL is one language intelligence aimed in three directions — Translate for converting others' words, Write for improving your own, Voice for translating speech as it is spoken

— unified by the single standard that runs through all of it: output a person would actually accept as natural, whether read or heard. Knowing the floor plan, you can walk straight to the room you need.

The next part takes the first and largest of those rooms. We begin where DeepL itself began — with translation — and with the practical business of getting set up and choosing the plan that fits how much of this work you actually do.

Part II: Translation

Audience: everyone. The original core of DeepL — and still the thing it does best.

"A translation you can use as written, without fixing it first, is worth more than a faster one you have to rewrite."

— A working principle

Chapter 4: Getting Started and Plans

The first time I paid DeepL anything, I did it backwards. I had been using the free tier for months — a paragraph here, a short email there — and one afternoon I tried to drop a forty-page contract into the document translator and got told, politely, that I had used up my document allowance for the month and the file was over the size cap besides. I upgraded on the spot, in a small panic, to the most expensive plan I could see, because I needed the thing done that day. It worked. It was also, I realized a week later, far more plan than I needed; a tier down would have covered me with room to spare. The lesson stuck, and it is the one this chapter is built around: spend ten minutes understanding the plans *before* the moment you are blocked, and you will buy the right one calmly instead of the wrong one in a hurry.

So before you put in a card, let's map the ground. Where DeepL lives, what the free tier really gives you, what the paid tiers unlock, the one billing concept that explains all of it — characters, not tokens — and which plan a sensible person should actually start on. Read this as the "before you spend" chapter it is meant to be.

A Warning About the Numbers

One caution that applies to this chapter with unusual force: **the specific prices, plan names, and quota figures are the most perishable facts in this book.** DeepL has renamed its tiers, adjusted what each one includes, and moved the prices more than once, and it will do so again. The amounts I give below are accurate to mid-2026 and quoted in euros, which is DeepL's home currency; what you pay in dollars, pounds, or anything else depends on the day's conversion and local tax. So treat every number here as the shape of the offer, not a quote. There is exactly one authoritative source for what you will actually be charged: DeepL's own pricing page, checked today, in your own currency. I will flag the figures as I go so you remember to verify them.

Where DeepL Lives

DeepL meets you in more places than the website most people picture, and the right surface depends on the moment.

The web app at the DeepL site is the home base — text translation, document translation, glossaries, and the Write tool all in the browser, nothing to install. It is where you will do most deliberate work and the place to start.

The desktop apps for Windows and Mac put DeepL a keyboard shortcut away. Select text in any application, press the shortcut, and DeepL pops up with the translation — no copying into a browser tab. For anyone who translates often while working in other programs, this is the quiet productivity win that justifies the install.

The mobile apps for iPhone and Android carry the same core into your pocket, with the additions that only make sense on a phone: translate text you photograph with the camera, and translate speech you speak aloud. For travel and on-the-spot translation, the phone is the tool.

The browser extensions for Chrome, Edge, Firefox, and others bring DeepL into the pages and webmail you are already reading and writing, so you can translate a page or improve an email without leaving it.

All of these draw on the same account and the same plan. Sign in once, and whichever surface you reach for, your tier and your glossaries come with you. The separate world is the **API**, for developers wiring DeepL into their own software — that has its own plans and its own meter, and I will point you there at the end.

A practical note on which surface to actually adopt, because "they all exist" is not the same as "use all of them." Most people get the most out of two: the **web app** for deliberate, sit-down work — translating a document, building a glossary, doing anything where you want the full interface in front of you — and the **desktop app** for the in-the-flow moments, where you are writing or reading in some other program and want a translation without breaking stride. The desktop shortcut is the one that quietly changes your habits: once selecting text and pressing a key gives you an instant translation anywhere on your machine, you stop the copy-into-a-tab dance, and the friction that used to make you skip translating a borderline-worth-it sentence disappears. The browser extension earns its place if a lot of your reading and writing happens inside web pages and webmail. The mobile app is situational — invaluable when traveling or translating something in front of you with the camera, easy to forget the rest of the time. The honest recommendation: install the web app and the desktop app first, live with them for a week, and add the others only when you feel the specific gap they fill.

One setup detail worth getting right early: sign in to every surface with the *same* account from the start. It sounds obvious, but a common stumble is creating a free account in the browser one day, then installing the desktop app another day and signing up afresh inside it — and now you have two accounts, your glossaries live on one, your subscription (when you buy one) attaches to whichever you happened to be in, and you spend an afternoon untangling it. One account, signed in everywhere, and the whole thing behaves as a single tool that follows you across devices.

The Free Tier: Genuinely Useful, Deliberately Bounded

DeepL's free tier is not a crippled demo. It is a real tool that a lot of people never outgrow, and it is the right place to start no matter who you are.

What you get, as of mid-2026 (verify these — they are exactly the kind of number that drifts): roughly **50,000 characters per month of text translation**, a small number of **document translations per month — on the order of three** — and a **file-size cap around 5 MB** on those documents. You also get access to the formality control and a limited taste of glossaries. That is enough to translate a steady stream of emails, messages, and short passages, plus the occasional file, without paying anything.

Where the free tier stops is precisely where heavier or more professional use begins. The monthly character budget is real and you can spend it faster than you'd think once you are pasting in long passages. The handful of document translations runs out quickly if files are your main use. The size cap rules out big presentations and long PDFs. And the glossary and team features that businesses lean on are thin or absent. None of that is a reason to avoid the free tier — it is the reason to *start* there and let your actual usage tell you whether you need more.

The most important thing the free tier buys you is not the translation — it is **information about your own usage**, which is the single best input to the plan decision and the one no comparison chart can give you. Spend a month on Free doing your real work, and at the end you will know, from experience rather than guesswork, three things: roughly how many characters a month you actually consume, whether documents or loose text are your main use, and how often you hit a wall. That month of honest data is worth more than any amount of staring at the pricing page, because it tells you which wall you'll hit *first* — and the wall you hit first is the one to buy your way past. People who skip this step tend to overbuy, the way I did, paying for allowances they never approach because they guessed instead of measured.

There is one subtlety about the free tier worth knowing before you lean on it for anything sensitive: the data-handling posture differs between free and paid. The strong commitments — not using your texts to improve the models, deleting text after translation — are part of the *paid* offering, and the free tier's terms are not the same. For casual, non-sensitive translation that distinction is academic. For anything confidential — a contract, internal documents, personal data — it is not, and it is a genuine reason to be on a paid plan rather than the free one even if your volume alone would not require it. Chapter 20 covers the data story in full; flagging it here so you don't paste a confidential file into the free tier on the assumption that all of DeepL handles data identically. It doesn't.

The Paid Tiers: What More Money Buys

DeepL's paid subscriptions climb a ladder, and what rises as you climb is consistent even as the names and prices shift. As of mid-2026, the individual tiers run roughly **Starter at about €8.99 a month, Advanced at about €28.99, and Ultimate at about €57.99** (verify every one of these — names and amounts move). Paying annually instead of monthly cuts the price by roughly a third, which is the lever to pull if you already know you'll keep the subscription.

What each step up actually unlocks, in plain terms:

Far more text translation. The 50,000-character monthly ceiling of the free tier lifts dramatically — paid tiers offer very large allowances, enough that most individuals stop thinking about the character meter at all.

More and larger document translations. Instead of three small files a month, you get many more per month and a much higher file-size cap, climbing as you go up the tiers. This is the single biggest reason most people upgrade: document work blows through the free allowance first.

Whole-document editing and download in more formats, so the translated file comes back fully usable rather than locked.

Real glossary capacity, rising by tier — more glossaries, more entries, more language pairs covered. If consistent terminology matters to you (Chapter 7), this is where it lives.

Stronger data handling — paid DeepL does not use your texts to improve its models and deletes them after translation, a posture that matters for any sensitive or professional material (Chapter 20).

There are also **Team and business plans** layered on top of the individual ones, adding centralized billing, more seats, admin controls, and shared glossaries for organizations. If you are buying for a group rather than yourself, that is the aisle to shop in, and Part V is written with you in mind.

The difference between stacking individual subscriptions and buying a proper team plan is worth understanding before you do the cheaper-looking thing and regret it. Three or four people could, in principle, each buy their own individual subscription, and for a tiny group that occasionally works. But the moment terminology consistency matters across the group, individual plans fall down: each person's glossaries live in their own account, so the product name that one colleague pinned does not exist for the next, and the team's output drifts apart exactly where it most needs to match. A team plan gives you **shared glossaries** the whole group draws on, so everyone's translations agree. It also gives you **centralized billing** (one invoice instead of chasing reimbursements), **admin controls** (add and remove seats as people join and leave, rather than orphaning a subscription when someone departs), and a single place to manage the organization's data-handling settings. The rule of thumb: the instant more than a couple of people need *consistent* output or the company needs to *administer* access rather than trust individuals to expense it, the team plan is not just convenient, it is the only setup that actually holds together. Don't reverse-engineer a team deployment out of individual seats; it looks cheaper on the spreadsheet and costs you in drift and administration.

The One Idea That Explains the Quota: Characters

Here is the concept that makes every plan legible. **DeepL meters text translation by characters — individual letters, spaces, and punctuation — not by words and not by the "tokens" you may have met in other AI tools.** A character is a character. "Hello" is five of them. A short email might be a few hundred; a dense page of prose, a couple of thousand; a long document, tens of thousands. When a plan says 50,000 characters a month, count it that way, and you'll have an honest sense of how far it stretches.

This matters for two reasons. First, it makes budgeting intuitive once you internalize it — you can eyeball roughly how much of your allowance a given task will cost. Second, it is *different* from how the chatbots in the rest of this series bill, which is by tokens, so if you are coming from those tools, retrain the instinct. With DeepL, the meter counts the raw text you send, plainly and predictably. Document translations are metered too, both against your character budget and against the separate per-month document count.

To turn the abstraction into a working intuition, calibrate against things you already have a feel for. A typical short business email is somewhere in the range of a few hundred to a thousand characters. A dense single page of prose — the kind of thing that fills a page in a normal document — runs roughly two to three thousand characters. A standard book page is in the same neighborhood. So a free-tier budget of around fifty thousand characters a month is, very roughly, on the order of fifty short emails, or fifteen-to-twenty dense pages, or some mix — and you can see immediately how a couple of longer documents would eat most of it. Count it that way and the allowance stops being an abstract number and becomes a quantity of *your* work, which is the only unit that helps you plan.

Two practical wrinkles to keep the intuition honest. First, **the source text is what's metered** — you are charged for what you send to be translated, by its character count, regardless of how long the translation comes back, which matters because some languages expand on translation (German is famously longer than English) without that expansion costing you anything extra. Second, **re-translating the same passage counts again.** If you translate a paragraph, tweak the original, and translate it once more, that is two charges against your budget, not one. People sometimes burn through an allowance faster than expected by re-running near-identical text repeatedly while fiddling; if you find yourself doing that, translate once, then edit the output directly rather than re-submitting the source over and over. For the free tier this is just good hygiene; for API usage at scale (Chapter 23) it becomes a real cost-management discipline.

A Separate Door for Builders: the API

Everything above is about using DeepL as a person, through a subscription, on the web or in an app. There is an entirely separate path for developers: the **DeepL API**, which you call from your own software and which bills on its own terms. It has a free API plan with a monthly character allowance and paid API plans that charge for usage on top, and it is the right route for automating translation, building DeepL into a product, or wiring it into a content pipeline. Its plans, limits, and costs are their own subject — Chapter 21 covers the API itself and Chapter 23 covers managing its cost and quota. I flag it here only so you know the subscription ladder is not the whole story; if you are a builder, the consumer plans may be beside the point and the API is your door.

Which Plan Should You Start On?

A direct recommendation, carrying the standing reminder to confirm current terms before you act on any of it:

If you are **trying DeepL at all**, start on **Free**. Translate real things — the emails and passages you actually need — and let a month tell you where you hit the wall. Most people learn more from one month of honest use than from any amount of plan-comparing.

If the wall you hit is **documents** — too few per month, or files too big — that is the most common reason to upgrade, and **Starter or Advanced** is usually the answer depending on how many files and how large.

If you translate **heavily, rely on glossaries, or handle sensitive material**, look at **Advanced or Ultimate**, where the allowances, glossary capacity, and data protections all open up.

If you are buying **for a team**, skip the individual ladder and look at the **Team and business plans**, and read Part V before you commit.

And if you are a **developer building on DeepL** rather than translating by hand, the subscription tiers may not be for you at all — go to the API in Part VI.

To show the logic in motion rather than as a list, walk through three people deciding. **Maria** is a freelance translator who works in DeepL all day, English to and from Spanish, and lives and dies by terminology consistency for her recurring clients. Free is never going to hold her; her character volume alone rules it out, and she needs real glossary capacity for client-specific term lists. She belongs on Advanced or Ultimate, and because she knows she'll keep the subscription for years, she pays annually and takes the roughly one-third discount without a second thought. **Tom** runs a small online shop and translates a few supplier emails and the occasional product sheet — light, sporadic, nothing confidential. He should stay on Free, possibly forever; upgrading would mean paying for allowances he'll never approach. If his volume ever climbs, the free-tier month will tell him, and he can move up then. **A four-person marketing team** at a growing company is localizing campaigns and needs the same brand terms across everyone's work. They should not buy four individual subscriptions; they should buy a team plan for the shared glossaries and centralized administration, and read Part V before committing. Same decision rule applied three times, three different right answers — which is the whole point of starting from your actual usage rather than from the price you'd prefer to pay.

One more piece of timing advice that the panic-upgrade story at the top of this chapter earns the right to give: **decide your plan when you are not blocked.** The worst moment to choose a tier is the afternoon a deadline collides with a quota wall, because under that pressure the rational move — measure first, buy the tier that clears the wall you actually hit — gets replaced by "buy the biggest thing visible and sort it out later." Spend the ten minutes now, while nothing is on fire, knowing roughly what each tier costs and which wall your work will hit first. Then when the wall arrives, the decision is already made and you upgrade to the right plan in thirty seconds instead of the wrong one in a panic.

Get that settled — a surface to work on, a starting tier (Free is a fine answer), and prices you confirmed in your own currency rather than took from this page — and the spending decision is behind you. What remains is the part the rest of Part II is about: actually translating, and translating well, starting with text.

Chapter 5: Text Translation

A French colleague once sent me a one-line reply to a proposal: a short sentence I dropped into DeepL out of habit before answering. The translation came back clean and unremarkable — until I noticed the alternative phrasing DeepL offered for the final clause, which carried a faint note of reservation the first rendering had smoothed away. That second version was the true one. My colleague was not enthusiastic; she was politely hedging, and the difference between "yes" and "yes, but" was the entire meaning of the message. I had nearly missed it by reading only the first answer. That is the whole discipline of using a translator well: the output is usually good, occasionally it hides the thing that matters most, and the skill is knowing how to read it so the difference doesn't slip past you.

This chapter is about the core act DeepL was built for — translating text — and how to do it in a way that gets you send-ready results when the stakes are low and catches the trouble when they are high. The mechanics are simple. The judgment is where the value is.

The Basic Loop

The act itself takes seconds. You paste or type text into the source box, DeepL detects the language automatically — and is reliable at it for the languages it supports well — you pick the target language, and the translation appears as you go, updating live. There is no "translate" button to wait on for short text; the result is just there. For most everyday work, that is the entire interaction: in goes the message, out comes a natural-sounding version in the other language, and you are done.

Two small habits make this loop better from the start. **Check the detected source language** before you trust the output — auto-detection is good but not infallible, and a mixed-language snippet or a short ambiguous phrase can fool it. And **give DeepL whole sentences, ideally whole paragraphs, rather than fragments.** Translation quality depends heavily on context; a complete sentence translates far better than the same words in isolation, because the surrounding words tell DeepL how to read the ambiguous ones. The more context you provide, the more the natural-language quality DeepL is known for has to work with.

To make the context point concrete, take the English word "charge." On its own it is a coin toss — it can mean a fee, an accusation, an electrical action, a military advance, or the act of putting something on a card. Paste "charge" alone and DeepL has to guess, and into a language that splits those meanings into entirely different words, the guess is often wrong. Paste "We will charge the deposit to your card on Friday" and there is no ambiguity left; the sentence resolves the word, and the translation comes back correct in one pass. This is why fragment translation is the single most common self-inflicted source of bad output. The model is not weak; it has simply been starved of the very thing it relies on. Whenever you find a translation reading oddly, the first thing to check is whether you handed DeepL enough sentence to work with.

There is a related habit worth forming for longer text: **paste the whole passage at once rather than feeding it line by line.** A bulleted list pasted as separate one-word lines translates worse than the same list pasted as a block, because the block lets DeepL see the relationships between items. The tool is built to work on coherent units of meaning. Give it those units and it rewards you; chop them up and you get the chopped-up quality back.

Where the Translating Actually Happens

It helps to know your options, because "text translation" lives in more places than the website, and the right entry point depends on what you are doing. The **web app** is the home base — the two-box interface most people picture, with the full set of controls (formality in Chapter 8, glossaries in Chapter 7, the alternatives covered below) sitting right there. The **desktop apps** for Windows and macOS put the same thing one keystroke away: select text in any application, hit the shortcut, and a translation window appears without your ever leaving the document you're in. For someone who translates dozens of times a day, that shortcut is the difference between a tool you reach for and a tool you forget. The **mobile apps** add the camera and voice entry points — point the phone at a menu or a sign and get the translation overlaid — which is a genuinely different mode of use, aimed at the traveler rather than the desk worker. And the **browser extension** lets you translate selected text or whole pages in place, which is where a great deal of casual reading-translation actually happens.

The point of naming all of these is not to catalog features but to make a practical claim: the *same* translation quality is behind all of them, so the right choice is whichever removes the most friction from your particular loop. If you are translating one passage, the web app is fine. If you are translating constantly throughout your day, learning the desktop shortcut will save you more time than any other single habit in this chapter. The mechanics are identical; only the friction differs.

Reading the Result Critically

Here is the part that separates people who use DeepL well from people who merely use it. **Machine translation errors are usually fluent.** When a translation goes wrong, it rarely produces obvious gibberish you would catch at a glance. It produces a smooth, confident, perfectly grammatical sentence that happens to mean something slightly — or entirely — different from the original. That fluency is exactly what makes the errors dangerous: there is no broken grammar to trip your eye, so a wrong translation reads as easily as a right one.

So the critical reading habit is not "scan for mistakes." It is to ask, at the points that matter, *does this say what the original meant?* A few specific things reward a second look. **Negations** — a misplaced or dropped "not" flips a sentence and reads perfectly either way. **Numbers, dates, names, and units** — these carry meaning the surrounding fluency won't reveal as wrong. **Pronouns and who-did-what-to-whom**, in languages where the grammar leaves that to context. And **anything where tone or hedging carries the message**, as my French colleague's reply did, because a translator optimizing for natural phrasing can quietly normalize away a deliberate note of caution or sharpness.

Each of these has a characteristic way of going wrong, and knowing the failure shape helps you catch it. Take **numbers and units.** DeepL will faithfully carry "5 lbs" across as the number five with a pounds label — but it will not convert pounds to kilograms, because that is arithmetic, not translation, and a translator should not silently rewrite your data. The fluent output hides this perfectly: the sentence reads naturally, the number is right, and only a reader who knows the target audience expects metric will notice the unit is foreign to them. The same goes for dates. "06/05/2026" means June 5th to an American and May 6th to most of Europe, and a translator cannot disambiguate a format the source itself left ambiguous. If your text leans on numbers, dates, or units that carry real consequence, read them as data, not as prose, and convert anything that needs converting yourself.

Negations are the quiet assassins. Consider a safety instruction: "Do not operate the machine without the guard in place." A dropped "not" or a mishandled double negative turns a warning into an invitation, and the resulting sentence is grammatically immaculate in the target language. There is nothing to catch your eye. The only defense is to read the negated sentences specifically, asking whether the *polarity* survived the trip — does the translation still forbid what the original forbade? On low-stakes text this is paranoia; on instructions, warnings, contracts, or anything where doing the opposite would be a problem, it is the single highest-value check you can run.

Pronouns and reference deserve their own note, because they trip people who think they've done the careful reading. Many languages drop subject pronouns that English requires, or carry gender on words that English leaves neutral, and the model has to reconstruct what the source left implicit. Translate a customer-service exchange from a pronoun-dropping language into English and you may find DeepL has guessed a "he" where the original was deliberately neutral, or attached an action to the wrong party in a sentence with two people in it. The sentence reads fine. It simply assigns the deposit refund to the wrong person. When a passage has more than one actor — two people, a company and a customer, a buyer and a seller — slow down and verify that each action landed on whoever did it in the original. This is the error most likely to survive a casual read precisely because it produces a perfectly sensible sentence that happens to be about the wrong person.

You do not need to interrogate every sentence; that would defeat the purpose. The skill is calibrating the scrutiny to the stakes. A casual message to a friend needs almost none. A sentence in a contract, a medical instruction, or a public statement needs all of it — and possibly a human translator besides (Chapter 24). Most text lives in between, and a quick read against the original meaning is enough.

A Worked Walkthrough: One Email, Start to Finish

Abstract advice gets slippery, so walk one realistic task end to end. You've received a German email from a prospective supplier and you need to reply in German, and you don't read German beyond a few words.

First, **translate their message into your language and read it for meaning.** Paste the whole email — not the subject line alone, not the first sentence — so DeepL has the full context. You read it and learn they can deliver in eight weeks, not the six you asked for, and there's a line about a price that holds "until the end of the quarter." That date qualifier is load-bearing, so you note it specifically rather than trusting the gist.

Second, **write your reply in clear source language.** Resist the urge to be clever. "We'd love to get the ball rolling but eight weeks is a stretch on our end" is full of idiom that will translate poorly; "Eight weeks is longer than we hoped. Can you deliver any sooner?" says the same thing and travels cleanly. You are writing for translation now, and plain beats colorful every time.

Third, **set formality before you translate** (Chapter 8). This is a first contact with a business stranger, so you want the formal register — in German, the difference between addressing them as *Sie* and *du* is a real social signal, and getting it wrong reads as either stiff or presumptuous. You set the dial to formal up front rather than translating casually and fixing it after.

Fourth, **translate, then read the result critically using the checks above.** You can't read German, so you work the levers you can. You check that the eight-weeks number survived (it did). You check the alternatives at the phrase that renders your request, choosing the version that reads as a polite ask rather than a demand. And before you send anything that matters, you run a round-trip check, covered next.

That's the whole loop, and it took perhaps three minutes. Notice what it is not: it is not blind trust, and it is not paranoid line-by-line interrogation. It is a handful of targeted checks aimed at the few things in this particular message that could embarrass you if they went wrong. Internalize that shape and you can run it on anything.

A Quick Sanity Check for the Languages You Don't Read

The hardest case is translating *into* a language you cannot read at all — the most common reason people use a translator, and the one where critical reading seems impossible. You cannot judge a German translation if you do not read German. There is a practical move that helps: the **round-trip check.** Translate your English into the target language, then translate that result back into English in a fresh translation. If the round trip comes back saying roughly what you started with, the core meaning probably survived. If it comes back mangled, distorted, or saying something you didn't intend, that is a flag worth acting on.

The round trip is a rough instrument, not a proof — a translation can be perfectly good and still come back slightly changed, because translation is not perfectly reversible, and a translation can be subtly wrong and still round-trip cleanly. Treat it as a smoke detector, not a guarantee. But for the everyday case of "I need to send something in a language I don't speak and I want to make sure I didn't say anything absurd," it is a thirty-second habit that catches the gross errors, which are the ones that embarrass you. For anything beyond gross errors in a language you don't read, the real answer is a native speaker (Chapter 24).

There is a smarter way to use the round trip than reading it whole. **Watch the load-bearing pieces specifically.** Did your number come back as the same number? Did the date survive? Did the one critical request — "can you deliver sooner" — come back as a request and not a statement? A round trip that garbles a throwaway pleasantry but preserves every fact and ask is more reassuring than one that reads smoothly but quietly drops your deadline. You are not grading the round trip on prose; you are checking whether the skeleton of meaning made it there and back. And when it doesn't — when the round trip reveals that your idiom became nonsense — the fix is almost never to fight the translator. It is to go back and rewrite the source plainer, which is the single most reliable lever you have and the subject of a later section.

Alternative Phrasings: DeepL's Quiet Superpower

The feature I'd most want a new user to discover is the one most easily overlooked. **Click a word or phrase in the translation, and DeepL offers alternatives** — other valid ways to render that piece, with the rest of the sentence adjusting to fit your choice. This is not a thesaurus. It is DeepL showing you the legitimate range of how a phrase could land in the target language, and letting you pick the shade you actually mean.

This matters for two reasons. First, it is how you catch the hidden-meaning problem: when DeepL offers a markedly different alternative for a clause, that is a signal the source was ambiguous or carried a nuance worth a second look — which is exactly what flagged my colleague's hedge. Second, it is how you tune tone and precision without speaking the language fluently yourself. If the default rendering feels too stiff or too casual, the alternatives often hold the register you want, and selecting one rephrases cleanly around it. Anyone doing real communication work in a second language should treat the alternatives not as a curiosity but as a core part of the workflow.

A worked example shows how the feature actually earns its keep. Suppose you are translating "I'd appreciate your prompt response" into French for a business email. DeepL's first pass might give you something perfectly serviceable. Click on the phrase that renders "appreciate," and you may be offered a range running from a warm, almost personal thanks to a clipped, formal acknowledgment. The choice between them is not about correctness — all of them are correct French — it is about how you want to *come across* to this particular reader. A new client you are courting might warrant the warmer option; a vendor who has missed two deadlines might warrant the cooler one. The alternatives let a non-native speaker make a native-level register decision, which is a genuinely remarkable thing for a tool to offer, and most users never click.

Here is a different kind of example, where the alternatives do diagnostic work rather than stylistic work. You translate a clause and DeepL's default and its top alternative are *not* near-synonyms — one says the meeting is "confirmed" and the other says it is "to be confirmed." That gap is not DeepL being indecisive; it is DeepL telling you the source was genuinely ambiguous and it had to pick. When the alternatives diverge that sharply in *meaning* rather than in *tone*, stop and reread your source. You have found a sentence that doesn't say what you thought it said clearly enough for a careful reader — human or machine — to be sure. The alternatives, used this way, are an ambiguity detector you didn't know you had.

The deeper point is that the alternatives turn translation from a one-shot output into a conversation. You are not stuck with what the model produced first; you are shown its reasoning made visible, the branch points where it had to choose, and given the choice back. Reading those branch points teaches you where your text was ambiguous in ways you didn't intend, which over time makes you write clearer source text — the single best thing you can do for translation quality, because a clear, unambiguous, idiom-light original translates well into everything.

Quick Edits and Refinement

The translation box is editable, and you should edit in it freely. If you know the target language even passably, fixing a word, adjusting a phrase, or tightening a sentence right there is faster than starting over, and DeepL keeps the rest coherent around your change. For the languages you don't read, lean on the alternatives instead — they give you legitimate options without requiring you to guess.

When the *source* is the problem, the better fix is upstream. If a translation keeps coming out wrong in the same place, the cause is often an over-clever original: a piece of idiom, a pun, a sentence that runs three clauses deep, a culturally specific reference that has no clean equivalent. Rather than fighting the output, **rewrite the source to be plainer and translate again.** "We're going to circle back on the low-hanging fruit" is a translation nightmare; "We'll start with the easy items" says the same thing and translates cleanly everywhere. This pre-editing habit — writing for translation — is the professional localizer's quiet trick, and it costs you nothing but the discipline of clear writing.

It's worth naming the specific shapes of source text that reliably cause trouble, because once you can spot them you can defuse them before they reach the translator. **Idiom and metaphor** — "ballpark figure," "moving the goalposts," "back to the drawing board" — translate literally and land as nonsense; say the plain thing instead. **Sarcasm and irony** carry meaning in the opposite direction from the words, and no translator can be relied on to invert it; if you mean it, say it straight. **Stacked clauses** — sentences that nest three or four ideas inside each other — give the model too many ways to misattach the pieces; break them into separate sentences. **Culturally specific references** — a sports metaphor, a holiday, a brand used as shorthand — have no clean equivalent and should be replaced with the literal point they were standing in for. And **deliberate ambiguity or wordplay**, the puns and double meanings that are sometimes the whole point of a line, simply cannot survive a single automatic pass; those are the lines that need a human who can re-create the effect rather than translate the words (Chapter 24). None of this means writing dully. It means writing *clearly*, and clear source text is the cheapest quality improvement available to anyone who translates.

Two refinement levers belong to other chapters but earn a mention here because they shape the text translation directly. **Glossaries** lock in your preferred translation of specific terms, names, and brand language so they come out consistently every time without manual fixing (Chapter 7). **Formality control** lets you ask for a formal or informal register up front, which for many languages changes the translation meaningfully and is worth setting before you translate rather than fixing after (Chapter 8). When you find yourself making the same edit repeatedly — the same term, the same level of politeness — that is the signal to reach for one of these rather than keep editing by hand.

If your aim is to improve text you wrote yourself rather than translate someone else's, that is a different tool entirely — DeepL Write — and it gets its own part of this book (Part III). Translation converts meaning across languages; Write polishes prose within one. Keep them distinct in your head.

Common Mistakes, and How to Avoid Them

A short field guide to the errors I see most, because naming them is most of avoiding them.

Translating fragments and blaming the tool. Covered above, and worth repeating because it's the most common of all: a one-word or half-sentence input gives the model nothing to disambiguate with. If output looks wrong, check the input length before anything else.

Reading only the first answer. The default rendering is one valid translation, not the only one. Skipping the alternatives means missing both the tone choices and the ambiguity signals they expose. Click at least the load-bearing phrases.

Trusting fluency as a proxy for accuracy. The smoothest-sounding translation is not necessarily the most faithful one. Polish and correctness are separate properties, and the whole danger of a good translator is that it makes the two feel like one.

Forgetting to set formality before translating into a marking language. Translating casually into German or French and only noticing the register problem after it's sent is a recurring, entirely avoidable mistake. Make the dial part of the loop (Chapter 8).

Pasting confidential text into a tool whose data terms you haven't checked. This is not a quality mistake but a judgment one, and it's more expensive than any mistranslation. For sensitive material, know your plan's data-handling terms before you paste (Chapter 20).

Assuming a strong-pair experience carries to every language. The send-ready quality you see in German does not guarantee the same in a less-resourced pair. Calibrate your trust to the language, not to DeepL in general (Chapter 9).

Send-Ready or Needs a Pass?

The practical question every translation comes down to is whether you can use it as-is or whether it wants a human pass first. A working rule, drawn from a lot of real use:

It is usually send-ready when the content is everyday and low-stakes, the language pair is one of DeepL's strong ones (Chapter 9), the text is straightforward prose without heavy idiom or wordplay, and a wrong translation would be a minor inconvenience rather than a real problem. Routine email, internal messages, informational text, getting the gist of something you received — for all of these, DeepL's first-pass output is genuinely usable, which is the entire point of its quality and the reason it saves you the cleanup a clumsier translator would demand.

It wants a pass when any of those flips: the stakes are real, the language pair is one of DeepL's weaker ones, the source is dense with idiom, humor, marketing voice, or legal precision, or the meaning hinges on exactly the kind of nuance that fluent errors erase. The pass can be light — read it against the original, check the alternatives at the load-bearing phrases, fix what's off — or it can mean handing it to a qualified human, which for the highest-stakes content is the right answer and no failure of the tool (Chapter 24).

It helps to picture the scale rather than a binary. At one end sits a text to a friend in a strong language pair: paste, send, done, no pass at all. A step up, a routine work email: a quick read against the original before it goes. Higher, a customer-facing message or a published blog post: the read plus a check of the alternatives at the phrases that carry the tone, and ideally a second set of eyes. Higher still, a contract clause or a dosage instruction: a qualified human in the loop, no exceptions, with DeepL doing the first draft and a professional owning the result. The same tool serves the whole scale; what changes is how much of your own judgment you spend on top of it.

The art is not in distrusting DeepL or in trusting it blindly. It is in knowing which kind of text is in front of you. Get that judgment right, and DeepL does what it is best at — turning the great volume of ordinary cross-language text into something you can simply use — while you reserve your scrutiny for the sentences that have earned it. That same discipline carries directly into the next thing most people reach DeepL for: handing it not a passage but a whole file, and getting the document back intact.

Chapter 6: Translating Documents: Files and Formatting

Translating a twelve-slide pitch deck the hard way eats an afternoon. You copy each text box into a translator, paste the result back, and then fight the layout as the longer German strings overflow their boxes and shove the design out of alignment; by the end the meaning is right and the deck looks broken. DeepL's document translator collapses that afternoon into the time it takes a coffee to cool. You upload the original PowerPoint, choose German, wait under a minute, and download a file that is the same deck — same slides, same images, same fonts, same layout — with the text in German. The feature that makes the difference is the one this chapter is about: whole-file translation that gives you back the *document*, not just the words.

This is, for a great many professionals, the single most valuable thing DeepL does. Text translation you can get adequately elsewhere. Handing over a formatted file and getting the same file back, intact, in another language is where DeepL earns its keep.

What Document Translation Actually Does

The mechanic is as simple as it sounds. You upload a file, pick the target language, and DeepL returns a new file in that language with the original formatting preserved. Not a wall of stripped text you then have to pour back into a layout — the actual document, structure and all. A Word file comes back a Word file with its headings, lists, tables, and styles in place. A PowerPoint comes back a PowerPoint with text sitting in the same boxes on the same slides. A PDF comes back laid out as a PDF. DeepL handles the common office formats — **Word, PowerPoint, plain text, and PDF among them** — which between them cover the overwhelming majority of what people actually need translated.

Why this is hard, and therefore worth something: a document is not just text. It is text wrapped in structure, and the two are entangled. Translation changes the length of the text — German runs long, many languages reflow differently — and naive tools break the structure trying to accommodate it. DeepL does the bookkeeping of pulling the text out, translating it with the same quality it brings to anything, and threading it back into the original structure so the file survives the trip. The result is something you can often use immediately rather than rebuild.

It's worth understanding, at a high level, what's happening under the hood, because it explains both the strengths and the failure modes you'll meet later in the chapter. A modern Word or PowerPoint file is not a printed page; it's a structured bundle of text runs, styles, and layout instructions. DeepL reads that structure, extracts the translatable text while keeping a map of where each piece belongs, translates it, and writes it back into the same slots. Because it's working with the document's own structure rather than a flattened picture of it, the headings stay headings and the bullets stay bullets. A PDF is a different animal — closer to a finished print job than an editable structure — which is exactly why PDFs are the hard case and the others are the easy ones. Hold that distinction; it's the single most useful thing to know about which files will come back clean.

The Basic Workflow, Step by Step

The whole thing is a handful of clicks, but walking it once makes the choices visible. **Open the document translation area** of the web app or desktop app — it sits alongside the text box, usually a clearly marked upload zone. **Drop or select your file. Pick the target language** the same way you would for text. If you've set up a glossary for this language pair (Chapter 7) or you want a specific formality (Chapter 8), **set those before you translate**, because they apply to the whole document and re-running with different settings spends another credit. DeepL processes the file — seconds for a short document, longer for a big one — and offers the **translated file for download** in the same format you uploaded.

Two settings are worth a deliberate pause rather than a reflexive click. The first is **glossary and formality**, just mentioned: a fifty-slide deck translated in the wrong register, or with your product name rendered three different ways, is fifty slides of rework, and both are one-time settings that prevent it entirely. The second is **which version of the file you're uploading.** If you have both an editable source (the .docx or .pptx) and a PDF export of the same document, upload the editable source — it will come back dramatically cleaner, for reasons the PDF section below makes plain. People reach for the PDF out of habit because it's the version they were sent; reach for the source if you have it.

The Limits: Size and Quota

Before you rely on this for a big job, know the two ceilings, both of which scale with your plan and both of which are exactly the kind of figure that drifts — verify the current numbers on DeepL's own page before you count on them.

A per-month document count. Document translations are metered separately from text. The free tier allows only a small number per month — on the order of three as of mid-2026 — and paid tiers raise that allowance substantially as you climb. If files are your main use, this count, not the character budget, is usually the first wall you hit, and it is the most common reason to upgrade (Chapter 4).

A file-size cap. Each file must come in under a size limit — around 5 MB on the free tier as of mid-2026, rising on paid tiers. This is what rules out large image-heavy presentations and long PDFs on the free plan. If a file is over the cap, you will need a higher tier or you will need to split or slim the file first.

The text inside the document also counts against your character allowance, so a long document spends from both budgets at once. None of this is cause for alarm; it is cause for checking your plan's limits against the job before you start, rather than discovering them halfway through a deadline.

A practical note on the document count, because it shapes how you should *batch* your work. Since each upload spends one credit regardless of length (within the size cap), there's a real difference between translating five short related files and combining them into one before uploading. If you have a deadline and a thin monthly allowance, consolidating several short documents into a single file before translating spends one credit instead of five — at the cost of having to split them apart again afterward. Conversely, don't re-translate the same file three times trying out different settings on the free tier; each attempt is a credit gone. Get the glossary and formality right before the first run. The metering rewards planning and punishes trial-and-error, which is the opposite of how the text box behaves, and that difference is worth internalizing before a deadline forces the lesson.

Slimming a File Under the Cap

When a file is over the size limit, you have two honest options: upgrade, or shrink the file. Shrinking is often easy and worth knowing. The bulk of an oversized office file is almost always **images**, not text, so the fastest win is compressing them — both Word and PowerPoint have a built-in "compress pictures" function that can take a presentation from well over the cap to comfortably under it without you noticing the quality drop on screen. A second move for a long PDF is to **split it into sections** and translate each separately, then reassemble; this also spends multiple document credits, so weigh it against simply upgrading for a one-off. And for a document that is mostly text with a few heavy embedded objects, **removing or temporarily stripping the heaviest images** before translation, then restoring them in the returned file, gets you under the cap while leaving the layout intact. None of these is elegant, but all of them beat being stuck, and the picture-compression trick in particular solves the size problem more often than people expect.

What Survives, and What Doesn't

The honest version, because "formatting preserved" is true but not absolute, and knowing the edges saves you a surprise.

What survives well is the structural backbone: headings and styles, paragraph and list structure, most tables, images and their placement, the slide layout of a presentation, the page structure of a clean document. For a well-built Word file or PowerPoint, the returned document usually looks like the original with the language swapped, and that is the experience most of the time.

What strains is anything where the *length* of the translated text fights the *space* it has to live in. When translation makes text longer — and it often does — tight layouts feel it: a line that fit on one row now wraps to two, a text box sized exactly to its English content overflows when the German runs longer, a slide that was visually balanced tips. The translation is correct; the container just wasn't built to flex. This is most visible in design-tight presentations and least visible in flowing prose documents that reflow naturally.

It's worth being concrete about *how much* longer text gets, because it explains where the strain shows up. Translating English into German or into the Romance languages commonly adds a noticeable fraction to the character count — German is the famous offender — while translating *into* English from those languages often shrinks the text. The direction matters: a deck designed in English and translated to German is where boxes overflow; the same deck translated from German to English usually has room to spare. If you're building a document that you know will be translated into a longer language, the kindest thing you can do for your future self is to leave slack in the layout — don't size text boxes to the exact pixel of the English, and don't pack slides to the edge. Designing with translation headroom is a localizer's habit that saves a great deal of cleanup later, and it costs nothing at design time.

Where it gets genuinely harder is the PDF. A clean, text-based PDF translates well. But PDFs are a finished, frozen format — some are essentially images of text, some have complex multi-column or graphical layouts, and reconstructing those faithfully in another language is the hardest case in document translation. Expect more variability with PDFs than with Word or PowerPoint, and expect that a scanned-image PDF will fare worse than a born-digital one. When a document exists in an editable source format, translating that source rather than a PDF of it almost always gives a cleaner result.

The distinction between a "born-digital" PDF and a "scanned" one is worth being able to make yourself, because it predicts the outcome. The quick test: open the PDF and try to select a sentence with your cursor. If the text highlights cleanly as text, it's born-digital and will translate reasonably. If your cursor selects a whole block as if it were a picture, or selects nothing, it's an image of text — a scan or an export that flattened the words into pixels — and DeepL has to recognize the characters before it can translate them, which is where quality and layout both suffer. For an image PDF that matters, the better path is almost always to get the original editable file from whoever made it, or to accept that the result will be a usable draft rather than a finished document. Knowing which kind of PDF you're holding tells you in advance how much review the result will need.

A Worked Example: The Multi-Slide Deck

Put the pieces together on the deck from the chapter's opening, because the document case rewards a concrete walk-through more than the text case does. You have a forty-slide sales deck in English, you need it in German for a Munich pitch on Friday, and the design is tight — branded, balanced, several slides with text sized exactly to its boxes.

Before uploading, you do two things. You **set the formality to formal**, because it's a client pitch (Chapter 8), and you **activate your product glossary** so the feature names come out the way your German materials already use them (Chapter 7). You check the file size; it's a hair over the cap because of the embedded product photos, so you run PowerPoint's compress-pictures function and it drops comfortably under. You upload, wait under a minute, and download the German deck.

Now the part people skip: the **visual scan.** You don't read forty slides of German for meaning if you don't read German — you look at them as a reader would. On three slides the German has overflowed its text box; on one a title has wrapped to a second line and collided with a graphic; on another a two-column comparison has gone lopsided because one side's text grew more than the other's. None of these is a translation error — the German is correct — they're length-versus-space problems, exactly the strain this chapter warned about. The fixes take ten minutes: nudge two font sizes down a point, let one title break differently, rebalance the columns. Then you send it to a German-speaking colleague for a final read on the language itself, because it's client-facing and the polish is part of the pitch.

That's the realistic shape of a document job: the translation is the fast part and the layout review is the part that determines whether the result looks professional. Budget for both. The afternoon DeepL saved you was real, but it bought you a deck that needs ten minutes of tidying, not zero — and ten minutes of tidying is a spectacular trade against rebuilding the thing by hand.

The Review Pass

A translated document needs the same critical reading as translated text (Chapter 5) — fluent errors hide just as well in a file as in a paste box — plus one extra layer the document form adds: **you have to look at it, not just read it.**

So the review pass for a document is two passes in one. **Read for meaning**, as always, paying attention to the load-bearing sentences, the negations, the numbers and names, and anything where nuance carries the message. And **scan for layout**, opening the returned file and looking at it as a reader would: Did any text overflow its box or table cell? Did a heading wrap awkwardly? Did a slide's balance break under longer strings? Did anything in a PDF land out of place? The fixes are usually small and mechanical — resize a box, nudge a font, let a line break differently — and far faster than rebuilding the document from scratch, which is the alternative DeepL spared you. But they are not automatic, and skipping the visual scan is how a perfectly translated deck still arrives looking broken.

There are a few document-specific things worth checking that have no equivalent in the text box. **Headers, footers, and page numbers** sometimes carry text that you forget is text — a running document title, a confidentiality notice — and you want to confirm it translated and didn't break the pagination. **Embedded charts and diagrams** may contain text that lives inside the graphic rather than in the document's text layer; depending on how the chart was built, that text may not have translated at all, and you'll need to handle it separately. **Tables** can shift when cell contents change length, pushing a column off the page or wrapping a header into an unreadable stack. And **automatic table-of-contents or cross-reference fields** may need refreshing in Word after translation, because the underlying text changed but the generated field didn't update on its own. None of these is common enough to dread, but all of them are the kind of thing that produces an embarrassing artifact in an otherwise clean document, and all of them are caught by a genuine look at the file rather than a skim of the prose.

For a low-stakes internal document, this pass can be a thirty-second glance. For a client-facing deck, a published report, or anything where the polish is part of the message, it deserves real attention, and a native speaker's eye on both the language and the layout is worth having before it goes out.

When to Reach for It

Document translation is the right tool whenever the *format* is part of what you need to preserve — a contract that must stay a properly structured contract, a deck that must stay a usable deck, a report whose layout carries meaning. For loose text where format doesn't matter, the plain text translator (Chapter 5) is simpler and spends only your character budget, not a document credit. The dividing line is whether you need the words or the whole artifact.

There's a sensible middle path people forget exists. If a document is mostly there but has one stubborn section — a complex table, an image-heavy page, a chart full of embedded text — you don't have to choose between perfect document translation and none. Translate the bulk as a document, then handle the awkward fragment as text and place it back by hand. Likewise, if you only need the *content* of a file and don't care about its layout at all — you're reading a foreign report to extract a few facts, not republishing it — copying the text into the text box is faster, cheaper on your quota, and gives you the alternatives and inline editing the document flow doesn't. Match the tool to whether you're consuming the document or reproducing it.

Used within its limits and followed by an honest review pass, document translation is the feature that turns DeepL from a convenience into a genuine time-saver — the afternoon-into-a-coffee-break difference. Get the file under the caps, mind your monthly count, read it for meaning and look at it for layout, and most of the time you will have something you can send. What it does not yet guarantee is that the *terms* inside that document — your product names, your brand language, the words you insist be translated your way — come out consistent every single time. That is what glossaries are for.

Chapter 7: Glossaries

Translate a product's documentation into Spanish across a dozen files, over several weeks, by several people, and you can end up with one flagship feature called four different things. Each rendering is individually defensible — the feature name is a common English word, and Spanish offers several reasonable translations of it — but collectively they are a mess, and a reader moving through the docs meets what looks like four distinct features that are in fact one. The fix is not better translators or more careful review. It is a glossary: a single instruction, set once, that tells DeepL exactly how that term should be translated, every time, in every file, for everyone. After that the name comes out the same way without anyone thinking about it. That is what a glossary buys you — consistency that holds automatically, so you stop fixing the same thing over and over.

This chapter is about that feature: what a glossary is, how to build and use one, and where it earns its place. It is one of the controls that separates DeepL from a casual translator, and for anyone doing real, repeated work in another language, it is among the most valuable.

What a Glossary Is

A glossary is a list of your own translation rules. Each entry says: when this term appears in the source language, translate it as *this* in the target language — not whatever DeepL would otherwise choose. You build it per language pair (English-to-German is a different glossary from English-to-Spanish), you fill it with the terms that matter to you, and from then on DeepL honors your choices automatically whenever you translate with that glossary active.

The key word is *automatically*. Without a glossary, keeping a term consistent means catching it and fixing it by hand every single time it appears — across paragraphs, across documents, across the months and the people doing the work. That is exactly the labor that fails, because it depends on everyone remembering the same decision forever. A glossary moves the decision out of everyone's head and into the tool. You make the call once; DeepL enforces it from then on.

It helps to be precise about what a glossary is *not*, because the name invites two wrong mental models. It is not a dictionary — it doesn't add vocabulary DeepL lacks, since DeepL already knows the language fully. And it is not a style guide — it doesn't capture tone, voice, or sentence preferences, only term-for-term substitutions. A glossary is narrower and sharper than either: it is a set of overrides for specific words and phrases where you have a settled preference that differs from DeepL's reasonable default. Everything outside those specific terms is translated exactly as it would be without the glossary. Understanding that boundary keeps you from expecting a glossary to fix problems it was never built to fix, and points you toward the right tool — formality settings, the alternatives, editing — for the problems it can't.

What Belongs in a Glossary

Not everything needs an entry — a glossary full of ordinary words would just fight DeepL's good judgment for no gain. The terms that belong are the ones where DeepL's default, however reasonable, isn't the one you specifically want. In practice, four kinds.

Product names, feature names, and brand language. The example that bit the software company. If your product or its features have names, you almost certainly want them rendered one consistent way — sometimes translated, sometimes deliberately left in the original language — and a glossary is how you pin that down across everything you produce.

Industry and technical terms with a house translation. Many fields have terms where several translations are valid but your organization, or your client, has settled on one. A glossary records that settlement so every document speaks the same dialect of your field rather than improvising per file.

Names and proper nouns you want handled a specific way — company names, place names, the names of people or programs — especially where you want them left untranslated or transliterated a particular way rather than rendered however the model guesses.

Terms DeepL gets predictably wrong for your context. Every now and then a word that means one thing generally means something specific in your domain, and DeepL, reasonably, picks the general meaning. A glossary entry is the clean way to correct a recurring miss without editing every output.

The discipline is to add entries where consistency or correctness genuinely matters and leave the rest to DeepL, whose ordinary translation is the thing you're paying for. A lean, deliberate glossary serves you better than a bloated one.

It's worth making the cases vivid, because the abstract categories blur together until you see them at work. Consider a financial-services firm translating into German. The English word "security" is a perfect glossary candidate: in everyday German it lands as something like safety, but in this firm's context it means a tradable financial instrument, a completely different word. Left to its default, DeepL will reasonably pick the everyday meaning, and every document will quietly mistranslate the firm's core vocabulary. One glossary entry fixes it forever. Or consider a consumer-electronics brand whose product is called "Pulse." They don't want it translated at all — "Pulse" is the name, in every language — but a translator will sometimes render it as the local word for a heartbeat. A glossary entry pinning "Pulse" to "Pulse" keeps the brand intact. Or a medical-device company whose materials use "indication" in its precise regulatory sense, not the loose everyday one. In each case the term is ordinary enough that DeepL's default is *defensible* and *wrong for this user* — which is exactly the signature of a term that belongs in a glossary.

The mirror-image discipline is knowing what *not* to add, and the temptation is real once you start. Don't add common words that DeepL already translates correctly just because you noticed them; you'll only constrain the model's grammar for no benefit. Don't add a term whose right translation genuinely depends on context — a word that should bend with its sentence — because a glossary can't make that judgment and will force one rigid form everywhere (more on this rigidity below). And don't add an entry to fix a one-time error you're unlikely to meet again; that's what inline editing is for. The glossary is for recurring, settled, term-level decisions. Anything that's a one-off, a judgment call, or a matter of tone belongs somewhere else.

Building and Using a Glossary

Building one is plain. In the web app you create a glossary for a specific language pair and add entries as source-term-and-its-translation pairs, either typing them in directly or importing a list you've prepared. You can maintain several glossaries — a different one per client, per project, or per language pair — and pick which is active for a given translation. Once a glossary is on, it applies to both text translation and document translation, so the terms stay consistent whether you're translating a paste box or a whole file.

The directionality is a detail worth dwelling on, because it trips people. A glossary entry maps a *source* term to a *target* term in one direction. An English-to-German glossary tells DeepL how to render English "security" in German; it does not automatically work the other way, German-to-English. If you translate in both directions — sending German documents to English and English documents to German — you may need a glossary for each direction, and the entries are not simply mirror images, because the term that needs pinning down going one way is often not the one that needs it coming back. Set this up deliberately rather than assuming one glossary covers both directions, or you'll find your terms locked down in one direction and wandering in the other.

A few practices that keep glossaries useful rather than burdensome. **Start small and grow from real misses** — don't try to anticipate every term up front; add entries as you notice DeepL rendering something the wrong way for you, and the glossary builds itself into exactly what you need. **Keep separate glossaries for separate contexts** when their preferred terms genuinely differ, rather than one sprawling list that mixes a casual client's voice with a formal one's. And **remember a glossary is a blunt instrument**: it forces your translation of a term regardless of surrounding grammar, so an entry that works perfectly in one sentence shape may read slightly stiff in another. For most terms — names, products, fixed jargon — this is exactly what you want. For a word that needs to bend grammatically with its sentence, a glossary entry can be too rigid, and you're better leaving it to DeepL's judgment.

That rigidity deserves a concrete illustration, because it's the one real downside of glossaries and the one that surprises people. Suppose you pin an English term to a specific German noun. German nouns change form with case and number — the word takes different endings depending on its grammatical role in the sentence. A glossary entry that forces one fixed form will be correct when the sentence happens to want that form and slightly off when the sentence wants another, producing a small grammatical stumble even though the *term* is the one you chose. For a product name like "Pulse," which doesn't inflect, this never happens. For an ordinary noun pressed into glossary service, it can. The lesson isn't to avoid glossaries; it's to reserve them for terms that are stable in form — names, fixed jargon, untranslatables — and to think twice before pinning a word that needs to flex with its grammar. When in doubt, watch a few real translations of the term in different sentences before committing it to the glossary.

A maintenance habit that pays off: **review the glossary when the thing it describes changes.** Products get renamed, house style gets revised, a client decides their feature should be translated after all rather than kept in English. A glossary is only as good as its currency, and a stale entry quietly enforces an old decision long after everyone has moved on. Tie a glossary review to whatever moment your terminology actually changes — a product launch, a brand refresh, a new client style guide — rather than letting it ossify. The whole value of the glossary is that it removes the term from everyone's attention, which is also exactly why an outdated entry can persist invisibly for months.

How many glossaries and how many entries you can keep **scales with your plan** — the free tier offers only a taste, and the paid tiers raise the capacity as you climb (Chapter 4). For anyone whose work turns on consistent terminology, glossary capacity is a real reason to choose a higher tier, and one of the cleaner ways a paid plan pays for itself.

A Worked Example: Building a Glossary From Scratch

Walk the software company's fix end to end, because the process is more instructive than the principle. They're translating product documentation from English to Spanish and they have the four-names-for-one-feature problem.

They start not by brainstorming every possible term but by **pulling the terms that have already caused trouble.** A quick pass through the existing translations surfaces the flagship feature name rendered four ways, the product name occasionally translated when it shouldn't be, and two technical terms where different writers chose different Spanish words. That's six entries — a real glossary, built from real misses, not a speculative list of a hundred guesses.

For each, they make the actual decision the glossary exists to encode. The flagship feature: they choose one Spanish rendering and commit to it. The product name: they pin it to itself, untranslated. The two technical terms: they pick the house translation and record it. Six decisions, made once, by the right people, and written down where the tool will honor them.

They **create the English-to-Spanish glossary**, enter the six pairs, and activate it. From the next translation onward, those six terms come out their way automatically — in the text box and in document translation alike, for everyone on the team who uses the shared glossary. Then they **let it grow.** Over the following weeks, as writers notice DeepL rendering some other recurring term inconsistently, they add it. Within a couple of months the glossary holds perhaps twenty entries — the exact twenty that matter to this product, in this language, for this team — and the four-names problem never recurs.

Notice the shape: small start, grown from real evidence, decisions made deliberately, capacity left to expand. That's the pattern that produces a glossary people actually trust, as opposed to the sprawling speculative list that fights DeepL and gets abandoned.

Where Glossaries Help Most

The value of a glossary scales with two things: how often the same terms recur, and how many people or documents are involved. That points to where it matters most.

For solo, one-off translations, a glossary is usually overkill — you can catch and fix a stray term by hand in a single short document faster than you can build the entry. The exception is when even your one document is long enough that a key term appears many times; then a single entry beats many manual fixes.

For repeated work in the same domain — translating a steady stream of material in your field, where the same vocabulary comes up again and again — a glossary starts paying off quickly, because each entry saves you a fix on every future document, not just this one.

For teams and organizations, a glossary stops being a convenience and becomes infrastructure. It is the mechanism that makes many people's translations agree with each other — the only practical way to guarantee that your product is called the same thing in Spanish no matter who translated which file, which is the exact failure that started this chapter. Shared, team-level glossaries are a core reason businesses choose DeepL's professional plans, and Part V returns to them in that context.

For localization and brand-consistent content, where the words *are* the product and a wandering term reads as carelessness, a glossary is not optional. It is how the voice stays the voice across every language you ship.

There's an ownership question that the team case forces and the solo case never raises: **who decides what goes in the glossary?** When a glossary is one person's, the answer is obvious. When it's shared infrastructure, an unowned glossary drifts — people add conflicting entries, terms get pinned by whoever happened to notice them, and the consistency the glossary was meant to guarantee quietly erodes from the inside. The teams that get lasting value from glossaries treat them like any other shared asset: someone owns the canonical list, changes go through that person or a light review, and the glossary reflects deliberate terminology decisions rather than the accumulated reflexes of everyone who ever touched it. This is a small amount of process, and it's the difference between a glossary that holds the line for years and one that becomes its own source of inconsistency. Pair it with the directionality and currency habits above and you have a glossary that does what the software company needed: makes the right decision, once, and keeps making it.

The through-line is that a glossary converts a decision into a default. You decide, once, how your terms should travel between languages, and DeepL carries that decision through every translation without being reminded. Consistency stops being a thing you police and becomes a thing the tool simply does. A glossary pins individual words; the next control reaches past any single term to the register the whole translation speaks in, formal or familiar — the province of style and tone.

Chapter 8: Style, Formality, and Tone Controls

I sent a German business contact a message once that DeepL translated perfectly — and that landed wrong. The grammar was flawless, the meaning exact. The problem was that DeepL had rendered it in the familiar register, addressing a senior person I'd never met with the German equivalent of casual "you," the *du* you'd use with a friend or a child. In English there is one "you" and the choice doesn't exist. In German it is a real social signal, and using the wrong one with a new business contact reads somewhere between overfamiliar and faintly disrespectful. The translation was correct. The register was a small social mistake. I learned to set the formality dial before I hit translate, and never made that particular error again. That dial — and the broader idea of matching a translation's register to its situation — is what this chapter is about.

It is a feature English speakers in particular tend to overlook, precisely because their own language barely has the distinction. But in much of the world, *how* formally you say something is as much a part of the message as what you say, and DeepL gives you control over it.

Why Register Matters More Than English Speakers Expect

English flattened its formality distinctions centuries ago. We have one "you," we lean on tone and word choice rather than grammar to signal respect, and we can often get away with the same phrasing whether we're writing to a friend or a minister. That is not how most languages work.

Many languages — German, French, Spanish, Italian, Japanese, and a great many others — build formality into their grammar. They have distinct words for "you" depending on your relationship to the person, distinct verb forms, distinct levels of politeness baked into the structure of the sentence. Choosing the wrong level is not a stylistic preference; it is a social fact the reader registers immediately. Too formal and you sound stiff, cold, or oddly distant with someone you should be warm to. Too informal and you sound presumptuous, careless, or disrespectful with someone you owe deference. The words can be perfect and the register still wrong, and the register is what the reader *feels*.

A short tour of how different languages mark this makes the stakes concrete, because the distinction isn't the same shape everywhere. **German** has the clean two-way split that bit me: *Sie* for the formal, *du* for the familiar, with everything downstream — verb forms, pronouns — following from the choice. **French** mirrors it with *vous* and *tu*, and the French even have a verb, *tutoyer*, for the act of switching someone to the familiar form, which tells you how socially loaded the move is. **Spanish** layers a regional dimension on top: *usted* is the formal across the board, but the familiar form varies between *tú* and *vos* depending on the country, and the plural formal *ustedes* behaves differently in Spain than in Latin America. **Japanese** goes furthest of all — politeness there is not a single dial but a whole grammatical system, *keigo*, with multiple registers encoding not just formality but the relative social standing of speaker, listener, and the people being spoken about. The point of the tour is not to teach these systems but to show that "formality" is a different and sometimes far richer thing in each language, which is exactly why no translator can pick the right level on its own and why the control matters more the further you get from English.

This is the gap a translator has to fill, and it's a gap it cannot always fill correctly on its own, because the right register depends on context the text doesn't contain — who you are, who you're addressing, and the relationship between you. DeepL can't know that your German correspondent is a senior stranger rather than an old friend. So it gives you the control to tell it.

The Formality Control

DeepL's **formality setting** lets you ask for a translation in a more formal or a more informal register, and for the languages that have the distinction, it changes the translation meaningfully — selecting the polite or the familiar forms, the deferential or the casual phrasing, throughout the text. You set it before translating, and DeepL renders the whole passage at the register you chose rather than guessing.

A few things to know about it. It applies to **text and document translation alike**, so you can set the register for a whole file, not just a snippet. It is **available for the languages where formality is a grammatical reality** — the European and other languages that actually mark the distinction — and it simply has nothing to do for a language like English that doesn't, which is exactly why English speakers forget the control exists. And it is the kind of thing best set

up front rather than fixed afterward, because changing register often touches many words across the text, not one; asking DeepL for the right register from the start is cleaner than translating in the wrong one and editing your way back.

What actually changes when you flip the dial is worth picturing, because "more formal" is vague until you see it. Set German to formal and the casual *du* becomes the respectful *Sie*, the verbs take their corresponding forms, and the phrasing leans toward the constructions a professional letter would use. Set it to informal and the whole thing relaxes in the other direction. The change is not cosmetic — it ripples through pronouns, verb endings, and often word choice across every sentence that addresses the reader. This is precisely why fixing register after the fact is so painful: it isn't one word to swap but a property of the entire text, and trying to edit your way from one register to the other by hand means catching every dependent form without missing one. Far easier to ask DeepL for the right register and let it render consistently from the start.

A practical detail that saves frustration: where DeepL exposes the setting can differ by surface. In the web app it's a visible control near the language selector; in the API it's a parameter you pass with the request (Chapter 21); in some integrations it may be set once in preferences rather than per translation. And the option only appears, or only does anything, for target languages that mark formality — so if you don't see it or it seems inert, check whether your target language is one that grammaticalizes the distinction before assuming something's broken. As with the other volatile specifics in this book, the exact placement of the control is the kind of thing that shifts with interface updates; if it's not where you expect, check the current docs.

The practical habit is simple: whenever you translate *to* a language that marks formality, pause and ask which register the situation calls for, and set the dial accordingly. A business email to a stranger: formal. A message to a friend: informal. A customer-service reply: usually formal, leaning warm. The cost of asking the question is two seconds. The cost of not asking it is the mistake I made.

A Field Guide to Choosing the Register

Since the dial only helps if you choose well, here is the judgment in concrete cases, because "it depends" is true but useless on its own.

First contact with anyone in a professional setting: formal. When you don't yet have a relationship, formality is the safe default — it can read as a touch stiff, but stiff is recoverable where presumptuous is not. The senior stranger, the prospective client, the official: formal, every time, until the relationship tells you otherwise.

Established peers and colleagues you know: follow their lead. In many workplaces and cultures, peers move to the familiar form once they know each other, and matching that is part of fitting in. If your counterpart has been writing to you in the familiar register, mirroring it is correct; continuing to be formal can itself read as cold or distancing. The signal is in their messages — read which register *they* use and generally match it.

Customer-facing communication: usually formal, deliberately warm. A support reply, a marketing email, a notice to users typically wants the respectful register, but warmth matters as much as formality here — you want to sound respectful without sounding bureaucratic. Formal handles the grammar; word choice and the alternatives (Chapter 5) handle the warmth on top.

Anything to a friend, or genuinely casual content: informal. A message to someone you'd address casually in person, social copy with a deliberately relaxed voice, internal banter — the familiar register is right, and forcing formality here reads as oddly distant or robotic.

When you genuinely don't know: formal-but-warm. This is the catch-all the next section returns to, and it's the right default whenever the relationship is unclear and the stakes are real. It rarely offends; over-familiarity sometimes does.

The meta-skill under all of these is *reading the relationship before choosing the register*, which is a thing only you can do because only you know who's on the other end. The dial executes your decision faithfully; making the decision is the part that stays yours.

Matching the Translation to the Context

Formality is the sharpest of the register controls, but the broader skill is matching the whole translation to its situation, and that takes a little judgment beyond flipping one switch.

Think about who reads it. The same content goes to different people in different registers — a notice to executives and the same notice to the general public are not phrased identically in a formal language. Decide who the reader is before you decide how to address them.

Think about the kind of document. A contract, a marketing headline, an internal memo, and a friendly message live at different points on the formal-to-casual range, and the register should match the genre as much as the reader. DeepL's formality control handles the grammatical part of this; the rest — word choice, warmth, directness — you tune through the alternative phrasings (Chapter 5) and through editing.

Think about the culture, not just the language. Norms for how formal to be differ between cultures even where the language is shared, and they differ from your own. What reads as appropriately friendly in American business English can read as too casual elsewhere; what reads as properly respectful in one culture can read as cold in another. When the stakes are real and you don't know the local norm, the formal-but-warm choice is usually the safer default, and a native speaker's read is worth having.

There's a layer beneath formality that the dial doesn't touch and that's worth naming, because it's where the most experienced users do their finest work: **tone within a register.** Two messages can both be formal and still feel completely different — one brisk and businesslike, one warm and personal; one apologetic, one confident. The formality setting picks the grammatical register; everything inside that register — how warm, how direct, how soft or firm — comes from word choice, and that's where the alternative phrasings earn their place. Translate at the right formality, then walk the load-bearing phrases and use the alternatives to dial the *warmth* up or down within the register you've chosen. A formal customer apology and a formal contract clause are both formal, but you want the apology warm and the clause neutral, and that distinction lives in the words, not the dial. This is the difference between a translation that's grammatically correct for the situation and one that actually *sounds* the way you'd want to sound — and it's available to a non-native speaker entirely through the alternatives, which is a genuinely remarkable thing.

These judgments are where translation stops being mechanical and starts being communication. DeepL gives you the controls — the formality dial, the alternatives, the glossary for locked terms — but the decision about what register the moment calls for is yours, because only you know the relationship and the situation the text is traveling into.

When the Tool Can't Decide and You Can't Either

There's an honest edge case worth naming: sometimes the right register genuinely isn't knowable from the text, and you're not sure either. A message addressed to a mixed audience — some of whom you'd be formal with and some casual — has no single correct register. A piece of marketing copy going to a culture whose norms you don't know forces a choice you're not equipped to make. A first message to someone whose seniority you can't determine leaves you guessing.

The honest moves in these cases are few and worth knowing. **Default to formal-but-warm**, as above, because it's the choice least likely to give offense across the widest range of readers. **Split the audience if you can** — if a notice is going to two very different groups, two versions in two registers will land better than one compromise that fits neither. And **ask a native speaker when the stakes justify it**, because register intuition is exactly the kind of thing a fluent local feels instantly and a checklist never captures. What you should *not* do is assume the absence of a clear answer means the choice doesn't matter; in a formality-marking language it always matters, and a non-decision is just an unexamined decision that defaults to whatever DeepL guessed. Make the call deliberately, even when the call is "I'm not sure, so I'll play it safe."

Where the Controls Live in Your Workflow

In practice, register handling folds into the loop from Chapter 5 with one added step. Before you translate to a formality-marking language, set the dial. After you translate, read not just for accuracy but for tone — does this *sound* the way I'd want to sound to this reader? — and use the alternative phrasings to adjust where it doesn't. For repeated work, lean on glossaries for the terms and the formality setting for the register, so the consistent parts stay consistent and you spend your attention on what genuinely varies.

For high-stakes or culturally sensitive material — the message that has to land exactly right with someone whose goodwill matters — treat the register with the same seriousness as the meaning, because to the reader they are not separate. A perfectly accurate translation in the wrong register is still a miss, just a quieter one than a mistranslation, and often a more damaging one socially. This is also a place where, when it truly matters, a native speaker's review earns its keep (Chapter 24): they will feel a register that's slightly off in a way no checklist catches.

The lesson under all of it is the one the *du* taught me: in most of the world, formality is not decoration on top of meaning — it *is* part of the meaning. DeepL is one of the few translators that hands you the control over it, and using that control deliberately is a large part of making your translations land the way you intend rather than merely say what you meant. How much DeepL can do here, though, depends on the language — which formality even exists to mark, which pairs it renders most naturally — and that unevenness is real enough to be worth a chapter of its own.

Chapter 9: Languages and Their Quirks

DeepL's quality is not one flat thing. Run an English business document into German and you get back something you'd happily send without a second glance — natural, idiomatic, exactly the register you asked for, the quality that made DeepL's name. Run a similar document into a far less commonly translated language, one DeepL supports but doesn't specialize in, and you get something usable but visibly thinner: more literal, occasionally stiff, the kind of output that gets the meaning across but would make a native speaker raise an eyebrow. Same tool, same care, two very different experiences — and the difference is not in how you used it. It is the language pair. Understanding *that* — that DeepL's quality varies, sometimes a lot, by which languages you're moving between — is what this chapter exists to give you.

This is the honest chapter. DeepL is excellent, and I've spent eight chapters saying so for good reason. But "excellent" is an average, and averages hide the spread. Using DeepL well over many languages means knowing where it's strongest, where it's thinner, and how to adjust your trust accordingly.

Why Quality Varies by Language

The unevenness isn't a flaw so much as a fact of how machine translation gets good. A translation model learns from data — vast quantities of text that humans have already translated between two languages. Where that data is abundant and high-quality, the model has a great deal to learn from and gets very good. Where it's scarcer, or where the two languages are structurally far apart, the model has less to work with and a harder problem to solve, and the output, while still useful, doesn't reach the same polish.

Two distinct forces are at work here, and separating them sharpens the whole picture. The first is **data abundance** — how much high-quality human translation exists between the two languages for the model to learn from. English-German is one of the most heavily translated pairs in human history; the model has an ocean to learn from. A pair involving a language with few speakers and little published translation gives the model a puddle. The second force is **structural distance** — how differently the two languages are built. Two related European languages share word order, grammar, and a great deal of vocabulary, so mapping between them is a comparatively gentle problem. English and a language with entirely different word order, a different writing system, and grammatical features English lacks is a genuinely harder mapping, even when data is plentiful. The two forces interact: a pair that is both data-rich and structurally close (English-German) is where DeepL is at its absolute best; a pair that is both data-poor and structurally distant is where it's thinnest; and the interesting middle is the well-resourced but structurally distant pairs — Japanese, Korean, Arabic — where DeepL has invested heavily against a hard problem and lands at "strong but reward a closer look." Holding both forces in mind explains not just *that* quality varies but *why* a particular pair sits where it does.

DeepL grew up as a European company focused first on European languages, and that history shows in its strengths. The languages it has invested in most, and had the most and best data for, are the ones where its quality is genuinely class-leading. The further you get from that core, the more variable the experience — not bad, often very good, but not uniformly the near-human quality the strongest pairs deliver. Holding that in mind keeps your expectations calibrated and your scrutiny in the right places.

Where DeepL Is Strongest

DeepL's home turf, and where it most clearly earns its reputation, is **European language pairs.** Translating between English and German, French, Spanish, Italian, Dutch, Polish, Portuguese, and the other major European languages is where DeepL shines hardest — natural phrasing, idiom that lands, register handled well, the formality controls (Chapter 8) fully meaningful, the alternative phrasings rich (Chapter 5). For these pairs, DeepL's first-pass output is send-ready across an enormous range of ordinary work, and the quality advantage over general translators that built its following is most visible here. This is the core, and if your work lives in these languages, you are using DeepL exactly where it's best.

It's worth noting that even within this strong core there's a gradient. The pairs DeepL built its name on — English with German and French above all — are the most polished, the product of the longest investment and the deepest data. The other major European languages are excellent and for most work indistinguishable in quality, but the very richest alternative phrasings and the surest handling of subtle idiom tend to track the pairs DeepL has worked on longest. This is a fine distinction, not a warning — all of these pairs are genuinely strong — but if you ever find yourself comparing, say, an English-German translation against an English-Polish one of equally tricky content, the difference you sense is real and explicable. The core is strong throughout; it's simply strongest at its oldest center.

DeepL also handles several **major Asian and Middle-Eastern languages well** — Japanese, Korean, and Chinese among the Asian, and Arabic and Hebrew among the Middle-Eastern. These are harder problems than the European pairs, structurally more distant from English and from each other, and the quality, while strong, can be a touch more variable than the European core. They are well-supported and genuinely useful, and DeepL has invested real effort in them; just expect that a Japanese or Arabic translation may reward a closer review pass than a German one of the same content.

The structural distance in these pairs shows up in specific, predictable places, and knowing where helps you target your review. **Japanese** leaves a great deal to context — subjects and even objects are routinely dropped and must be reconstructed — so the place to check a Japanese translation is whether the model rebuilt the right who-did-what, and whether the level of politeness (the *keigo* register from Chapter 8) matches the situation. **Chinese** carries no inflection and minimal explicit grammar of the kind English leans on, so number, tense, and definiteness are inferred rather than marked; check that singular/plural and past/present landed as you meant. **Arabic and Hebrew** are written right-to-left and are richly inflected, which means both the language *and* the layout (Chapter 6, for documents) reward a closer look — text direction in a translated file is its own thing to verify. None of this makes these pairs unreliable; it makes their characteristic error spots knowable, which is exactly what lets you review them efficiently rather than anxiously.

Where DeepL Is Thinner

DeepL supports well over a hundred languages, and that breadth is real and valuable — but support and specialization are not the same thing. The further down the list of less commonly translated languages you go, the more you should expect the experience of that second document: usable output, meaning conveyed, but more literal, occasionally stiffer, and more likely to need a human pass before it's truly ready. Feature support can thin out too — the formality control only exists where the language grammatically marks formality, and the richness of alternative phrasings tends to track how well-resourced the pair is.

What "thinner" actually looks like, in practice, is worth describing so you can recognize it rather than just brace for it. The output tends to be **more literal** — closer to a word-by-word mapping, less willing to restructure a sentence into the shape the target language would naturally use. It can be **stiffer in register**, defaulting to a neutral middle even where the situation wants warmth or deference, partly because the formality machinery may not exist for that language. Idiom comes out **flatter** — rendered for meaning where a strong pair would have found an idiomatic equivalent. And the alternatives, when you click for them, are **fewer and less varied**, because the model has a narrower sense of the legitimate range. None of these is gibberish; all of them are the signature of a model working a harder problem with less to learn from. Spotting the signature tells you immediately that you're off DeepL's strong turf and should raise your scrutiny accordingly.

This is not a reason to avoid those languages in DeepL; for many of them it's still a fine choice and may be as good as anything else available. It is a reason to *adjust your trust*. The same first-pass output that you'd send without thinking in German deserves a careful read, and ideally a native speaker's eye, in a language DeepL supports but doesn't specialize in. The tool is honest enough to be useful across a hundred-plus languages; you have to be honest with yourself about which ones it's merely good at versus the ones it's great at.

Quirks Worth Knowing

A few specific things that come up across languages, worth carrying in your head.

Formality only exists where the grammar marks it. The control from Chapter 8 does meaningful work in German, French, Spanish, Japanese, and the many languages that grammaticalize politeness, and nothing at all in languages like English that don't. Don't expect a formality dial to change a translation into a language that has no formal-informal distinction to change.

Gender forces choices English leaves open. Many languages mark grammatical gender on nouns, adjectives, and past-tense verbs where English stays neutral. Translate "I'm grateful" into a language where the adjective carries the speaker's gender, and the model has to pick one — and it may pick wrong if nothing in the text signals who's speaking. The same bites with professions and roles. When you're translating into a gendered language and the gender of a person matters, check that the translation didn't silently assign the wrong one, because the sentence will read perfectly while being about the wrong gender.

Structurally distant pairs are harder than structurally close ones. Translating between two related European languages is an easier problem than translating between English and a language with completely different grammar, word order, and writing system. Even where DeepL is strong, the structurally distant pairs are where the subtle errors are likeliest to hide, so weight your review there.

Writing system and direction add their own layer. Languages in non-Latin scripts, and especially right-to-left languages, carry concerns beyond the words — text direction, how the script renders in a document, how it interacts with surrounding Latin-script content. For text this is mostly invisible; for documents (Chapter 6) it's another thing to look at in the review pass.

Idiom, humor, and wordplay travel worst, everywhere. This is true in every language pair, but it bites hardest in the weaker ones. A pun, a cultural reference, or a turn of phrase that depends on the source language's particular shape is the most likely thing to come out flat or wrong, in any pair, and the most likely to need a human who can re-create the effect rather than translate the words.

Less common pairs may route through a stronger one. For some less-resourced combinations, the cleanest result can come from going through a language DeepL is strong in rather than direct — though for most users, most of the time, the direct translation is fine and worth trying first.

A Worked Comparison: The Same Email, Three Pairs

Make the spread concrete by imagining one English message — a warm, slightly idiomatic customer-service apology with a deadline and a product name in it — translated into three targets, and what the review pass looks like for each.

Into German. The output comes back natural and idiomatic, the apology genuinely warm, the formality dial doing real work to keep it respectful, the product name held in place by your glossary. Your review is light: confirm the deadline survived, glance at the load-bearing apology phrase against the alternatives to make sure the warmth landed, send. This is the send-ready experience DeepL is famous for, and it's earned here.

Into Japanese. The output is strong but asks more of you. The politeness level needs checking — did it land at the deference a customer apology wants, or default to something flatter? The idiomatic touch in the English apology may have come out more literal. A subject the English stated explicitly may have been handled differently in a language that drops them. The deadline and product name are fine, but the *tone* of the apology deserves a deliberate read, and for a customer-facing message you'd want a Japanese-speaking colleague's eye before it goes. Still fast, still useful — but not the glance-and-send of the German.

Into a less commonly translated language. The meaning is all there and the message is usable, but the warmth has flattened toward neutral, the idiom has gone literal, and the register may be doing less than you'd like because the formality machinery is thinner here. You treat this output as a strong draft, not a finished message: it's gotten you most of the way, saved real work, and conveyed the facts — but for anything customer-facing you plan on a human pass, because the difference between "conveys the meaning" and "lands the way you intended" is exactly the difference that thins out down the language list.

One email, one tool, three genuinely different review obligations. The work didn't change; the pair did. That's the whole chapter in a single example, and it's why the next section reduces to a rule about calibrating trust to the pair rather than to DeepL in general.

Practical Guidance: Trust, but Verify by Language

The whole chapter reduces to a single working rule: **calibrate your trust to the pair, not to DeepL in general.** A few concrete defaults follow from that.

For **English and the major European languages**, trust the first pass for ordinary low-stakes work and reserve scrutiny for the high-stakes sentences (Chapter 5). This is where DeepL most deserves the confidence its reputation suggests.

For the **well-supported Asian and Middle-Eastern languages**, trust it for the gist and for everyday use, but give important content a more deliberate review than you would the European pairs, and lean on a native speaker for anything that matters.

For the **less commonly translated languages**, treat every output as a strong draft rather than a finished product. Use it to get the meaning, to get most of the way there, to save real work — but plan on a human pass before anything important goes out, and don't assume the send-ready quality you've seen in German.

There's a corollary that catches people who work across many pairs: **don't let your trust in one pair set your trust in another.** The fluency of your daily English-German work quietly trains you to expect that quality everywhere, and that expectation is exactly the trap — it's most dangerous precisely when you switch to a pair you use rarely and read poorly, where you have neither the calibrated trust nor the language skill to catch a slip. Treat each new pair as its own thing with its own review obligation, and re-set your scrutiny deliberately when you change targets rather than carrying yesterday's confidence into today's unfamiliar language.

And across **all** languages, remember the constant from Chapter 5: the errors are fluent, so they hide best exactly where you're least able to catch them — in the languages you don't read. That is the deepest reason to know which pairs are DeepL's strong ones. In a language you command, you'll catch a slip yourself. In one you don't, your only protection is knowing whether you're on DeepL's strong turf or its thin turf, and reviewing accordingly.

None of this diminishes what DeepL is. It is, across its strong pairs, the best mainstream translator most people will use, and across its full range a genuinely capable tool for a hundred-plus languages. But the unevenness is real, and using the tool well means meeting it honestly: superb where it specializes, good where it doesn't, and worth a closer look precisely where you can least tell the difference yourself. Keep that map in mind, and you'll trust DeepL where it has earned trust and verify where it hasn't — which is the whole of using any translator wisely.

Part III: DeepL Write

Audience: everyone who writes — especially in a language that isn't their first.

"Translate converts someone else's words. Write turns the same quality on your own — and makes a fluent draft of an imperfect one."

— A working principle

Chapter 10: What Write Does

A colleague of mine once sent me a paragraph she had agonized over for twenty minutes — a short note declining a speaking invitation — and asked, half-joking, whether I could "make it sound less like I was apologizing for existing." She was a native English speaker, a sharp writer, and the words on the page were all correct. There was nothing to translate. The grammar held, the spelling was fine, and yet the thing sat there limp and over-soft, three hedges deep, saying *no* in a way that somehow sounded like a plea. What she needed was not a translator. She needed an editor who could take her own words and make them carry the weight she meant them to carry. That is what DeepL Write is, and it is the part of DeepL that the most people misunderstand the fastest.

This chapter introduces Write as a thing genuinely distinct from Translate, and getting the distinction right is the whole foundation of Part III. Once you see clearly what Write is *for*, the chapters that follow — fixing and rephrasing, tuning tone for the workplace, drafting fluently in a second language — all fall into place. Get the distinction wrong, and you will keep reaching for the wrong tool.

The One Distinction That Matters

Translate takes someone's words in one language and gives you the equivalent in another. Write takes *your own* words and makes them better in the same language. That is the line, and it is sharper than it sounds.

When you use Translate, you are converting meaning across a boundary — German in, English out. You are not the author of the source; you are moving someone's meaning, or your own, from a language you have into a language you need. When you use Write, there is no boundary to cross. You wrote the text. It is already in the language it is going out in. What you want is not conversion but *improvement* — the same thought, said better, with the errors gone and the phrasing cleaned up and the tone where you want it. Write never hands you a different language. It hands you a better version of what you already said.

This is why "DeepL Write" confuses people who know DeepL only as a translator. They assume Write must be the writing-side of translation — maybe a place to draft text that will then be translated. It is not. Write is a self-contained tool for one job: improving prose you produced yourself, in the language you produced it in. You can use Write and never translate a word. Plenty of people do exactly that — native speakers polishing their own native-language writing, the way my colleague did with her decline note.

The cleanest way to feel the distinction is to run the same source text through both products and watch what comes back. Take a single English sentence that is clumsy: "The reason for the delay was due to the fact that the vendor did not send us the parts on time." Put that into Translate with English chosen as the target — and you get the same sentence back, untouched, because Translate's job is to cross a language boundary and there is no boundary to cross. Put the identical sentence into Write, and you get something like "The delay happened because the vendor sent the parts late." Same language, same meaning, fewer words, better rhythm. That is the entire difference in one experiment: Translate moves text *between* languages; Write moves text *toward better* within one. If your text is already in the language it needs to be in, Translate has nothing to offer you and Write has everything.

What Write Actually Fixes and Improves

Hold the philosophy and look at the work. Write operates on text you paste or type, and it does roughly three kinds of things to it.

It corrects the mechanical errors. Grammar, spelling, punctuation — the layer of writing where there is a right answer and a wrong one. A misplaced comma, a subject-verb disagreement, a misspelled word, a run-on that should be two sentences: Write catches these and proposes the fix. This is the least glamorous part of the tool and the part most writing aids stop at, but Write treats it as the floor, not the ceiling.

It rephrases for clarity and flow. This is where Write earns its keep and where it goes past a spell-checker. Give it a sentence that is technically correct but clumsy — overlong, tangled, repetitive, buried in qualifiers — and it offers a cleaner way to say the same thing. Often it offers several, so you are choosing among alternatives rather than accepting a single verdict. The clumsy-but-correct sentence is exactly the case my colleague was stuck on, and it is the case no spell-checker can help with, because nothing is technically *wrong*. It just is not good. Write works on the gap between correct and good — the same gap Chapter 1 said the whole company is built around, now turned on your own prose.

It adjusts tone and style. Write gives you controls to shift the register of your text — more formal, more casual, more concise, more business-appropriate. The same paragraph can be made tighter, or warmed up, or stiffened into something fit for a regulator. This is the lever my colleague actually needed: not a fix to any error, but a shift from apologetic to assured. Chapter 12 is devoted to using these tone controls well in professional settings; for now, the point is simply that they exist and that they are a core part of what Write does, not an afterthought.

It helps to see the three working on one piece of text in sequence, because in real use you rarely want only one of them. Imagine you have typed, fast and unedited, a note to a coworker: "hey so i was thinking maybe we could possibly move the meeting because i dont think everyone is going to be able to make it at 3 which is kind of a problem honestly." The mechanical pass fixes the missing apostrophe in *don't*, the missing capital, the absent punctuation. The clarity pass collapses the throat-clearing — "i was thinking maybe we could possibly" is four hedges doing the work of one — into "Can we move the meeting?" The tone pass, if you push it toward something more polished, gives you a version fit to send to someone senior: "Could we move the 3 p.m. meeting? I don't think everyone can make that time." Same intent, three different layers of improvement, and you chose how far up the ladder to climb. That is the shape of a typical Write session: not a single correction but a short, deliberate refinement, with you deciding where to stop.

A Worked Walkthrough

Because the abstraction can stay abstract, walk through one realistic pass start to finish. Say you have drafted a two-sentence reply to a customer who has complained that a shipment arrived damaged: "We are sorry that your order was not in good condition when it arrived to you and we will be sending a replacement that should be there within the week hopefully." Read it as the customer. It is apologetic enough, but it is shapeless — "in good condition," "arrived to you," and that limp "hopefully" at the end undercut the one thing the customer wants, which is confidence that the problem is handled.

You paste it into Write. The first thing you notice is that it does not silently overwrite your text. It shows you the original and the suggested version together, with the changes marked, so you can see exactly what moved. The mechanical layer is small here — "arrived to you" becomes "arrived" — but the rephrasing layer does the real work: "We're sorry your order arrived damaged. We're shipping a replacement that should reach you within the week." Tighter, cleaner, and the apology now reads as competent rather than nervous.

But you stop on that word *hopefully*, which Write has dropped entirely. Sometimes you want the hedge. If you genuinely cannot promise a week, deleting "hopefully" turns a soft estimate into a firm commitment you may not be able to keep — and that is your call, not the tool's. So you might accept the rest of the rephrasing and restore a softer time frame yourself: "should reach you within about a week." This is the rhythm of using Write well. It proposes; you read the proposal against what you actually meant and what you can actually promise; you take what is right and override what is not. The walkthrough's real lesson is in that last move — the moment you overrode a fluent suggestion because you knew something the tool did not. Chapter 11 builds an entire discipline around exactly that moment.

Why It Sounds Like a Person

The reason any of this matters — the reason Write is worth a chapter rather than a shrug — is the same reason DeepL Translate earned its following. The suggestions sound natural. They sound like something a fluent, careful human writer would actually produce, not like the stilted output of a grammar tool optimizing for rules.

This is not a small thing. There is a long history of writing aids that technically improve your text while quietly draining the life out of it — flattening your voice into generic correctness, swapping a vivid word for a safe one, turning a sentence with a pulse into a sentence with none. Write is built on the same language quality DeepL is known for, the quality that made its translations read like a person wrote them, and that foundation shows in the suggestions. They tend to preserve what is good about your sentence while fixing what is not. You are far less likely to feel that the tool has sanded your writing down into anonymous mush.

It is worth being clear about how Write differs from the general-purpose AI assistants the rest of this series covers, because people increasingly ask one of those to "fix my email" and assume Write is the same thing. There is a real difference in posture. A general chatbot, asked to improve a paragraph, tends to *rewrite* it — to produce its own version of what it thinks you should have said, sometimes adding sentences you never wrote, changing your claims, restructuring your argument, and quietly substituting its judgment for yours. Write is narrower and, for this job, more respectful of your authorship: it stays close to your sentence, fixes and refines what is there, and does not go off and invent new content. When you want a careful editor who keeps your meaning and your structure, that narrowness is the feature. When you actually want a collaborator to brainstorm or draft from scratch, Write is the wrong tool and a general assistant is the right one. Knowing which job you have is half of choosing the right tool.

The Honest Flip Side

I want to be honest about the flip side, because it runs through all of Part III and the whole book. *Sounds natural* is a property of the prose, not a guarantee about the meaning. A suggestion can read beautifully and still have nudged your point a half-step off from what you intended — and because it reads so well, that drift is easy to miss. Chapter 11 makes the discipline explicit. For now, hold both halves: the naturalness is real and it is the reason to use Write, and the naturalness is also exactly why you have to read the result rather than trust it.

There is also a more ordinary failure worth naming up front, because it catches people who expect the tool to do more than it does. Write will not catch an error of *fact*. If you write "the contract renews on March 1st" and you meant April, Write will happily polish the sentence into elegant, fluent, confidently wrong prose. It operates on the language, not on the truth of the claim. It does not know your contract, your numbers, your dates, or your intentions; it knows English (or German, or French). So the layer of checking that only you can do — is this *true*, is this what I meant, did I get the date right — is still entirely yours. Write makes your writing read better. It cannot make your writing correct about the world.

Who Write Is For

Three groups get the most out of Write, in my experience, and they overlap.

Anyone writing in a second language. This is the standout use, important enough that Chapter 13 is given entirely to it. You write imperfect text in a language that is not your first, and Write makes it read like a fluent native produced it — without translating, so you keep your own meaning and your own authorship. It is the closest thing I know to a fluent colleague reading over your shoulder, and for non-native writers it is genuinely transformative.

Native speakers who want their writing to land better. My colleague was not struggling with English. She was struggling with the same thing every writer struggles with: getting the words to do what she meant. Write helps with the clumsy sentence, the email that reads colder than intended, the paragraph that is correct and lifeless. You do not have to be writing in a foreign language to need an editor.

Professionals whose words carry weight. When the email represents you, the proposal represents your company, and the message will be read by someone whose opinion matters, the difference between correct and good is not cosmetic — it is the difference between being taken seriously and not. For people doing enough of this writing to feel that difference, Write pays off the same way Translate's quality does: in the cleanup it saves and the impression it protects.

To make those groups concrete, think of three people on the same afternoon. A Spanish product manager writes a release announcement in English and runs it through Write so it reads as if a native colleague drafted it — that is the second-language case. A native-English support lead writes a delicate email to an angry account and uses Write to take the defensiveness out of it without going mushy — that is the native-speaker case. And a partner at a small firm pastes in the executive summary of a proposal worth real money, because at that level the difference between *correct* and *polished* shows up directly in whether the client takes the firm seriously — that is the high-stakes professional case. None of the three is translating anything. All three are using the same tool for the same underlying job: making prose they wrote read the way they wish they had written it the first time.

Where you reach Write — web, the apps, browser integration — and what the different tiers unlock by way of volume and features is the subject of Chapter 4; the controls are the same wherever you use it. What matters here is the shape of the tool, not the doorway.

Where Write Fits in How You Actually Write

Knowing what Write is leaves one practical question open: *when*, in the act of writing, do you reach for it? Get the timing wrong and you blunt the tool. There are two common mistakes, and they pull in opposite directions.

The first mistake is reaching for Write too early — opening it on a blank page and expecting it to help you produce a first draft. It will not, because there is nothing yet to improve. Write operates on text that exists; it is an editor, and an editor needs a draft. If you sit waiting for Write to give you words, you have mistaken it for a different kind of tool entirely. The honest move is to get your thought down first, however roughly — bad sentences, wrong words, tangled order, all of it — and only then hand it over. The rough draft is your job. Write's job starts after.

The second mistake is reaching for Write too late, or too totally — pasting in a finished piece you are emotionally done with and accepting whatever comes back so you can be rid of it. That is when meaning drift slips through, because your attention has already left the building. The sweet spot is in between: you have a complete-enough draft that says roughly what you mean, you are still engaged with it, and you use Write to close the gap between *roughly right* and *right*. Engaged refinement, not exhausted rubber-stamping.

In practice the rhythm that works for most people is draft, refine, decide, in that order and with clear seams between the steps. Draft in your own voice without worrying about polish. Refine a section at a time with Write, looking at each suggestion. Decide what to keep, override, or write yourself. Keeping the steps separate matters more than it sounds, because the failure mode is letting them blur — drafting and refining at once, so you never commit a real thought before sanding it, or refining and deciding at once, so you accept changes you have not actually read. The discipline that makes Write pay off is mostly a discipline of *sequence*: do your thinking first, let the tool improve the result, and keep the final judgment as a distinct, deliberate act rather than a reflex.

One more practical note, because it changes how the tool feels day to day: Write rewards being used in small, frequent doses far more than in rare, large ones. A sentence here, a paragraph there, a quick pass on the email before you hit send — used that way it becomes a near-invisible part of writing, the editorial pass you would otherwise skip because you are busy. Saved up for the occasional big document, it is still useful, but you lose the compounding benefit of having every routine message land a little better than it would have. The leverage is in the routine, not the exceptional.

The Through-Line

One idea to carry forward: Write is not Translate pointed at a different language. It is DeepL's language quality pointed inward, at your own prose, in your own language, to do the one job an editor does — take what you said and help you say it better. It fixes the mechanical errors, rephrases the clumsy-but-correct sentences, and shifts the tone to fit the moment, and it does all of it in suggestions that sound like a person rather than a rulebook.

And it suggests. The text is still yours, it still goes out under your name, and the final say is still a decision you make rather than one the tool makes for you. The rest of Part III is about making that decision well — which is, in the end, the same skill as writing well in the first place.

Chapter 11: Fixing and Rephrasing

I once watched a perfectly good sentence get worse in the act of being improved. I had written, in a draft, that a feature "saves you the cleanup a worse tool would demand." Clear enough. I ran it through Write looking to tighten it, accepted a smooth-sounding suggestion without really reading it, and ended up with a sentence saying the feature "demands cleanup a worse tool would save you" — the exact opposite of what I meant, in prose that read better than my original. Nothing was misspelled. The grammar was flawless. The rhythm was nicer. And the meaning had flipped a hundred and eighty degrees while I was admiring the flow. That small disaster taught me the one discipline this chapter is built around, and I will get to it. But first, the two things Write is doing when you hand it a sentence — because understanding the two moves is what lets you catch it when one of them goes wrong.

The Two Core Moves

Everything Write does to a piece of text is one of two operations, and they are different enough that it helps to think of them separately.

The first move is correcting errors. This is the deterministic half — the part of writing with right answers. A comma in the wrong place, a *their* that should be a *there*, a verb that does not agree with its subject, a sentence missing a word. Write finds these and proposes the correction, and for the most part you can accept its mechanical fixes with a quick glance, because there is genuinely a correct answer and Write generally knows it. This is the layer a competent spell-and-grammar checker also handles. It is table stakes, and Write does it well, but it is not where the tool distinguishes itself.

The second move is rephrasing. This is the part with no single right answer — the part that makes Write more than a checker. You give it a sentence that is correct but not good, and it offers a different way to say the same thought: shorter, clearer, less tangled, better-flowing. There is no objective "correct" rephrasing the way there is a correct comma. There are only better and worse versions, and judgment about which is which. This is also, not coincidentally, where the meaning can drift — because changing *how* something is said always risks changing *what* is said, and rephrasing is nothing but changing how something is said.

Keeping these two moves distinct in your head is practically useful. When Write fixes a comma, the stakes are low and a glance suffices. When Write rephrases a whole sentence, the stakes are higher and the sentence deserves a real read, because that is the move that flipped my meaning while I wasn't looking.

There is a third category that lives between the two and is worth recognizing as its own thing: the *word-level swap*. Write will often replace a single word with one it judges more natural or precise — "utilize" becomes "use," "in order to" becomes "to," "a large number of" becomes "many." These feel mechanical, almost like corrections, but they are quietly rephrasings, and they carry the same small risk. Most of the time the swap is pure improvement. But a word you chose deliberately — a technical term, a word with a precise legal or emotional shade — can get traded for a casual near-synonym that reads more smoothly and means slightly less. The swap is the easiest change to wave through and one of the more common places a precise meaning leaks out. Treat single-word substitutions as small rephrasings, not as corrections, and the leak mostly stops.

Using the Alternatives

Write usually does not hand you one rephrasing and call it settled. It offers alternatives — several ways to recast a sentence or a phrase — and this is a feature worth using deliberately rather than skimming past.

The value of alternatives is that they put you back in the author's chair. Instead of a tool issuing a verdict you accept or reject, you get a small menu of options, and choosing among them is an act of writing, not just editing. One version might be crisper but lose a nuance you care about. Another might keep the nuance but run a little long. A third might be the obvious winner. The point is that *you* are weighing them against what you actually meant — which is exactly the judgment a tool cannot make for you, because only you know what you meant.

I have found the alternatives most useful on the sentences I am genuinely stuck on. When I know a sentence is clumsy but cannot see my way to a better one, seeing three options breaks the logjam — sometimes I pick one outright, and sometimes none of them is quite right but one of them shows me the move I needed to make myself. Treat the suggestions as a brainstorm you are curating, not a correction you are approving. The best outcome is often a version Write didn't offer, prompted by a version it did.

A practical refinement: the size of the chunk you hand Write changes the quality of the alternatives you get back. Select a single tangled sentence, and the alternatives stay tightly focused on that sentence — usually what you want when you are unsticking one clumsy line. Select a whole paragraph, and Write reworks the flow between sentences too, which is powerful when the paragraph as a whole is lumpy but riskier, because more is moving at once and more can drift. My habit is to work sentence by sentence on anything that matters and to reserve paragraph-level rephrasing for early drafts where I am still finding the shape and the meaning is not yet load-bearing. The smaller the selection, the easier it is to check, and checkability is the whole game once the stakes rise.

Here is a small worked example of the alternatives doing their best work. I was stuck on: "We should probably consider the possibility of maybe revisiting the pricing at some point." Hedge upon hedge. Write offered three: "We should revisit the pricing." (clean, but firmer than I felt). "We may want to revisit the pricing eventually." (kept the softness, lost the dither). "It might be worth revisiting the pricing." (neutral, noncommittal). None was exactly right — but seeing the second one showed me the move: keep one hedge, kill the other three. I wrote my own final version, "We should probably revisit the pricing before long," which Write never offered. That is alternatives used well: not a menu you order from, but a set of prompts that show you the shape of your own better sentence.

The Discipline: Watch the Meaning Didn't Shift

Now the lesson from my flipped sentence, stated plainly, because it is the single most important habit in this chapter and the one most likely to be skipped.

A rephrasing can sound better and mean something different. This is not a rare malfunction; it is a structural property of the task. Rephrasing changes words, word order, and emphasis, and any of those changes can move the meaning — subtly, into a near-synonym that carries a slightly different shade, or grossly, into the opposite of what you wrote, as in my case. And here is the trap: the better the suggestion sounds, the less scrutiny it invites. Fluent, confident prose reads as trustworthy whether or not it is faithful to your intent. The smooth version that flipped my sentence got *less* of my attention than a clunky one would have, precisely because it sounded good. Naturalness is a kind of camouflage.

So the discipline is simple and non-negotiable: after you accept a rephrasing, read it against your original intent, not against your original wording. The question is not "does this read well?" — it almost always does — but "does this still say what I meant?" Those are different questions, and the gap between them is where meaning drift lives.

There is a concrete trick that makes the second read actually work, because "read it again" is easy advice to nod at and skip. The trick is to read the *new* sentence cold, without looking at the original, and ask yourself what it claims — then check that claim against what you intended. Reading the two versions side by side fools you: your eye slides over the new one and your brain supplies the meaning from the old one, so the two appear to agree even when they don't. That is exactly how I missed my flipped sentence — I read it next to my original and my mind filled in the meaning I expected. Read the new version alone, force it to tell you what it says on its own terms, and the drift surfaces. It is a thirty-second habit and it is the difference between catching the flip and shipping it.

A few specific things I have learned to watch for:

Negation and direction. The highest-stakes drift, because it is the most consequential and the easiest to miss. A rephrasing that quietly drops or inverts a *not*, a *without*, a *fails to*, or flips who is doing what to whom, can reverse your meaning entirely while reading perfectly. My flipped sentence was exactly this. When a rephrasing touches a negative or a direction of action, read it twice. The "who does what to whom" version is sneaky in the passive-to-active conversions Write loves: "the report was reviewed by legal" becoming "legal reviewed the report" is fine, but "the vendor was charged by us" becoming "we were charged by the vendor" reverses who paid whom, and both read smoothly.

Specificity and hedging. Watch whether a rephrasing has firmed up something you deliberately left soft, or softened something you meant firmly. "May increase" is not "increases." "Often" is not "always." "Should arrive Tuesday" is not "will arrive Tuesday." Rephrasing for concision loves to shave off the qualifier that was carrying your caution, and the result reads cleaner while claiming more than you meant to claim. In anything that could be held against you later — a commitment, an estimate, a guarantee — the missing hedge is not a style improvement, it is a liability.

Numbers, names, and dates. Rephrasing is mostly safe around hard data, but not always — Write can fold "between fifteen and twenty" into "around twenty," or smooth "the third of March" into "early March," and the looser version reads fine while quietly losing the precision that mattered. Whenever a sentence carries a figure, a date, or a proper name, confirm it survived the rephrasing exactly. These are the cheapest things to check and the most expensive to get wrong.

Loaded and technical words. If your sentence turned on a precise term — a legal word, a technical term, a word you chose for its exact shade — check that the rephrasing kept it or replaced it with a true equivalent rather than a casual near-synonym. The natural-sounding swap is sometimes the slightly wrong one. "Terminate" and "cancel" are not interchangeable in a contract; "diagnosis" and "assessment" are not interchangeable in a medical note; "estimate" and "quote" are not interchangeable in a sales document.

Your voice. Less about correctness, more about ownership. If a rephrasing has scrubbed out the phrase that made the sentence sound like you, you are allowed to reject an objectively smoother version to keep your own register. The text goes out under your name; it should still sound like you wrote it.

Common Mistakes, and How to Avoid Them

A few patterns I have watched people fall into, and the fix for each.

Accepting everything in one click. Some interfaces make it easy to take all suggestions at once, and the temptation on a long document is enormous. The problem is that a bulk-accept turns off exactly the per-change reading the discipline depends on — you trade ten minutes of review for one click and a small chance of a buried meaning flip you will never notice until a reader does. On anything that matters, accept changes individually, even though it is slower. Reserve bulk-accept for low-stakes text where a stray drift costs nothing.

Running the same text through twice and losing the thread. Write's output is good enough that people sometimes re-run an already-refined paragraph for a second polish. Each pass drifts a little further from your original, and after two or three the text can be fluent, professional, and no longer quite yours or quite what you meant. Refine once, check it, stop. If you genuinely want a second pass, check against your *original* intent, not against the once-refined version, or the drift compounds invisibly.

Confusing "I would never have written this" with "this is wrong." Sometimes a suggestion is better than what you would have produced and also feels foreign because it is not your habit. That discomfort is not a reason to reject it — only the *meaning* is. Separate the two reactions. "This changes what I said" is a veto. "This isn't how I'd phrase it but it's accurate and good" is often worth accepting, and is part of how you learn to write better.

Editing for fluency in a language you can't fully judge. This is the second-language trap, and it is serious enough that Chapter 13 is built around it. If you cannot reliably tell whether the fluent version still means what you meant, you cannot enforce the meaning-drift discipline, and "it sounds great" becomes the only signal you have — which is exactly the signal that camouflages the error. Know when you are in that situation and raise your guard, or get a fluent human into the loop.

Calibrating the Review to the Stakes

If every accepted change demanded a careful second read, Write would be exhausting and you would stop using it. It does not, and you should not. The discipline is real but it is not uniform — the right amount of scrutiny scales with what the text will do in the world, and learning to triage is what keeps the habit sustainable.

At the low-stakes end sits the bulk of everyday writing: the quick internal message, the note to yourself, the casual reply where a slightly drifted meaning costs nothing because the reader will ask if anything is unclear and nothing is riding on the exact words. Here a glance is genuinely enough. Lean on the tool, accept freely, move on. Treating a grocery-list-grade message with contract-grade caution is not discipline; it is wasted effort, and it trains you to resent a tool that should feel light.

The middle band is where most working writing lives — the client email, the team update, the proposal section, the message that represents you to someone whose opinion matters. Here the second read earns its keep, especially on the rephrased sentences and the negations, but it is a read, not an audit. Thirty seconds reading the result against your intent, with extra attention on the specific traps from the last section, catches nearly everything that matters at this level.

The high-stakes end is narrow but it is where the cost of drift is worst: the contract clause, the regulatory filing, the public statement, the number in a financial document, the sentence that could be quoted back at you in a dispute. Here the posture changes in kind, not just degree. You read every accepted change individually and deliberately; you confirm every figure, name, and date survived untouched; you treat any rephrasing that touches a negation, an obligation, or a precise term as guilty until proven innocent; and for the genuinely consequential text you get a second human's eyes on it, because your own reading of your own writing is the least reliable check there is — you see what you meant, not what you wrote.

The skill, then, is not "always scrutinize" — it is recognizing which band a given piece of text falls into and matching your attention to it. Spend your vigilance where the stakes are, conserve it where they are not, and the discipline becomes something you can actually sustain for years rather than a counsel of perfection you abandon by Friday.

Why This Bites Harder Than It Looks

It would be easy to read all this as overcaution about a tool that is, most of the time, simply helpful — and it is most of the time simply helpful. Most of Write's suggestions are faithful, and the meaning survives the polish intact. The reason to hold the discipline anyway is the asymmetry of the failure. The cost of reading a rephrased sentence one extra time is a couple of seconds. The cost of sending out a sentence that says the reverse of what you meant — to a client, in a contract, in a message that represents you — can be large and is sometimes irreversible. Cheap insurance against an expensive mistake is a good trade, and that is exactly what the second read is.

This is the same posture Chapter 10 set up and the whole book returns to: Write suggests, you decide. The fixing half of the tool you can lean on with a light hand. The rephrasing half you lean on with your eyes open — using the alternatives as a genuine aid to writing, and reading every accepted change against what you actually meant before it goes anywhere. Do that, and Write makes your prose meaningfully better. Skip it, and Write will eventually, smoothly, confidently, help you say something you never meant to say.

Chapter 12: Styles and Tones for the Workplace

The most useful thing Write does at work is often not fixing an error. Picture a reply you've written to an unreasonable request — a reply that is, if you're honest, a little sharp. The facts are right. The *no* is right. What's wrong is the temperature: it would be satisfying to send and costly to have sent. A single shift toward "more diplomatic" gives you a version that says the same thing in a way that keeps the relationship intact. The content was never the problem. The tone was, and tone is exactly the lever this chapter is about.

Chapter 11 covered fixing and rephrasing — the work of making a sentence correct and clear. This chapter is about the layer above that: making your writing *fit*, matching its register to the audience and the moment. In professional contexts that fit is not a finishing touch. It is often the whole game, because at work the same accurate message can succeed or fail entirely on how it sounds.

The Controls You Have

Write gives you controls to shift the tone and style of your text, and for workplace writing three directions matter most.

More formal. Takes prose that is fine for a quick internal note and lifts it to the register a memo to leadership, a message to a regulator, or a note to a client you don't yet know well calls for. It firms up casual phrasing, removes the conversational shortcuts, and gives the text the weight that formal contexts expect. Useful when "fine for Slack" is not fine for the actual recipient.

More concise. Cuts the prose down — removes the throat-clearing, the redundancy, the qualifiers stacked three deep — and leaves a tighter version that respects the reader's time. This is the control I reach for most, because the default failure mode of professional writing is not being too blunt; it is being too long. A busy reader skims, and concise writing survives skimming.

More diplomatic. Softens the edges. This is the control for that sharp reply — it keeps the message while smoothing the delivery, finding the phrasing that says the hard thing without the hard tone. In a working life full of pushback, declines, corrections, and disagreement, the ability to be firm without being cold is worth a great deal, and this is where Write directly helps.

These are not separate machines; they are directions you can move your text, sometimes in combination — a note made both more formal and more concise, or more diplomatic without losing its firmness. The skill is not in operating the controls. It is in knowing which way a given piece of writing needs to move, which is a question about your reader, not about your text.

It is worth being honest that the directions can pull against each other, and the tension is where judgment lives. *More diplomatic* and *more concise* are natural enemies: diplomacy works by adding cushioning — the soft preamble, the acknowledgment, the gentle framing — and concision works by removing exactly that kind of material. Push a message hard toward concise and it can come out curt; push it hard toward diplomatic and it can come out padded and evasive. *More formal* and *more concise* can also conflict, because formality often means longer, more careful constructions. There is no setting that maximizes all three at once, and the moment you feel a rewrite has gone wrong it is usually because you asked for two directions that fight. The fix is to decide which one the situation needs *most* — for a tense client, diplomacy wins and you accept a few extra words; for a busy executive, concision wins and you accept a plainer tone — and let the other yield.

A Worked Example: One Message, Three Readers

Take a single piece of substance and watch how the right tone changes with the reader, because this is the muscle the controls are meant to support, not replace. The substance: a project is going to miss its deadline by a week because a dependency slipped, and you need to say so.

To a peer on your own team, the message can be plain and direct: "Heads up — we're going to slip about a week. The API work came in late and it cascaded. Nothing on fire, just wanted you to know." Direct, casual, no cushioning needed, because the relationship carries it.

To your manager, the same facts want a touch more structure and a little more reassurance that you have it handled: "Quick update: we're tracking about a week behind because the API dependency came in later than planned. I've adjusted the downstream tasks and the new target is the 14th. No other risks at this point — happy to walk through it if useful." Same slip, same cause, but now framed to answer the questions a manager will ask before they ask them.

To the client who is paying for the work and waiting on the launch, the register shifts again — warmer, more careful, leading with what you are doing rather than what went wrong: "I want to keep you fully in the loop on timing. A technical dependency took longer than expected, which moves our delivery to the 14th — about a week later than planned. We've already reworked the schedule around it and don't anticipate any further changes. I'm glad to hop on a call if you'd like to talk it through." Identical facts, third register.

The point of the example is what the tool can and cannot do here. Write can take your plain peer-message and push it toward the formality and warmth the client version needs; it can take your client-message and strip it down toward the peer version. What Write cannot do is *choose* which reader you are writing to or what they need to feel — that the manager needs reassurance about control, that the client needs to hear the recovery before the problem, that the peer needs nothing but the facts. You make those calls. The control moves the dial; you decide the setting.

Matching Tone to Audience

The reason tone controls matter is that there is no single "correct" tone — there is only tone appropriate to *this* reader in *this* situation. The same content genuinely should sound different depending on who is receiving it, and getting that match right is most of what professional communication skill actually is.

A status update to a peer can be direct and casual; the same update to a nervous client needs warmth and reassurance built in. A correction to a junior colleague should land gently; the same correction to a vendor who has missed three deadlines can afford to be firm. A pitch to an internal team can assume shared context; the same pitch to an outside executive has to earn its formality. The facts are constant across all of these. The tone is not, and a message in the wrong register fails no matter how accurate it is — too casual and you seem to not take the reader seriously, too stiff and you seem cold or evasive, too sharp and you damage a relationship you needed.

So the move is to decide who you are writing to and what they need to feel, and then use Write to push your draft in that direction. I find it helps to picture the specific person reading the first line. Will the client feel reassured or managed? Will the colleague feel corrected or attacked? Write can take you toward "warmer" or "firmer" or "more formal," but only you know which of those this particular reader requires — the tool moves the dial, you choose the setting.

A cross-cultural wrinkle is worth flagging, because workplace writing increasingly crosses borders and the "right" register is not the same everywhere. Directness that reads as efficient and respectful in one business culture can read as brusque or even rude in another; the elaborate politeness that is expected in some contexts reads as evasive or insincere in others. If you are writing to a German counterpart, a Japanese client, and an American colleague, the "appropriately professional" tone differs for each, and a tone control set to one global notion of "formal" will not capture that. Write tunes the register competently within a language, but it does not know the cultural expectations of your specific recipient. When you are writing across a culture you do not know well, that is exactly the moment to ask someone who does — and, if the message is also crossing a language, to remember that Translate's formality settings (Chapter 8) are a separate lever from Write's tone controls, aimed at a different part of the problem.

One honest caution about the controls themselves: a tone shift is a kind of rephrasing, and everything Chapter 11 said about meaning drift applies here too. When you push a message toward "more diplomatic," check that the diplomacy didn't dissolve your actual point — softened so far that the *no* turned into a *maybe*, or the firm deadline turned into a gentle suggestion. The most common failure of a diplomatic rewrite is not that it offends; it is that it goes mushy and stops saying the thing you needed to say. Read the softened version for whether your message survived the softening.

That failure has a recognizable shape, and once you can spot it you can fix it fast. A point that has been over-softened reads as if it could be answered with "okay, noted" and no action. The test is to ask: after reading this, does the recipient know exactly what I am asking them to do or accept? If "the invoice is sixty days overdue and payment is required by Friday" has become "we wanted to gently check in on the status of the outstanding balance when you have a moment," diplomacy has eaten the message. The fix is not to abandon diplomacy but to restore the spine: keep the warm framing and put the hard fact and the clear ask back in plain words. Firm and kind are not opposites; mushy and kind only look alike.

The Direction People Forget: Warming Up

The three directions above — formal, concise, diplomatic — all describe ways to *raise* or *constrain* a message. There is a fourth move that working writers underuse, which is warming a message *up*: making it sound more human, more personable, less like a transactional notice. It does not have a single labeled button the way the others do, but you reach it through the casual and personable directions, and it solves a problem the others cannot.

The problem is that efficient professional writing trends cold. When you are busy, you strip a message to its function — "Approved. Proceed." "Received, will review." "Not available that day." — and each one is perfectly clear and faintly chilling. Done repeatedly, to the same people, it accumulates into a reputation for being curt or hard to read, even when you feel nothing of the kind. The cost is relational and slow, which is why people miss it: no single terse message does damage, but a year of them does.

Warming a message up is the antidote, and it matters most exactly where the content is thinnest. The one-line approval becomes "Approved — nice work pulling this together, go ahead." The decline becomes "I can't make that day unfortunately, but I'd really like to find a time — does the following week work?" The substance is unchanged; what changed is that the reader now feels regarded rather than processed. For anyone who manages people, works with clients over the long term, or simply wants to be someone others find pleasant to deal with, deliberately warming the thin functional messages is among the higher-return uses of the tone controls — and the easiest to forget, because those messages feel too trivial to bother editing. They are precisely the ones worth the ten seconds.

The caution is the obvious mirror of the diplomatic one: warmth can tip into something that reads as fake, gushing, or unprofessional, and over-warmed business writing has its own cringe. The test is whether the warmth sounds like you on a good day or like a greeting card. Aim for the former; if the rewrite gives you the latter, dial it back toward plain and keep just enough warmth to take the chill off.

The Beat That Matters Most: It Owns Your Name

Here is the part of professional writing that no tone control can take off your plate, and it is the reason to read every shifted draft before it goes out.

The message goes out under your name, and the reader holds you accountable for how it lands. Nobody on the receiving end knows or cares that Write helped you tune it. They read the email, the memo, the proposal, and they form an impression of *you* — your competence, your judgment, your regard for them — from how it sounds. If the tone is wrong, that wrong impression attaches to you, not to the tool, and you do not get to add a footnote explaining what you really meant. The tone *is* the message, as far as the reader is concerned.

This is why the review discipline bites especially hard on tone. With a factual error, at least there is a fact to check. With tone, the only instrument is your own judgment reading the draft as its actual recipient — and that reading is something only you can do, because only you know the relationship, the history, and the stakes. Write can offer you a more diplomatic version. It cannot know that this particular client is touchy about exactly this subject, or that this colleague will read brevity as coldness, or that the formality you added will come across as a chill where you needed warmth. The tool tunes the register; you confirm the register is right.

There is a particular danger in the high-stakes message written in anger, because that is precisely where the tone controls feel most like a rescue and are most likely to be trusted too far. You write the furious reply, you push it toward "more diplomatic," it comes back civil and professional, and the relief of having a sendable version is so strong that you send it. Resist that. The diplomatic rewrite of an angry message often still carries the anger underneath the politeness — a coldness in the structure, a pointedness in the framing that the recipient feels even though no individual word is hostile. The genuinely safe move with an angry message is older than any software: push it diplomatic, then leave it, and read it again an hour later as the person who will receive it. The tool gives you a calmer surface. Time gives you the judgment to know whether the calm is real.

The practical habit is the one that has never failed me: before you send anything that carries weight, read it once more as the person receiving it, not as the person who wrote it. Authors read for what they meant. Recipients read for how it sounds. The gap between those two readings is where relationships get damaged, and closing it is a thirty-second job that the tool cannot do for you and that you cannot afford to skip.

Putting It Together

Used well, Write's tone controls are one of the most quietly valuable things in a working life, because they let you separate two problems that usually get tangled: *what to say* and *how to sound saying it*. You write the honest substance first — the real *no*, the real correction, the real pushback — and then you use the controls to dress it in the register the moment requires, firm or warm or formal or brief, without having to grind out the right tone by hand from a blank page.

What the controls don't do, and were never going to do, is make the judgment about your reader or take responsibility for the result. That stays with you, because the writing stays yours. Decide who you're writing to, push the draft toward what they need, check that the tone shift didn't hollow out your meaning, and read it one last time as the person who will receive it. Do that, and the message lands the way you intended — which, at work, is most of what landing at all requires.

Chapter 13: Writing in a Second Language

A German engineer I worked with wrote excellent English — clear, precise, technically flawless — and hated every email he sent in it. He could make himself understood without trouble. What he couldn't do was sound like *himself*: the dry wit that made him good company in German came out stiff in English, the easy warmth flattened into something formal and a little cold, and he knew it. "I sound like a manual," he told me once. He wasn't wrong about his English, which was genuinely good. He was right about the gap between *understood* and *fluent*, and that gap — invisible to most native speakers, painfully visible to the people living in it — is exactly what this chapter is about. It is also, I think, the single most valuable thing DeepL Write does.

The Standout Use

Here is the use that makes Write more than a polish tool. You write imperfect text in a language that is not your first — text that is roughly right, gets the meaning across, but carries the small tells of non-native writing: the slightly off preposition, the word order a native would never choose, the phrasing that is correct in the grammar book and wrong in the ear. You run it through Write. What comes back reads like a fluent native wrote it. The errors are gone, the phrasing is natural, the rhythm is right, and the text now sounds like it belongs in the language rather than visiting it.

For anyone who works across a language barrier on the *output* side — writing in English when it isn't their first language, or in German, or in any tongue they have learned but not lived in — this is genuinely transformative. It closes the gap my German colleague was stuck in: the gap between writing that is correct and writing that is fluent. Correct, he could manage. Fluent, he could not, not reliably, not without help. Write gave him fluent on demand, and it changed how he felt about every message he sent.

It helps to be concrete about what the "small tells" actually are, because naming them is the first step to noticing what Write fixes. There is the *preposition problem*: non-native writers reach for "discuss about the issue," "married with her," "depends of the weather," "good in math" — each one a single wrong word that no grammar rule quite forbids but every native ear catches. There is the *false friend*: the German speaker who writes "I become a coffee" because *bekommen* means "to get," or the Spanish speaker who is "embarrassed" when they mean pregnant. There is the *register mismatch*: vocabulary learned from textbooks comes out either too formal ("I would hereby like to inquire") or oddly casual for the moment. And there is the *word-order tell*: structures carried over from the first language — the verb arriving where a German would put it, the adjective trailing where a French speaker would leave it. None of these breaks comprehension. All of them quietly flag the writer as non-native, and all of them are exactly what Write smooths away. Watching which of these Write corrects in your own writing is the fastest map of where your second language is still leaking through.

Why This Is Not Translating

It is worth being precise about why this is different from translation, because the difference is the whole point and it is easy to blur.

When you translate, you write in the language you *have* — your native one — and the tool converts your meaning into the language you *need*. The thinking happens in your first language; the second language is something the machine produces from it. That works, and Chapter 5 is about doing it well. But it has a cost: the result is a translation of your native-language thought, and it can carry the shape of the original language, the structure you would never have chosen had you been writing in the target language directly.

Writing in a second language with Write is a different act. You write in the target language *yourself* — imperfectly, with mistakes, with the wrong word here and the clumsy construction there — and Write refines that into fluent prose. You did the thinking in the target language. You chose the framing, the emphasis, the words, the structure, in English or German or whatever it was. Write only fixed the execution. The meaning is yours in a way a translation's meaning never quite is, because you authored it in the language it goes out in, rather than authoring it elsewhere and having it carried over.

This matters for ownership and it matters for quality. The text reads as more authentically *of* the language because it was conceived in that language. And it stays more genuinely yours, because you made every meaningful choice and the tool only cleaned up the surface. You kept authorship. Write polished. That is the trade, and it is a better trade than translation for the writing you want to feel like your own.

There is also a practical reason to prefer drafting-then-refining over translating, and it shows up most clearly in idiom and tone. When you write directly in the target language, you naturally reach for the constructions you have absorbed by reading and hearing it — and even when you reach imperfectly, you are reaching in the right direction, toward how the language actually moves. Write nudges that imperfect reach the rest of the way home. When you write in your first language and translate, you reach for *your* idioms, and the tool must render them into something equivalent — which it does well, but the result is a faithful carrying-over of a foreign idiom rather than a native one chosen from the start. For a contract, faithful carrying-over is exactly right. For an email you want to feel warm and natural to its reader, the version you authored directly and then refined usually lands better. The two methods are not competitors so much as tools for different jobs: translate when fidelity to a source matters most, draft-and-refine when sounding native matters most.

How to Use It Well

A few habits make this work in practice, drawn from watching people who do it daily.

Write the imperfect draft anyway. The instinct, when you are unsure of a language, is to keep it simple and safe — short sentences, basic words, nothing you might get wrong. Resist it. Write what you actually mean, in the full complexity you would attempt in your first language, even if you are sure parts of it are wrong. Write has far more to work with when you give it your real attempt than when you give it a timid, dumbed-down version. The richer your imperfect draft, the more fluent and complete the refined result. Reach past your comfort and let the tool catch you.

There is a real mechanism behind that advice, not just encouragement. When you give Write a thin, cautious sentence — "The meeting was good. We agreed. I will send the document." — it can only polish what is there, and what is there is flat, so the result is flat-but-correct. When you give it your genuine, ambitious, slightly broken attempt — "The meeting went really well, I had the feeling we are finally on one line about the direction, and I will send over the document until end of week so we can keep the momentum" — Write has actual intent and texture to work with, and it can produce "The meeting went really well — I felt we're finally aligned on direction. I'll send the document by the end of the week so we can keep up the momentum." ("On one line" and "until end of week" are classic carry-overs from German; Write fixed both.) The fluent version exists *because* you swung for it. Play it safe and you get safe, forgettable prose; reach, and you get prose that sounds like a capable native wrote it.

Read the refined version as a learner, not just a sender. When Write fixes your second-language text, the corrections are a free language lesson if you let them be. Notice what it changed — the preposition it swapped, the word order it fixed, the phrase it replaced — and over time you absorb the patterns. People who pay attention to Write's corrections get better at the language itself, not just better at this one email. The tool is a crutch you can also learn to walk without.

To turn that from a nice idea into actual learning, look for the *repeat* corrections. If Write keeps fixing the same preposition for you week after week — always changing your "discuss about" to "discuss," always swapping your "since two years" to "for two years" — that recurring fix is the single most valuable signal the tool gives you, because it is pointing straight at a stable gap in your knowledge. Most people fix the error in the document and move on. The ones who actually improve note the pattern, not just the instance, and the next time they catch themselves before they type it. Write will correct your "since two years" forever without complaint; the point is to need the correction less. A second-language writer who treats Write's recurring fixes as a curriculum can close real gaps in months that would otherwise persist for years.

Don't over-reach into registers you can't yet judge. Here is the limit, and it is real. Write can make your text sound fluent, but you may not be able to *tell* whether the fluent version says exactly what you meant — because judging fine shades of meaning in a second language is precisely the skill you are still building. A native speaker catches when a rephrasing has drifted; a learner may not. So the meaning-drift discipline from Chapter 11 is sharper here, not softer, and you have less ability to enforce it yourself. This bites hardest in the registers furthest from your daily use: humor, irony, deliberate understatement, and emotional nuance are the last things you master in a language, and exactly the places where a fluent-sounding rewrite can land somewhere you did not intend — a joke that reads as a slight, a polite softening that reads as sarcasm. When you are reaching for a tone you cannot yet hear well in the language, that is the moment to keep it plainer than you would in your first language, or to get a native ear.

What Fluency on Demand Actually Changes

It is worth dwelling on what my German engineer actually got from Write, because the real benefit is larger than "fewer errors" and it explains why people who adopt this become so attached to it. What he got back was *confidence* — and confidence changes behavior in ways that compound.

Before, the friction of writing in English shaped what he was willing to do. He kept his emails short, because longer meant more chances to sound wrong. He avoided writing to senior people in English when he could route around it. He stayed quiet on email threads where, in German, he would have weighed in, because composing the reply felt like a performance he might fail. None of this was about his actual competence; it was about the tax that writing in a second language levies on every act of communication, and the way that tax quietly narrows what a person attempts. Capable people make themselves smaller to avoid sounding less capable than they are.

Remove enough of that friction and the behavior opens back up. Once he trusted that his real thoughts would come out reading like a fluent colleague's, he wrote more, weighed in more, took on the client-facing writing he had been avoiding. The tool did not make him more competent — he was always competent — it stopped his second language from hiding his competence. That is the deeper transformation, and it is why this use earns the word *transformative* honestly rather than as marketing. For a non-native professional, the gap between *understood* and *fluent* is not cosmetic; it is the difference between being read as the capable person you are and being read as someone slightly less sharp than you are, every single time you write. Closing that gap changes how you are perceived, which changes the opportunities that come to you, which is a much bigger deal than a tidier email.

There is a discipline that keeps this benefit from curdling, though, and it connects to the cautions ahead: confidence is good, *over*-confidence in a language you have not mastered is exactly the trap. The same fluency that lets you write more also lets you write more in registers and stakes where you cannot fully verify the result. So the right version of the confidence Write gives you is not "I can now write anything in this language without help" — it is "I can now write far more without help, and I have a clear sense of the narrowing set of cases where I still need a fluent human." Confidence about your range and humility about its edges are not in tension; together they are exactly the judgment that makes a second-language writer effective rather than merely bold.

Honest Limits and the Keep-Your-Voice Caution

Two cautions, and they are the heart of using this well rather than naively.

You can't fully check what you can't fully read. When you refine native-language prose, you can vouch for the result — you know the language well enough to confirm the meaning survived. When you refine second-language prose, you partly can't. Write hands you fluent text, and fluent text reads as trustworthy, but if your command of the language isn't strong enough to catch a subtle shift in meaning, you are accepting on faith that the fluent version says what your clumsy version meant. For low-stakes messages, that faith is usually fine. For anything consequential — a contract clause, a sensitive negotiation, a message where a wrong shade of meaning carries real cost — you want a fluent human in the loop, the same DeepL-plus-a-human posture Chapter 1 named for high-stakes translation. Fluent-sounding is not the same as verified-correct, and in a second language you are less equipped to tell the difference.

There is a partial self-check worth knowing for the cases where no human is available. Write a sentence in your second language, refine it with Write, and then run the refined version through Translate *back into your first language* and read what it says. This is not foolproof — translation can paper over the very drift you are hunting for, and a faithful back-translation does not prove the forward version is natural — but it catches the gross errors, the flipped negations, the false friend that changed your meaning entirely. It is a smoke alarm, not a guarantee: useful for noticing that something is badly wrong, useless for certifying that everything is subtly right. For the genuinely high-stakes message, it does not replace the fluent human; for the everyday message you are slightly unsure of, it is a cheap and worthwhile sanity check.

Keep your voice, even as Write smooths the language. My German colleague's problem was that he sounded like a manual; the goal was to sound like *him*. But there is a version of "fluent" that is also generic — correct, natural, and utterly characterless, the same smooth English everyone's refined text turns into. Watch for that. The aim is not to erase that you are a non-native writer with your own way of putting things; it is to make your own way of putting things read fluently. When Write offers a version that is fluent but has scrubbed out whatever made the sentence sound like you, you are allowed to keep your version, or to push back toward it. A little of your own grain is not a defect to be polished away. It is the thing that makes the writing yours rather than the tool's, and the whole point of writing in a second language with Write — rather than having a machine translate for you — was to stay the author. Don't trade that authorship back for a fluency so smooth it could be anyone's.

The way to protect your voice in practice is to refine in small bites rather than handing Write a whole message and accepting the wholesale rewrite. Take a sentence, see the fluent version, and ask not only "is this correct?" but "does this still sound like a thing I would say?" The smaller the unit, the more of your own framing survives, because Write is fixing your construction rather than replacing your paragraph with its own. Writers who paste in an entire email and take the full rewrite get fluent text that reads like the platonic average of all business email; writers who go line by line get fluent text that still has their fingerprints on it. The grain you keep is deliberate, and keeping it is work — but it is the difference between writing fluently in a second language and disappearing into it.

Used with those cautions, Write does something I genuinely find a little remarkable: it lets people work in languages they have learned but not mastered, and sound like they belong there, while keeping their own meaning and their own voice. For the millions who write every day in a language that isn't their first, that is not a convenience. It is a door — into work, into relationships, into being taken as the fluent, capable person they actually are. Just walk through it as the author, not the passenger.

Part IV: DeepL Voice

Audience: everyone who meets, calls, or talks across a language barrier.

"For all of history, two people who shared no language could not simply talk. That is the wall Voice was built to lower."

— A working principle

Chapter 14: Real-Time Voice Translation

The supplier in Lisbon spoke almost no English, and my Portuguese stops at ordering coffee. We had a forty-minute call scheduled and a contract to sort out, and in the past that meant one of two things: a stilted exchange where both of us typed into a translator between every sentence, or the expense and scheduling pain of a human interpreter on the line. This time we tried DeepL Voice. He spoke a paragraph of Portuguese; a beat later I heard it in English, in my ear, clearly enough to follow. I answered; a beat later he heard me in Portuguese. It was not telepathy and it was not flawless — I will be honest about the seams in a moment — but for the first time a real working conversation happened across a language we did not share, live, without a third person in the room. That is what this chapter is about.

DeepL Voice is the third of the company's product lines (Chapter 3), and Part IV is where we meet it properly. This chapter covers what Voice actually is, how live spoken translation works under the hood, and — most importantly — what to realistically expect from it, because the gap between the demo and the daily reality is where people get disappointed if no one tells them the truth first. The two-person, voice-to-voice case and meeting integrations get their own treatment in Chapter 15; here I want to establish the foundation.

What DeepL Voice Is

DeepL Voice is real-time spoken translation, built on the same translation quality that made DeepL's name. You speak in one language; Voice listens, translates, and delivers the result in another language as the conversation happens — not after, not in a separate step you trigger, but live, in the flow of talking. The thing to hold onto is that this is not a new, lesser translator bolted onto a microphone. It is DeepL's translation engine, the one Part II is about, now fed by speech instead of typed text and run fast enough to keep up with a conversation.

That lineage matters. Plenty of tools can transcribe speech and shove the words through some translation layer; what distinguishes Voice is that the translation underneath is the quality DeepL is known for, the difference between *correct* and *good* that Chapter 1 opened on. When the words come back in your ear, they are meant to sound like something a person would actually say, not a word-for-word swap that technically parses.

The headline capability launched in stages. The piece that landed in **April 2026** is the one most people mean when they say "voice translation": true **voice-to-voice** — you speak, and it speaks the translation back, audibly, rather than only showing it as text on a screen. (Flag that date and the staging as perishable; by the time you read this the rollout will have moved on, and the exact surfaces and tiers will have shifted.) Voice-to-voice is the heart of Chapter 15, so I will not belabor it here, but it is the feature that turns Voice from a captioning aid into an actual interpreter you can talk through.

It is worth being clear about what Voice is *not*, because the category is crowded with similar-sounding tools and the distinctions matter when you choose one. Voice is not a transcription service that happens to translate — though it transcribes along the way (Chapter 16 takes up transcription as its own subject). It is not a dubbing tool for finished video, where there is no live conversation and you can afford to take your time. And it is not, despite the surface resemblance, the same as typing into Translate and reading the result aloud — the whole point is that it removes the typing and the screen-staring from the loop so two people can actually talk. Voice occupies a specific niche: *live, two-way or one-way spoken translation in the moment*, optimized for the conversation rather than the artifact. Keep that niche in mind and you will reach for it at the right times.

How Live Spoken Translation Works

It helps to know what is happening between your mouth and the other person's ear, because the mental model explains both the strengths and the lag.

Three things happen in sequence, fast. **First, your speech is transcribed** — converted from sound into text in your source language, the same speech-to-text problem Chapter 16 is devoted to. **Second, that text is translated** by DeepL's engine into the target language. **Third, the translation is delivered** — shown as an on-screen caption, spoken aloud in a synthesized voice, or both, depending on how you are using it. Hear, translate, deliver: a pipeline, running continuously, chasing your speech in near-real time.

That word *near* is doing real work. Each of the three stages takes a moment, and they cannot fully start until you have produced enough speech to work with — the system needs a phrase, often a clause or a full sentence, before it can transcribe and translate it well. So there is an inherent, unavoidable delay between what you say and what the other person receives. It is usually a beat or two, short enough that conversation stays workable, long enough that you feel it and have to adjust your rhythm. This is not a bug to be patched away; it is the physics of translating speech you have not finished speaking. The better you understand it, the less it trips you up.

There is a deeper reason the lag cannot simply be engineered to zero, and it is worth understanding because it shapes how you should speak. Many languages put critical information at the *end* of a sentence — German famously parks the verb there, so "I have the contract yesterday finally signed" only resolves into a meaningful action when that last word arrives. A translator, human or machine, often cannot commit to the translation of the opening of a sentence until it has heard the end, because the end can change what the beginning meant. This is the same problem human simultaneous interpreters wrestle with, and they manage it with experience, anticipation, and the occasional graceful correction. Voice manages it by waiting for enough of the sentence to be sure — which is precisely the latency you feel. Understanding this tells you the single most useful speaking habit for Voice: finish your thoughts. A complete sentence followed by a small pause gives the system a clean, fully resolved unit to work with; a sentence you abandon halfway and restart gives it a tangle it has to throw away.

Voice also offers **on-screen captions and transcripts** alongside or instead of the spoken output. For a lot of real use — a meeting, a presentation, a conversation in a noisy room — seeing the translation in text is as valuable as hearing it, and a transcript you can scroll back through covers the moments where your ear missed something. We will come back to transcription as its own subject in Chapter 16.

And there is a **Voice API** for builders who want this capability inside their own software rather than only in DeepL's apps: you stream audio in, and you get back the source-language transcription plus the translation, into up to around five target languages at once. That last detail — the multi-target capacity — is perishable and worth verifying, but the shape is durable: Voice is exposed to developers, not locked to DeepL's own surfaces (Part VI, Chapter 21).

Realistic Expectations

Here is the part an honest guide owes you, because Voice is genuinely useful *and* genuinely imperfect, and pretending otherwise sets you up to be let down.

There is latency, and you have to talk around it. As I said, the pipeline needs a moment. In practice this means speaking in complete thoughts and then pausing — giving the system a clean unit to work with — rather than trailing off, interrupting, or talking over each other. Conversations through Voice have a slightly more turn-taking, walkie-talkie cadence than a native-language chat. Once both people settle into it, it works; the friction is mostly in the first few minutes before you find the rhythm.

It helps to brief the other person before you start, because the cadence only works if both sides adopt it. On the Lisbon call, the few seconds I spent at the top — "let's each finish a thought and pause, and not talk over each other" — saved us five minutes of stepping on each other's translations. The most common cause of a Voice conversation going badly is not the technology; it is two people trying to converse at their normal interrupt-heavy pace and drowning the pipeline in crosstalk. Treat the first thirty seconds as calibration: speak a little slower than feels natural, leave a beat after each turn, and resist the urge to fill the silence while the translation is still arriving. The silence is the system working.

It mishears, and mishearings propagate. Voice is only as good as the transcription underneath it, and transcription struggles with the things human ears also struggle with: heavy accents, fast or mumbled speech, crosstalk when two people speak at once, background noise, and unfamiliar jargon or names. The catch is that an error in what Voice *heard* flows straight into what it translates — a mistranscribed word becomes a confidently mistranslated word. When a translation comes out strange, the culprit is more often a mishearing than a failure of translation. This is the same propagation problem voice interfaces have everywhere, and it is worth keeping in the front of your mind.

The practical upshot is to control what you can control. A surprising amount of Voice's accuracy is decided before anyone says a word, by the audio conditions. A decent headset microphone close to your mouth beats a laptop's built-in mic across a conference table every time, because the close mic captures your voice clean and the room mic captures your voice plus the air conditioning, the hallway, and the person two seats down. A quiet room beats a café. Facing the microphone beats turning away from it mid-sentence. None of this is glamorous, but if you use Voice for anything that matters, the half-hour spent getting a good headset and a quiet space buys you more accuracy than any setting in the app. Garbage audio in, garbage translation out — and the translation will sound confident either way, which is exactly what makes the bad audio dangerous.

Names and special terms are a known weak spot — so DeepL gives you a lever for them. A feature called **Spoken Terms** lets you supply the words Voice is most likely to fumble: industry jargon, product and company names, and people's given names. By telling the system in advance that "Finnoybu" or "Tannenbaum" or some piece of in-house vocabulary is a real word it should expect, you head off the most maddening errors before they happen. If you use Voice for recurring meetings with the same cast of names and terms, setting up Spoken Terms is the single highest-value bit of preparation you can do. (It is conceptually a cousin of the glossaries in Chapter 7, aimed at the spoken channel.)

The reason Spoken Terms matters so much is the propagation problem again. A name or a piece of jargon is exactly the kind of word the transcriber has never reliably heard, so it guesses — and it guesses with something that sounds similar, which then gets translated as if it were that other word, producing nonsense at the far end. "We'll route this through Finnoybu" becomes "we'll route this through Finn, oy, boo" becomes whatever that mess translates to. Pre-loading the real terms breaks the chain at the first link. Build the list from the words that are unavoidable in your context: your company and product names, the names of the people who will be on the call, the technical vocabulary specific to your industry, and any acronyms you say out loud. Five minutes assembling that list before a recurring meeting eliminates the errors most likely to derail it.

It is a communication aid, not a flawless interpreter. This is the line to underline. For lowering a language barrier in everyday and business conversation — a supplier call, a colleague who speaks another language, a traveler asking directions, a customer you would otherwise not be able to help — Voice is a genuine breakthrough, and the right expectation is "we can now talk, imperfectly but usefully." For high-stakes interpreting, where a subtle error carries legal or medical consequence, a qualified human interpreter remains the standard, and Voice does not replace one. Chapter 24 draws that line carefully; Chapter 18 looks at the regulated contexts specifically. Know which side of the line your conversation sits on before you rely on the machine.

The way to use Voice honestly on the borderline is to build in confirmation rather than assuming the channel was clean. When something important is said — a price, a date, a commitment, a yes or no — say it back: "So to confirm, you can deliver by the fourteenth, correct?" This is not a workaround for a broken tool; it is exactly what careful people do even with human interpreters and even in their own language, and through Voice it is essential, because the mishearing-and-propagation problem means an error can be both invisible and consequential. The conversations that go wrong through Voice are rarely the ones where someone confirmed the key points; they are the ones where a misheard number sailed past unremarked and surfaced later as a dispute. Treat read-back as the seatbelt of voice translation. It costs a sentence and prevents the failures that actually hurt.

Where Voice Genuinely Shines

Set against those limits, the wins are real and worth naming, because they are the reason to reach for Voice at all.

Live business conversations across a language gap are the clearest case — the supplier call I opened with, the cross-border negotiation, the international colleague, the moment where the alternative was a clumsy typed exchange or no real conversation at all. **In-person encounters** are another: standing with someone, both of you speaking into a phone, hearing each other in your own languages. And Voice slots into **meetings and collaboration tools**, so a multilingual call can carry live translation for everyone on it, with captions and a transcript afterward — the subject Chapter 15 takes up in full.

What unites the cases where Voice shines is that they are all situations where the realistic alternative was *worse*, not where the alternative was a perfect human interpreter. That framing is the key to being happy with the tool. If you compare Voice to a seasoned simultaneous interpreter, it will disappoint you on the hard cases. If you compare it to what you would actually have done otherwise — typing into a translator between every sentence, struggling through in broken shared vocabulary, postponing the conversation until you could book an interpreter, or simply not being able to talk to that person at all — Voice is often transformative. The Lisbon supplier and I were never going to hire an interpreter for a forty-minute contract call. Our real choice was Voice or a painful typed exchange, and against that choice Voice won easily. Judge it against your real alternative and it earns its place; judge it against perfection and it never will.

The languages. Voice supports **40-plus languages**, anchored by the 24 official EU languages and reaching well beyond them — Vietnamese, Thai, Arabic, Norwegian, Hebrew, Bengali, Tagalog, and a growing list more. Treat the exact roster as perishable; the supported set expands, and the languages available for *spoken output* may differ from those available for captions or text. Appendix A carries a snapshot, but before you commit to Voice for a particular language pair, verify the current list against DeepL's own documentation. That is the one piece of this chapter most likely to be out of date by the time it matters to you.

One nuance inside that caution deserves emphasis because it is easy to get burned by: support is not uniform across the pipeline. A language can be available as a transcription source but not as a spoken-output target, or available for captions but not yet for the synthesized voice, or strong in one direction of a pair and weaker in the other. So "is language X supported?" is the wrong question. The right question is "is the specific thing I need — speaking *into* it, hearing it spoken *back*, captioning it — supported for my exact pair, right now?" Before you build a workflow or promise a client a multilingual call, test your actual language pair end to end, in the actual mode you will use, rather than trusting a headline number. The forty-plus figure tells you Voice is broad; only a test tells you whether it covers the one combination you care about.

A last note on the horizon: DeepL has a **voice-preservation** feature planned for **end of 2026** — translated speech that keeps something of the *speaker's own* voice rather than a generic synthesized one. It is not generally available as I write, so treat it as forthcoming rather than a feature to plan around; I will return to it in Chapter 15, where it belongs.

We have established what Voice is and what to expect of it: a real, latency-bound, occasionally mishearing, frequently remarkable aid to talking across languages. The natural next move is the case that makes it sing — two people who share no language, talking live — and the meeting tools that carry it.

Chapter 15: Voice-to-Voice and Meetings

My neighbor runs a small import business, and last spring he closed a deal with a workshop in Osaka where exactly one person spoke English and she was out sick the week it mattered. He called me, half-joking, to ask whether the AI books I write had a trick for this. They did. He put DeepL Voice between himself and the workshop's owner, set it to translate his English into Japanese spoken aloud and the owner's Japanese into spoken English, and the two of them talked for half an hour about lead times and tolerances. Neither understood a word the other actually said; both understood each other. He told me afterward that the strangest part was how *ordinary* it started to feel ten minutes in — that he stopped noticing the machine and just had the conversation. That is the thing voice-to-voice does at its best, and it is what this chapter is about.

Chapter 14 laid the foundation: what DeepL Voice is, how the hear-translate-deliver pipeline works, and what to realistically expect from it. This chapter takes the capability that foundation makes possible and looks at it closely — two people who share no language talking live, the meeting and collaboration tools Voice plugs into, the captions and transcripts that come with them, the voice-preservation feature on the horizon, and the etiquette and limits that separate a conversation that works from one that falls apart. This is the human heart of Part IV.

Two People, No Shared Language, Talking Live

Voice-to-voice is the feature where you speak and DeepL speaks the translation back, audibly, so a conversation between two people who share no common language can actually happen out loud. It launched in **April 2026** (perishable date), and it is the difference between a tool that *shows* you a translation and one that lets you *talk*. When both directions are spoken — your words rendered as audible speech in their language, theirs rendered as audible speech in yours — the screen drops away and what is left is a conversation.

The setup is symmetric. Voice handles both directions at once: it listens for your language and speaks the other person's, and listens for theirs and speaks yours, switching as the turns pass. My neighbor's call is the canonical shape — two people, two languages, one device or one connection between them, each hearing the other in their own tongue a beat after it is said. For in-person encounters you can do this with a single phone between you; for remote ones it rides on a call. Either way the experience is the one he described: after the first few minutes of finding the rhythm, you stop managing the tool and start talking to the person.

The honest caveat from Chapter 14 still applies and is worth repeating here, because voice-to-voice is exactly where people are tempted to forget it. The latency is real, so you take turns and speak in complete thoughts rather than overlapping. The mishearings are real, so accents, crosstalk, and noise still cost you, and a strange translation usually traces back to a misheard word. And **Spoken Terms** — the customization from Chapter 14 that teaches Voice your names, products, and jargon — earns its keep most in exactly this two-person setting, where a fumbled name can stall a conversation that has no human interpreter to recover it. Set those terms before an important call. It is five minutes that prevents the most frustrating failures.

Two Ways to Run a Two-Person Conversation

The phrase "voice-to-voice" covers two physically different setups, and it is worth being explicit about both, because they fail in different ways and reward different preparation.

The **in-person setup** is the one where you and the other person are standing or sitting together with a single device between you. You speak into the phone; the other person hears your words in their language come out of the same phone a beat later; they answer into it; you hear theirs. This is the configuration that feels most like science fiction — two strangers passing a phone back and forth and conducting an actual conversation — and it is also the one most exposed to the audio hazards from Chapter 14. A single device sitting on a café table is hearing both of you plus the room, and the room is the enemy of clean transcription. If the encounter matters, the small moves pay off disproportionately: hold the phone closer to whoever is speaking, turn slightly away from the noise, and resist the very human urge to both lean in and talk at once. The device cannot separate two voices arriving simultaneously into one microphone the way your ear can.

The **remote setup** rides on a call — a phone call, a video call, a meeting platform — where each person is in their own space with their own microphone.

This is generally the *better* audio situation, because each side can have a decent headset close to their mouth and a quiet room around them, and because the two voices arrive on separate channels rather than colliding in one mic. My neighbor's Osaka call was this kind: two people, two countries, two headsets, one connection carrying the translation between them. The trade is that you lose the shared physical presence that makes the in-person version feel so natural, and you depend on the call quality underneath — a dropping connection garbles the audio before Voice ever gets to hear it, and no translation engine can recover words that never arrived intact. Match the setup to the situation, and in both cases remember that the quality of what Voice *hears* sets the ceiling on everything downstream.

A worked example makes the difference vivid. Imagine you are buying a used car from a private seller in another country, in person, in their driveway. The in-person setup is your only realistic option, and the conditions are working against you: an outdoor space, traffic noise, a seller who speaks quickly and uses local slang for car parts. Here the preparation that matters is Spoken Terms loaded with the vocabulary you expect — model names, the words for "mileage," "service history," "registration" — and the discipline of reading back every number out loud: "So, ninety thousand kilometers, and the timing belt was replaced last year, correct?" The read-back is doing the work the noisy audio cannot guarantee. Now imagine instead you are negotiating a supply contract over a scheduled video call. The remote setup gives you clean audio on both ends, but the stakes are higher and the language more abstract, so the preparation shifts: Spoken Terms loaded with the company and product names, a quiet room, and a spoken agreement at the top to take turns. Same feature, two settings, two different sets of habits — and in both, the failures come from skipping the preparation, not from the tool.

Voice in Meetings

The two-person case is the vivid one, but a great deal of real-world Voice use is in **meetings**, where the dynamics are different and the tooling matters more.

Voice integrates with meeting and collaboration tools, which means a multilingual call does not have to bend around the translation — the translation lives inside the meeting everyone is already in. Participants can follow along in their own language while others speak in theirs. The exact list of supported platforms and how the integration is set up is perishable and varies by plan, so verify the current state against DeepL's documentation and Chapter 22, which covers integrations broadly; the durable point is that Voice is built to drop into the meeting software teams already use rather than forcing everyone into a separate app.

In a meeting, **on-screen captions and transcripts** often carry more of the weight than spoken output does. A room or a call with several people cannot easily have synthesized speech talking over the live speaker for everyone at once, so the common pattern is live captions in each participant's chosen language, scrolling as people talk, with a full transcript available afterward. This turns out to be a quietly powerful mode. Captions let someone catch a phrase they missed by ear, follow a fast speaker at their own pace, and stay oriented in a conversation moving through a language they only partly know. The transcript then becomes the meeting's record — searchable, reviewable, and translated, which is a genuine work artifact, not just an accessibility nicety. Chapter 16 goes deep on transcription as its own subject; here it is enough to know that in meetings, the text channel is a first-class part of how Voice helps, not an afterthought to the audio.

The reason captions outperform spoken output in a multi-person setting is worth spelling out, because it changes how you should set a meeting up. With two people, synthesized speech works: one person talks, the other listens to the translation, and the turn-taking is clean. Add a third and fourth participant in two or three languages and the audio model breaks down — you cannot have three synthesized voices speaking three translations over one live speaker without producing chaos. Text scales where audio does not. Each participant reads the captions in their own language at their own pace, silently, without anyone's translation colliding with anyone else's. So the practical default for a real multilingual meeting is captions-first: let people *read* the translation while the speaker talks normally, and reserve spoken translation for the moments or the pairs where it genuinely helps. This also sidesteps the most awkward failure of synthesized speech in a group — the translation arriving a beat late and stepping on the next speaker who has already begun.

Running a Multilingual Meeting Well

A meeting with live translation is a different kind of meeting, and a little structure makes the difference between one that flows and one that stalls. Several habits are worth building in deliberately.

Appoint a light facilitator. Someone needs to manage the rhythm — calling on people one at a time, watching for the moment when the captions have fallen behind, and gently slowing a fast speaker. In a same-language meeting this happens informally; with translation in the loop it benefits from one person consciously holding the pace. The facilitator's main job is preventing the overlap that drowns the pipeline.

Brief everyone at the start. Just as you would tell a single conversation partner that a translation tool is in the loop, tell the whole room. Say that captions will appear in each person's chosen language, that there is a slight delay, that people should finish their thought and pause, and that the transcript will be available afterward so nobody needs to scramble to capture everything live. Thirty seconds of framing changes how the whole meeting behaves.

Pre-load the shared vocabulary. A recurring multilingual meeting almost always has a stable cast of names and a fixed set of project terms, product names, and acronyms. This is exactly what Spoken Terms is for, and a meeting is where its payoff compounds — set it once and every future session of that meeting transcribes and translates the load-bearing words correctly. The proper noun that comes out garbled every single time is the most demoralizing failure in a group setting, because it makes the tool feel unreliable even when the rest of the translation is excellent.

Decide what the transcript is for before the meeting, not after. If the transcript is going to be the official record of decisions, tell people that, because it changes how they speak — they will state conclusions clearly and confirm action items out loud, which both improves the record and improves the live translation. If the transcript is just a convenience, treat it as a draft. Either way, knowing its role in advance is better than discovering after the fact that the one decision you needed captured was the one that got garbled.

Lean on the asymmetry of comprehension. In most multilingual meetings, participants understand the shared business language better than they can *produce* it. The common and effective pattern is to let people speak in their strongest language and read the meeting in the shared one through captions — production in the native tongue, comprehension in translation. This plays to exactly the strength Voice has and away from the place it is weakest, which is real-time back-and-forth at full conversational speed.

The Voice-Preservation Feature (Forthcoming)

One of the odder frictions of synthesized translation is that everyone comes out sounding like the same neutral voice. You say something warm and emphatic; the other person hears your meaning in a flat, generic synthetic tone that carries none of *you*. For a transaction it does not matter. For a relationship — a negotiation, an ongoing partnership, a difficult conversation where tone is half the message — it costs something.

DeepL has a **voice-preservation** feature planned for **end of 2026** aimed squarely at this: translated speech that retains characteristics of the *speaker's own* voice, so the person on the other end hears the translation in something closer to how you actually sound rather than a stock synthetic voice. If it lands as described, it would make voice-to-voice meaningfully more human — preserving not just your words but a little of your manner across the language gap.

Flag this clearly, because it is the kind of thing that is easy to over-promise: **voice preservation is forthcoming, not generally available as I write.** Treat it as a direction the product is heading, not a feature to build a plan around today. If it matters to you, check whether it has shipped before you count on it, and verify how it actually behaves rather than trusting the roadmap. The durable observation is the one underneath the feature: the seam in voice-to-voice today is that the translated speaker sounds like a machine, and DeepL knows it and is working on it.

How Voice-to-Voice Conversations Actually Fail

It is more useful to know the specific ways these conversations go wrong than to be told vaguely that they "can be imperfect." There are a handful of recurring failure modes, and each has a countermeasure.

The first and most common is **crosstalk collapse.** Two people who are getting along start to converse at their natural pace, finishing each other's thoughts and jumping in — and the pipeline, which needs a clean unfinished-then-finished unit to translate, receives a tangle of overlapping speech and produces garbage. The conversation feels like it suddenly "stopped working," when what actually happened is the people stopped taking turns. The countermeasure is the turn-taking discipline, and the tell that you have slipped is when the translations start arriving wrong all at once. Slow down, pause, and the quality returns.

The second is the **propagated mishearing.** A single misheard word — usually a name, a number, or a piece of jargon — gets transcribed wrong, then translated faithfully as the wrong word, and arrives at the other end as confident nonsense. The other person, trying to be polite, often does not flag it, and the conversation drifts off the rails because both sides are now working from a different fact. The countermeasure is read-back on anything load-bearing: prices, dates, quantities, commitments, spellings. Say it back and let the other person confirm it. This single habit prevents the failures that actually cost something.

The third is the **dropped negation or flipped polarity** — the same fluent error that haunts text translation, now in speech, where you cannot scroll back to check. "We can deliver by Friday" and "we cannot deliver by Friday" differ by one word, and if that word is misheard or mistranslated, the sentence still sounds perfectly natural. The countermeasure again is confirmation, phrased to surface the polarity: not "got it" but "so you *can* make Friday — yes?"

The fourth is **expecting it to handle a three-way conversation by audio.** Voice-to-voice is built for two people and two languages at a time. The moment a third person or a third language enters, the spoken model strains, and you should switch to the captions-first meeting pattern rather than trying to make synthesized speech serve a crowd. Reaching for the wrong mode is itself a failure mode.

Notice that three of the four countermeasures are the same move: confirm the things that matter out loud. The read-back habit from Chapter 14 is cheap — a sentence — against the cost of a misheard number surfacing later as a dispute.

Etiquette and Limits

A few practical norms separate a Voice conversation that works from one that frustrates everyone in it. Most of these I learned by getting them wrong.

Tell the other person what is happening. Starting a translated conversation without a word of explanation is disorienting — the beat of latency, the synthetic voice, the slightly formal cadence all read as strange if the other person does not know a machine is in the loop. A short "I'm using a translation tool, so there will be a small delay — let's take turns" resets everyone's expectations and makes the whole thing feel collaborative rather than uncanny.

Speak in clean, complete units, then pause. The pipeline needs a finished thought to work well. Short-to-medium complete sentences, delivered clearly and followed by a beat, translate far better than long rambling runs or trailed-off fragments. This is a learnable habit, and it is the single biggest thing you control.

Mind the setting. Crosstalk and background noise are the enemy of accurate transcription, and accurate transcription is the foundation of the whole thing. A quiet room and one-speaker-at-a-time will give you dramatically better results than a loud café with people talking over each other.

Know what the conversation can bear. This is the limit that matters most, and it is the same line Chapter 14 drew and Chapters 18 and 24 draw in detail. Voice-to-voice is a superb aid for everyday and business conversation, for relationships you could not otherwise have, for getting real work done across a language barrier. It is *not* a substitute for a qualified human interpreter where a subtle error carries legal, medical, or other high-stakes consequence. For those situations a human stays in the loop, and Voice, if it is present at all, is a convenience around the edges rather than the thing you rely on. Match the tool to the stakes.

Used within those bounds — explained to the other person, spoken cleanly, in a reasonable setting, for conversations whose stakes it can carry — voice-to-voice does something that was science fiction not long ago. It lets two people who cannot understand each other have a real conversation, and after the first few minutes, mostly forget the machine is there.

We have now heard Voice translate, and watched it carry a meeting. The text it produces along the way — the captions, the transcripts, the searchable record — deserves a chapter of its own, because transcription is useful well beyond translation.

Chapter 16: Transcription

Picture a project kickoff where four people talk for an hour and nobody takes notes, and for once that is fine. Voice is running for the captions — two people on the call work in German, two in English — and when it ends, there is a transcript: the whole meeting in text, every speaker's words, with the German turns rendered in English alongside them. The action items someone would normally have scribbled and half-lost are sitting there, searchable, by the time the call drops. Nobody had to choose between participating and recording; the machine kept the record while the people kept their attention on the conversation. That quiet shift — from frantically transcribing to simply having the transcript — is what this chapter is about.

We arrive at transcription having come through the spoken side of DeepL Voice: Chapter 14 on real-time translation and Chapter 15 on voice-to-voice and meetings. Transcription is the text those features produce and a capability worth understanding on its own terms, because the words-on-a-page output of Voice is useful for a great deal more than translation. This chapter covers what transcription is, where it genuinely earns its place, the accuracy caveats you must keep in view, and how it pairs with translation to become something more than either alone.

What Transcription Is

Transcription is speech turned into text — the spoken word captured as written words you can read, search, save, and share. It is the first stage of the Voice pipeline from Chapter 14 (hear, translate, deliver) surfaced as a product in its own right: the *hear* step, made visible and kept.

There are really two flavors, and it is worth separating them. The plain version is a **same-language transcript** — someone speaks English, you get the English in text. The version that is distinctively DeepL is the **translated transcript** — someone speaks German, and you get the text in English, or in both, so a meeting conducted across languages leaves behind a single readable record everyone can use. That second flavor is where DeepL's translation quality (Chapter 1) flows into transcription and makes it more than a commodity. Anyone can give you words on a page; DeepL can give you the *other* language's words on a page, rendered the way a person would actually have written them.

Treat the precise mechanics as perishable — which surfaces produce transcripts, what file or export formats you get, how live versus after-the-fact transcription is offered, and which languages are supported for transcription as opposed to spoken output. All of that drifts, and you should verify the current state against DeepL's documentation and Appendix A. The durable capability is simple: Voice can hand you the conversation as text, in the source language, the target language, or both.

It is worth pulling apart two timings, because they shape how you use transcription and they fail differently. **Live transcription** is the text that scrolls as people speak — the captions of Chapter 15, captured rather than discarded. It runs under real-time pressure, which means it makes the same speed-versus-certainty trade that real-time translation makes: it has to commit to a word before it has heard the whole sentence, so it occasionally guesses and occasionally has to revise on the fly. **After-the-fact transcription** of a recording faces no such clock. It can take a recorded conversation, process it without the latency constraint, and generally produce a cleaner result, because it can use more context to resolve ambiguous audio. The practical implication is simple: if a transcript matters and you have the choice, transcribing a clean recording afterward tends to beat relying on the live caption stream — and if you only have the live stream, treat it as the slightly rougher artifact it is. Which of these DeepL offers, and on which surfaces, is exactly the kind of perishable detail to confirm in the current docs.

Speaker attribution is a third axis worth checking for a given use. A transcript that says only *what* was said is useful; a transcript that also says *who* said it — separating the four people in the kickoff into four labeled voices — is far more useful for meeting notes, because decisions and commitments attach to people. How reliably any tool separates speakers depends heavily on the audio: separate microphones make it much easier than four people sharing one room mic. Do not assume clean attribution from a single shared microphone in a noisy room; verify it on your actual setup before you rely on a transcript to tell you who agreed to what.

Where Transcription Earns Its Place

The value shows up in a handful of recurring situations, and they are worth naming because each one removes a specific, familiar pain.

Meeting notes. This is the headline use and the one in that kickoff. A transcript frees the people in a meeting to actually be *in* it rather than splitting their attention between listening and writing. Afterward you have the full record to pull decisions and action items from, search for the moment someone committed to a date, and send to whoever could not attend. For a multilingual team the translated transcript does double duty — everyone gets the meeting in their own language, and nobody is stuck reconstructing what the half of the call they did not understand actually agreed to. Chapter 19 looks at multilingual teams in depth; transcription is one of the load-bearing tools there.

A durable record. Some conversations need to be kept — an interview, a customer call, a stakeholder discussion, a verbal agreement you want documented. A transcript turns ephemeral speech into a reviewable artifact, which is useful for memory, for handoff, and for the simple ability to go back and check what was actually said rather than what everyone remembers. (When the conversation is itself high-stakes or regulated, the accuracy caveats below and the cautions in Chapter 18 matter a great deal — a transcript is a draft record, not a certified one.)

Accessibility. This one is easy to undersell and important not to. Live captions and transcripts make spoken content reachable for people who are deaf or hard of hearing, for people following a conversation in a language they read better than they hear, and for anyone in a setting where they cannot use audio. In meetings and presentations, captions are not a courtesy add-on; for some participants they are the difference between being included and being shut out. Building them in is one of the genuinely good things Voice does.

There are quieter uses too — turning a voice memo into editable text, capturing a phone call you would otherwise have to remember, getting the gist of an audio recording without sitting through all of it. The common thread is the same: speech is hard to search, hard to skim, and easy to lose, and text is none of those things. Transcription converts the one into the other.

A few of these quieter uses deserve a closer look, because they are the ones working people reach for most and underestimate most.

Drafting by speaking. Some people think far faster than they type, and a great deal of first-draft writing — an email, a set of notes, the bones of a document — comes out more naturally spoken than typed. Transcription turns a two-minute spoken ramble into editable text you can then shape, and when the spoken language is not your first, pairing transcription with translation means you can think out loud in your strongest language and get the draft in another. The transcript is rough, but a rough draft you can edit beats a blank page you have to fill.

Skimming long audio. A forty-five-minute recorded briefing, an interview, a recorded webinar — sitting through the whole thing to find the five minutes you need is a poor use of an hour. A transcript lets you skim, search for the term you care about, and jump to the relevant passage. You are trading perfect fidelity for the ability to *navigate* the content, which for triage is exactly the right trade.

Capturing the call you could not record by hand. A phone conversation where something was agreed, a verbal briefing you received while your hands were full — the kind of exchange that normally survives only as a fading memory and a few scribbled words. A transcript captures the whole of it, so that "what did she actually say about the timeline?" has an answer you can check rather than reconstruct. Note the caveats below, and note too that recording a conversation may carry legal and ethical obligations to inform the other party; transcription does not exempt you from the rules about recording in the first place, which vary by jurisdiction.

Accuracy Caveats

An honest guide has to be clear here, because transcription *looks* authoritative — clean text on a page carries an air of being exactly what was said — and that confidence is precisely where it can mislead you.

Transcription is good, not perfect, and it fails on predictable things. The same hazards that trouble real-time translation (Chapter 14) trouble transcription, because it is the same listening step: heavy accents, fast or mumbled speech, crosstalk when people talk over one another, background noise, and unfamiliar names, jargon, or acronyms. A transcript of a clear, one-at-a-time conversation in a quiet room can be remarkably accurate. A transcript of a noisy four-way call with strong accents and industry shorthand will have errors, sometimes meaningful ones.

Errors hide in plain sight. A mistranscribed word does not announce itself — it sits in the text looking just as confident as the correct words around it. A misheard name, a flipped number, a technical term rendered as the ordinary word that sounds like it: these are easy to read straight past. The practical discipline is to **treat an important transcript as a draft to verify, not a finished record to trust blindly**, especially for the specific things transcription gets wrong — names, numbers, and terms. If a decision or a figure rides on a line in a transcript, confirm that line.

Spoken Terms helps, within limits. The same Spoken Terms customization from Chapter 14 — where you supply the names, products, and jargon Voice is likely to fumble — improves transcription of exactly those weak spots. It will not fix accents or crosstalk, but it meaningfully reduces the most maddening category of error, the proper noun that comes out wrong every single time. For recurring meetings with a stable cast of names and terms, set it up once and benefit on every transcript after.

Translated transcripts inherit two layers of risk. When the transcript is also translated, remember that a transcription error feeds into the translation — a misheard source word becomes a confidently mistranslated one. The translation itself may be excellent (this is DeepL, after all), but it can only be as good as what it was given to translate. Two stages, two places for a slip. This is not a reason to avoid translated transcripts; it is a reason to keep the verification habit when the stakes warrant it.

There is a useful trick when both the source and the translated text are available to you: **read them against each other on the lines that matter.** Because a transcription error usually produces a source word that does not quite fit the surrounding sentence, and a translation then renders that ill-fitting word faithfully, a passage that reads slightly oddly in *both* languages is a flag worth a second look. If the German transcript says something that does not quite parse and the English translation faithfully reproduces the same not-quite-sense, the problem is almost certainly upstream — a mishearing — and the source audio is the thing to recheck. You will not do this for every line, but for the figure or commitment a decision rides on, comparing the two versions is faster than relistening to the whole recording and catches exactly the kind of error this two-stage pipeline produces.

A concrete illustration. Suppose a recorded supplier call is transcribed and translated, and the English transcript reads: "We can ship the order by the fourteenth, pending the deposit." Clean, confident, actionable. But the speaker actually said "by the *fourth*teenth" with the stress that, in the source language, distinguished it from a different date entirely — and the transcriber, hearing a fast speaker, settled on the wrong number. Nothing in the English transcript reveals the error; the sentence is grammatical and plausible. Only checking the line against the source audio, or against the source-language transcript where the misheard word may sit oddly, surfaces it. This is precisely why a transcript of a number-laden negotiation is a draft to verify, not a record to file and trust. The places to look are always the same three: names, numbers, and the words that flip a meaning — the negations and conditionals.

Common Mistakes, and How to Avoid Them

A few errors come up again and again with transcription, and naming them is the fastest way to stop making them.

Trusting clean formatting as a proxy for accuracy. The single most common mistake is treating a tidy, well-punctuated transcript as if neatness implied correctness. It does not. The formatting is generated automatically and looks the same whether the words underneath are right or wrong. A transcript can be beautifully laid out and contain a flipped number on line forty. Read for meaning on the lines that matter, not for tidiness.

Skipping the audio setup and blaming the tool. When a transcript comes back full of errors, the instinct is to conclude the transcription is bad. Far more often the *audio* was bad — a shared room mic, crosstalk, a noisy space — and any transcriber would have struggled. The fix is upstream: a close microphone, a quiet room, one speaker at a time. As with everything in the Voice pipeline, garbage audio in produces garbage text out, and the text will look just as confident either way.

Not setting Spoken Terms for recurring content. People set up Spoken Terms once for a single important call and then forget it exists for the weekly meeting that mangles the same three names every single time. For any recurring transcript, the names and terms are stable; loading them once and benefiting on every future transcript is among the highest-value five minutes you can spend.

Treating a draft record as a final one. A transcript is a draft of what was said, not a certified account of it. For casual purposes that distinction does not matter. For anything where the record will be relied upon — a decision log, an agreement, anything that might be disputed — the transcript is the starting point for a verified record, not the verified record itself. Chapter 18 takes this up where the stakes are highest.

Forgetting the privacy weight of a transcript. A transcript is a durable, searchable, copyable text version of a conversation that was previously ephemeral. That is exactly its value and exactly its risk. A spoken conversation in a meeting leaves no artifact; a transcript leaves a complete one that can be forwarded, leaked, or subpoenaed. Treat a transcript of a sensitive conversation with the same care you would treat any sensitive document — which means the data-handling questions of Chapter 20 apply to it, and a confidential conversation does not belong on a tool whose data terms are an afterthought.

Pairing Transcription with Translation

The two capabilities are at their strongest together, and the combination is really the point of putting transcription in a translation company's product.

A monolingual transcript is a convenience. A **translated transcript is a bridge** — it lets a meeting happen in several languages and still leave behind one shared, readable record that every participant can use in their own tongue. That is something neither plain transcription nor plain translation delivers alone. It is also what makes Voice genuinely useful for the multilingual workplace: the live captions carry the conversation as it happens (Chapter 15), and the translated transcript carries it afterward, so the language barrier is lowered both in the moment and in the record.

The "one shared record" point is easy to skim past and worth dwelling on, because it solves a problem that quietly plagues multilingual teams. Before translated transcripts, a meeting held across two languages left behind either two partial records — each person remembering the half they understood — or one record in one language that the other half of the room could not fully use. Decisions got remembered differently on the two sides of the language line, and the disagreements that surfaced weeks later were often not real disagreements at all but two faithful memories of two different halves of the same conversation. A single transcript, available to everyone in their own language, collapses that gap: there is now one artifact, and "what did we decide?" has one answer that everyone can read. For a distributed team that meets across languages routinely, this is the difference between a record and a recurring source of confusion.

There is also a compounding benefit over time, which connects this chapter to the localization material ahead. Translated transcripts of recurring meetings accumulate into a searchable history of a relationship or a project, in whatever language each person reads. Six months in, "when did the client first raise the pricing concern?" is a search, not a memory test — and the answer comes back in your language regardless of which language it was originally spoken in. The transcript stops being a per-meeting convenience and becomes an institutional memory that happens to be multilingual.

The honest framing to carry out of this chapter is the one that runs through all of Part IV. Transcription, like the translation it pairs with, is a powerful aid that you supervise rather than a flawless scribe you can ignore. Use it to free your attention in meetings, to keep records you would otherwise lose, and to include people audio alone would exclude. Verify the parts that matter — the names, the numbers, the commitments — because the clean-looking text can be confidently wrong. Within that discipline, transcription quietly removes one of the oldest frictions of working across languages and across the spoken word: that conversations vanish the moment they end, and vanish hardest of all when you only half-understood them.

That completes Part IV and the spoken side of DeepL. From here the book turns to DeepL at work — the professional and organizational uses of everything we have covered.

Part V: DeepL at Work

Audience: professionals and teams operating across languages — where quality, consistency, and privacy stop being conveniences and become requirements.

"At one email, quality is a nicety. At ten thousand, it is the whole economics of the thing."

— A working principle

Chapter 17: Localization Workflows

A software company I advised wanted to launch in eight new markets, which meant translating roughly a quarter of a million words — a product, a website, a help center, a stack of legal pages — into eight languages, on a deadline that made the traditional approach impossible. The traditional approach was professional human translators working through every word from scratch, and priced and scheduled accordingly, it would have blown the budget and missed the launch by months. What they actually did was put DeepL at the center of the work and human translators around the edges of it: the machine produced the first full draft of all two million target words in an afternoon, and the humans spent their time *fixing and judging* rather than typing from zero. They launched on time, at a fraction of the cost, and — this is the part that matters — at a quality their markets accepted. That is localization done well, and it is the subject of this chapter.

This chapter opens Part V, DeepL at Work, which is about the professional and organizational uses of everything the book has covered so far. Localization is the discipline of producing high-quality translated content at scale, and it is where DeepL stops being a website you paste into and becomes an *engine* inside a larger production process. I want to show you that process honestly: where DeepL genuinely accelerates real localization, how the pieces — glossaries, document flows, CAT-tool integration, translation memory — fit together, and where human beings remain not optional but essential. The headline, which I will spend the chapter earning, is that quality localization is a human-in-the-loop discipline, and DeepL's job is to make the loop dramatically faster, not to remove the human from it.

What Localization Actually Is

It is worth separating *translation* from *localization*, because they are not the same thing and the difference shapes everything that follows.

Translation converts words from one language to another. **Localization adapts content so it works for a specific market** — which includes translation but goes well beyond it. It means consistent terminology across thousands of pages, the right formality and tone for the audience (Chapter 8), formats and conventions that fit the locale, product and brand names handled correctly every time, and a final result that reads as though it were created for that market rather than imported into it. Localization is translation plus consistency plus adaptation plus scale, run as a repeatable process rather than a one-off task.

That "at scale" and "repeatable process" part is the key. Translating one email is a task. Localizing a product into eight languages and then keeping all eight in sync as the product changes every week is an *operation*, and operations need an engine, a workflow, and quality control. DeepL supplies the engine. The rest of this chapter is about the workflow and the control around it.

To make the difference concrete, consider what "adaptation beyond translation" actually means in practice, because it is the part newcomers underestimate. A date written 03/04/2026 means March in one market and April in another; localization fixes the format, not just the words. A price needs the right currency, the right symbol, and the right placement of that symbol — €1.234,56 in one locale and $1,234.56 in another, with the decimal and thousands separators *swapped*. A form that asks for a "first name" and "last name" assumes a naming convention that does not hold everywhere. An idiom or a cultural reference that lands in the source market may be meaningless or even offensive in the target one. A screenshot in a help article shows the interface in the wrong language until someone retakes it. None of these are translation in the narrow sense; all of them are localization, and a translated-but-not-localized product reads, to a native user, as something built elsewhere and shipped over — exactly the impression localization exists to prevent. DeepL handles the language layer of this superbly. The locale layer — formats, conventions, cultural fit — is a job for the workflow and the human judgment around the engine, which is the recurring theme of the chapter.

There is also a distinction worth drawing between two kinds of localization content, because they call for different handling. **Running text** — marketing copy, help articles, legal pages, documentation — is prose, and prose is where DeepL's quality shines and where MTPE (below) is the natural pattern. **User-interface strings** — the buttons, labels, error messages, and menu items inside software — are a harder, stranger problem: they are short, context-poor (the translator often sees "Open" with no idea whether it is a verb or an adjective), length-constrained (a word that fits a button in English may overflow it in German), and full of variables and placeholders that must survive untouched. Both are localization, but the first is a prose problem and the second is closer to an engineering problem. Knowing which kind of content you are dealing with tells you how much human attention each segment needs and where the machine will need the most help.

MT-Then-Post-Edit: The Core Pattern

The dominant pattern in professional localization today, and the one my software company used, has a clumsy name and a simple shape: **machine translation followed by human post-editing**, or MTPE. You let the machine produce the full first draft, and then a qualified human edits that draft to final quality rather than translating from a blank page.

The reason this pattern won is arithmetic. Editing a good draft is far faster than producing one from scratch, and DeepL's drafts are good — the *correct-versus-good* quality from Chapter 1 means the post-editor is often making light touches rather than heavy repairs. A human translating from zero might manage a few thousand words a day; the same human post-editing strong machine output can move several times that, because most sentences need only a glance and a nudge. Multiply that across a quarter-million words and eight languages and the difference is the launch happening or not.

Two things make MTPE work, and both are worth saying plainly. **First, the quality of the raw machine output sets the ceiling on how much the pattern helps** — a bad first draft is slower to fix than to redo, which is exactly why the engine choice matters and why DeepL's quality is not a vanity metric but the thing that makes the economics work. **Second, the human post-edit is not a formality** — it is where mistranslations get caught, tone gets corrected, terminology gets enforced, and the cultural and contextual judgment a machine cannot supply gets added. Skip the post-edit and you have machine output, not localization. The loop is the discipline.

It helps to know that post-editing comes in two recognized depths, because choosing the right one for each kind of content is where a lot of the cost savings actually live. **Light post-editing** aims for "good enough" — accurate, understandable, no serious errors — without polishing every sentence to publication shine. It suits high-volume, lower-stakes, or short-lived content: internal documentation, knowledge-base articles, user-generated content, anything where correctness matters more than elegance. **Full post-editing** aims for output indistinguishable from a from-scratch human translation — every nuance, every stylistic choice, fully native register. It is what you use for marketing copy, brand-facing material, and anything where the writing itself is part of the product. The mistake teams make is applying one depth uniformly: lavishing full post-editing on a transient internal FAQ wastes expensive attention, while applying only light post-editing to the homepage ships something that reads slightly off to every visitor. Match the depth to the content's stakes and lifespan, and the same localization budget goes much further.

A worked picture of how the arithmetic plays out: take a 250,000-word project across eight languages, the scenario this chapter opened with. From-scratch human translation at a few thousand words a day per translator turns each language into a multi-week effort and the whole project into months of elapsed time and a correspondingly large bill. With MTPE, DeepL produces the entire two-million-word draft (250,000 words times eight languages) in an afternoon, and the human work shifts to post-editing strong drafts, which moves several times faster than translating from zero. The eight post-editors are now steering rather than authoring, the timeline compresses from months to weeks, and the cost drops to a fraction — not because anyone cut a corner, but because the expensive human hours are spent on judgment instead of typing. The quality the markets accept is the same; what changed is where the human effort went. That redistribution is the whole point of the pattern.

The Pieces DeepL Brings to the Loop

DeepL contributes more than raw translation to a localization workflow. Several features from earlier in the book are, in this context, the apparatus that makes scaled production consistent and controllable.

Glossaries (Chapter 7) are arguably the single most important. At localization scale, the enemy is inconsistency — the same product feature translated three different ways across three documents, the brand name rendered however the model guessed that day. A glossary locks in your approved translation of every term that matters, so it comes out the same way every time, across every document and every translator. This is the difference between content that reads as one coherent product and content that reads as a committee. Set the glossary first; it pays off on every word after.

Document and file flows (Chapter 6) matter because real localization content is not loose text — it is Word files, presentations, PDFs, and structured formats with layout and markup that must survive translation. DeepL's ability to take a document, translate it, and hand it back with formatting intact removes an enormous amount of manual reconstruction. The post-editor works on a real document, not a wall of stripped text they then have to reformat.

Formality and tone controls (Chapter 8) let the machine output start closer to the register the market needs — formal where formality is expected, casual where it is not — so the post-editor is steering rather than rebuilding tone from scratch.

The API (Chapter 21) is what lets all of this run inside an automated pipeline rather than by hand. At real scale, nobody is pasting documents into a website. The localization system pulls content, sends it through DeepL programmatically, and routes the drafts to the post-editing stage — DeepL as infrastructure, the subject of Part VI.

These pieces are not independent; they reinforce each other, and the order in which you put them in place matters. The glossary should exist *before* the first batch goes through, because every word translated without it is a word that may need re-editing for terminology later — fixing inconsistency after the fact is far more expensive than preventing it. The document flow and the formality setting shape what the post-editor receives, so getting them right means the draft arrives closer to final and the editing is lighter. And the API ties the whole thing together so the pipeline runs without a human shuttling files around. A mature setup looks like this: content management system detects new or changed text, sends it to DeepL through the API with the project glossary and the appropriate formality applied, receives the draft, checks it against translation memory (below) to reuse anything already approved, and routes only the genuinely new segments to a post-editor in their CAT tool. The human touches only what needs a human. Everything else flows.

A short worked example of glossaries earning their keep: a company localizing a project-management product has a feature it calls "Sprints." Left to its own judgment, a translation engine will sometimes render that as the athletic term for a short fast run, which is correct as language and wrong as product terminology — and worse, it may render it that way *inconsistently*, the sports word in one screen and a transliteration in another. A glossary entry pinning "Sprints" to the company's approved target-language rendering (often the English word left intact, for a coined product term) makes the output identical across every screen, every help article, and every translator, on the first pass, forever. Multiply that by every feature name, every menu label, and every piece of brand vocabulary, and the glossary is the difference between a product that reads as one coherent thing and one that reads as if eight different people translated it without talking to each other — which, in a sense, is exactly what happened without it.

CAT Tools and Translation Memory

Professional translators do not, by and large, work in DeepL's website. They work in **CAT tools** — computer-aided translation environments built for exactly this job — and DeepL is designed to live inside them. Chapter 22 covers the integrations in detail; here I want to explain *why* this matters for the workflow, because two CAT-tool concepts are central to how localization actually runs.

The first is the integration itself: DeepL plugs into the major CAT tools so the translator gets DeepL's draft *inside the environment they already work in*, alongside all their other tooling, rather than copying between a website and their workbench. The machine draft becomes one more input in the professional's cockpit.

The second is **translation memory**, and it is the concept that makes localization compound over time rather than starting fresh with every project. A translation memory is a database of previously translated and human-approved segments — every sentence you have localized before, paired with its finalized translation. When new content matches or resembles something already in the memory, the prior human-approved translation is reused or suggested, so you never re-translate and never re-edit what you have already perfected. Over a long-running localization program, the memory grows into a deep asset: more and more of each new batch is already handled, the machine and post-editor only touch what is genuinely new, and consistency with everything you have shipped before is automatic. DeepL's role is to draft the *new* segments well; the translation memory carries the accumulated human judgment of everything before. Together they are why a mature localization operation gets faster and more consistent the longer it runs.

Common Pitfalls in a Localization Operation

A few failure patterns recur often enough across real localization programs that they are worth flagging directly, because each one is avoidable once named.

Building the glossary too late. Teams frequently start translating to "make progress," intending to add the glossary once they see how the terminology is shaking out. By then thousands of segments carry inconsistent terms that have to be found and fixed. The glossary is cheapest to build first and most expensive to retrofit. Front-load it.

Confusing translation memory with a glossary. They solve different problems and you need both. A glossary enforces how individual *terms* are translated; a translation memory reuses whole *segments* you have already finalized. A glossary without a memory re-edits the same sentences project after project; a memory without a glossary lets terminology drift within those sentences. They are complementary, not alternatives.

Treating context-free strings like prose. Sending a software interface's strings through the pipeline as if they were paragraphs produces predictable trouble: the lone word "Open" translated as the wrong part of speech, a button label that overflows its space in a longer language, a placeholder variable mangled. UI strings need context notes for the translator, length awareness, and protected placeholders — handling them like running text is a recurring source of embarrassing launch bugs.

Skipping the human loop to save time, then paying for it. Under deadline pressure, the tempting shortcut is to ship lightly checked or unchecked machine output and "fix it later." The errors that ship are the fluent ones a market notices, and fixing them after launch — under scrutiny, across already-published pages — costs more than the post-edit would have. The loop is not the slow part of localization; skipping it is.

Forgetting that the product keeps changing. A first launch is a project; keeping eight locales in sync as the product ships weekly is the real work, and it is where the compounding assets — glossary, translation memory, automated pipeline — pay off most. Teams that treat localization as a one-time push rather than an ongoing operation rebuild the same effort every release. Set up the operation, not just the project.

Where DeepL Speeds Real Localization — and Where Humans Stay Essential

Let me draw the line cleanly, because it is the honest center of the chapter.

DeepL genuinely accelerates the parts of localization that are about volume and consistency. Producing the first full draft of enormous amounts of content, fast and at a quality that makes editing efficient; holding terminology steady across thousands of pages through glossaries; preserving formatting; feeding automated pipelines through the API; supplying the draft inside the translator's CAT tool. These are real, large, measurable gains, and they are why localization that used to take months and a fortune now takes weeks and a fraction of it. For the bulk of the words in most localization projects, DeepL plus a post-editor is faster, cheaper, and entirely good enough.

Humans stay essential for the parts that are about judgment. The post-editor catches the mistranslation that reads plausibly but means the wrong thing. They supply the cultural adaptation — the joke that does not travel, the example that does not fit the market, the phrasing that is technically correct and locally tone-deaf. They make the call on the high-stakes content where a subtle error carries legal or reputational consequence (Chapters 18 and 24). They own the final quality, because the responsibility for what ships cannot be delegated to a model. The machine handles volume; the human handles judgment, and serious localization needs both.

The mistake to avoid in both directions is the same: treating it as all-or-nothing. Hand-translating everything from scratch wastes the engine and usually misses the deadline. Shipping raw machine output without the human loop produces content that *reads* localized and is full of the quiet errors a market will notice. The discipline that actually works is the loop — machine for the draft, human for the judgment, glossaries and memory for the consistency, automation for the scale. DeepL is built to be the engine in that loop, and used that way it does not replace the localization team. It makes a small team do the work of a large one, and frees the humans to spend their expertise where expertise is actually required.

Part V continues from this foundation into the settings where the stakes climb and the rules tighten. The first of those is the content where an error is not merely embarrassing but consequential — legal, medical, and regulated material — and where the human-in-the-loop principle this chapter introduced becomes not just wise but mandatory.

Chapter 18: Legal, Medical, and Regulated Content

A localization manager at a medical-device company once showed me a single mistranslated line in a set of patient instructions. The source had said a dose should be taken "every other day." The machine output, fluent and confident in the target language, had rendered it as "every day." Nothing about the translated sentence looked wrong. It read naturally, the grammar was clean, and a reviewer skimming for awkwardness would have sailed right past it — because the error was not awkward, it was *fluent*. That is the whole hazard of high-stakes translation in one example. The dangerous mistakes are rarely the clumsy ones you can spot. They are the smooth ones that say something subtly, consequentially different from the original, and carry the authority of good prose while they do it.

This chapter is about the content where that hazard has teeth: legal documents, medical and clinical material, and anything regulated — finance, pharmaceuticals, safety, compliance — where a translation is not just read but *relied on*, and a quiet error can become a lawsuit, a harmed patient, or a regulatory finding. DeepL is genuinely useful for this work. It is also, on its own, never sufficient for it. Holding both of those truths at once is the entire skill.

Where DeepL Genuinely Helps

Start with the good news, because it is substantial and easy to undersell once you have been frightened about the risks.

Volume and speed. High-stakes domains drown in language. A litigation matter can involve thousands of pages of foreign-language documents that someone has to *understand* before anyone decides which ones matter. A regulatory submission may need to exist in a dozen markets. DeepL turns a wall of unreadable material into something a qualified person can actually triage, fast, at a cost that makes the work possible at all. For sheer throughput — getting the gist, sorting the relevant from the irrelevant, knowing what you are looking at — it is transformative.

First drafts. For content that *will* get expert human review anyway, starting from a strong DeepL draft rather than a blank page is a real accelerant. The translator or domain expert shifts from authoring to reviewing and correcting, which on most documents is faster, and DeepL's quality means the draft they start from is already close on the routine 90 percent, letting them spend their expensive attention on the 10 percent that actually needs it. The glossary controls from Chapter 7 matter enormously here, because they let you lock regulated terminology — the exact rendering of a defined contract term, a drug name, a statutory phrase — so the draft is consistent before a human ever touches it.

Comprehension for decisions. Sometimes you do not need a publishable translation at all; you need to *know what a document says* so you can act. A contract you are deciding whether to sign, a foreign regulation you must comply with, an adverse-event report you need to assess — DeepL gets you to understanding quickly. That is a legitimate, valuable use even in the most regulated settings, as long as you are clear that comprehension is the goal and not a substitute for an authoritative version.

Across all three, notice the pattern: DeepL is doing the heavy lifting of *volume*, and a human is supplying the *judgment*. That division is the right mental model for this entire chapter.

It is worth making the legal use cases concrete, because the abstract "DeepL helps with volume" undersells how transformative the triage case is in practice. In cross-border litigation or due diligence, a team may face tens of thousands of pages in a language no one on the deal can read — emails, contracts, internal memos, regulatory filings — and the first question is not "what does each page say precisely?" but "which of these pages even matter?" Reading every page through a human translator before knowing which are relevant is economically impossible; it would cost more than the matter is worth. DeepL inverts the problem: run the whole corpus through translation, let a qualified person skim the lot to find the dozen documents that are actually load-bearing, and *then* commission careful human translation of only those. The machine made the haystack searchable so the human could find the needles. That workflow — machine for breadth, human for the depth that breadth revealed was needed — is the single most valuable thing DeepL does in legal work, and it is entirely compatible with the hard line drawn in the next section, because the documents that end up mattering still get the human treatment. The triage just made it affordable to find them.

The same shape recurs in medical and regulatory settings. A pharmacovigilance team monitoring adverse-event reports from many countries needs to understand each report quickly enough to spot a safety signal; DeepL gets them to comprehension at the speed the volume demands, and the reports that indicate something serious then get the careful, expert, verified treatment they warrant. A compliance officer trying to understand a foreign regulator's new guidance needs the gist now and the authoritative reading from counsel before acting. In every case the structure is identical: comprehension fast and broad from the machine, authority and accountability narrow and slow from the human, with the machine's speed being precisely what makes the human's careful attention affordable to focus where it counts.

Where Human Review Is Non-Negotiable

Now the hard line. For high-stakes content, **the model is DeepL-plus-a-human, never DeepL alone** — and the human is not a proofreader checking for typos but a qualified expert checking for meaning.

The reason is exactly the patient-instruction example. Machine translation's failure mode in regulated content is not gibberish; gibberish is harmless because you catch it. The failure mode is the *fluent error* — a sentence that is grammatically perfect and reads naturally while saying something the source did not. A negation dropped or added. A dosage, a deadline, a liability cap, a defined term rendered plausibly but wrong. A conditional turned into an absolute. These slip past anyone who is reviewing for style rather than for fidelity, and in legal and medical contexts the gap between what the source said and what the translation says is precisely where the harm lives.

So the review has to be done by someone who can read both languages *and* understands the domain — a legal translator who knows what the contract term has to mean, a medical translator who knows the clinical stakes of the dosage line. They are not polishing DeepL's prose. They are verifying, against the source, that the meaning survived the crossing. That is irreducibly human work, and no amount of fluency in the output reduces the need for it. If anything, DeepL's high quality makes the review *more* important to insist on, because good prose is more persuasive, and a reviewer is more likely to trust output that reads well — which is exactly when the fluent error gets through.

It is worth cataloguing the specific kinds of fluent error that recur in high-stakes content, because knowing what to hunt for is what makes a review effective rather than a reassuring skim. **Negation errors** are the most dangerous: a dropped or added "not," "no," or "without" inverts a clause while leaving it grammatically perfect — "the warranty does not cover water damage" becoming "the warranty covers water damage." **Number and unit errors** are next: a transposed figure, a misread decimal, a confusion of units (milligrams for micrograms, the patient-instruction "every other day" becoming "every day"), a date shifted. **Defined-term drift**, where a word that has a precise meaning in the source — a term defined in a contract's definitions section, a statutory phrase, a drug's exact name — gets translated as its ordinary-language cousin, which reads naturally and means something legally or clinically different. **Modality and conditionality errors**, where "may" becomes "must," "should" becomes "shall," or a conditional ("if the buyer defaults") loses its condition and becomes an absolute. And **scope errors**, where a qualifier attaches to the wrong noun, changing what a clause governs. None of these are awkward; all of them are fluent; every one of them can carry real consequence. A domain reviewer who knows this list reads *for* these failure modes specifically, against the source, rather than reading the translation alone for smoothness — which is exactly the reading that lets them through.

A practical note on how to structure that review so it actually catches these. The reviewer should read the *source and the translation side by side*, not the translation alone, because the fluent error is invisible in the translation by definition — it is only visible as a *divergence* from the source. A reviewer handed only the polished target text has no way to see that a negation went missing; they can only judge whether the target reads well, and it does, which is the trap. Sentence-by-sentence comparison against the original is slower than a smoothness skim, and it is the entire point: the speed you saved by starting from a machine draft is meant to be reinvested in this comparison, not pocketed. A team that uses DeepL's draft to skip the comparison has not accelerated the work; it has removed the only step that made the work safe.

Certified Translation Is Its Own Thing

A point that trips people up: **a certified translation is a legal and procedural category, not a quality level.** When a court, a government, an immigration authority, or a regulator demands a certified translation, they are demanding a translation accompanied by a formal attestation — typically a qualified or sworn translator's signed statement, sometimes notarized, sometimes apostilled — that the translation is accurate and complete. The requirements vary by jurisdiction and by purpose, and they are about *accountability*: a named, qualified human putting their professional standing behind the document.

DeepL cannot certify anything. No machine can, because certification is precisely the act of a responsible human vouching for the work. DeepL can produce the draft that the certifying translator works from, and often does in professional practice — but the deliverable is the human's certified product, with the human's name and liability on it. If your document needs certification, your workflow needs a qualified human translator from the start, with DeepL as a tool inside their process rather than a replacement for it. Confirm the exact certification requirements with the body that is demanding the translation, because they differ and they are not negotiable by you.

Liability and Who Owns the Error

This is the part that turns an abstract risk into a concrete reason to be careful. When a translation in a regulated context is wrong and someone is harmed — a patient, a counterparty, a regulator's expectation — **the liability does not attach to the tool. It attaches to the organization and the people who relied on it.** DeepL is software you used; you are the one who put the output into the world and stood behind it.

That reframes the whole decision. The question is never "is DeepL good enough?" in the abstract. It is "who is accountable if this specific document is wrong, and have they actually reviewed it?" For internal comprehension, the accountable person is the one making the decision, and the bar is whether they understand the document well enough to decide — DeepL often clears that bar alone. For anything that goes out under your organization's name with legal, clinical, or regulatory weight, the accountable person is a qualified human who must have verified the meaning, and unreviewed machine output simply cannot be allowed to reach that role. Deciding which bucket a given document falls into, before you start, is the single most important judgment in this chapter.

Sorting a Document Into the Right Bucket

Because that sorting decision carries so much weight, it is worth a concrete procedure rather than a vibe. Three questions, asked before you touch the tool, place almost any document correctly.

Who relies on this, and for what? If the only person relying on the output is you, internally, to inform a decision you are accountable for, the document is in the comprehension bucket — DeepL alone is often appropriate, and the bar is simply whether you understand it well enough to act. If anyone *outside* will rely on it, or if it will be acted upon as an authoritative statement of what the source says, it has crossed into the bucket that requires verified human translation.

What is the cost of a fluent error here? Run the worst plausible case. If a dropped negation or a flipped number in this document caused harm, what would it be — an inconvenience, or a harmed patient, a lost case, a regulatory finding, a contract enforced against you on terms you never agreed to? The size of that downside, not the difficulty of the translation, decides how much human verification the document needs. A simple sentence can carry catastrophic stakes; an enormous document can be low-stakes triage.

Does an external body dictate the form? If a court, regulator, immigration authority, or contract requires a certified, sworn, or otherwise formally attested translation, the bucket is decided for you regardless of the other answers — you need a qualified human translator from the start, with DeepL as a tool inside their process. This is a procedural requirement, not a quality judgment, and it is covered in the next section.

A worked sort makes the procedure tangible. A pharmaceutical company receives a foreign-language regulatory inspection report. *Reading it to understand what the inspectors found and brief the team* is comprehension — DeepL alone, fast, appropriate. *The official response the company files back with the regulator* is external-reliance, maximal-consequence, possibly form-dictated — qualified human translation with full verification, DeepL at most a drafting aid inside that process. Same company, same language pair, two documents, two completely different buckets, sorted in under a minute by the three questions. The discipline is doing the sort deliberately and in advance, rather than discovering after something shipped that you had quietly trusted unreviewed output with weight it could not bear.

The Privacy Dimension Sensitive Documents Demand

High-stakes content is almost always *confidential* content. Legal documents carry privilege and trade secrets. Medical material carries protected health information. Regulated filings carry material non-public data. So the privacy question is not separate from the high-stakes question — it is part of it, and the wrong tool can turn a translation task into a data breach.

This is where DeepL's posture becomes a practical reason to choose it rather than a footnote. On its paid and API products, DeepL does not retain your texts after translation and does not use them to train its models, and it is built on European data protection with enterprise-grade security — the full treatment is Chapter 20, and for sensitive legal and medical material that chapter is not optional reading. The actionable point here is twofold. First, the *consumer free* tier and the *Pro and API* products differ in their data handling, and confidential documents belong only on the products with the stronger guarantees — never pasted into a free consumer tool whose data terms are an afterthought. Second, if you operate under a specific regime — HIPAA in the United States, GDPR in the European Union, or a sector regulator's rules — you must confirm that your DeepL deployment and contract actually meet that regime's requirements before you route protected data through it. The capability is there; whether your specific configuration satisfies your specific obligation is something to verify with the current terms and, where it matters, your counsel and compliance team.

A few of those regime-specific requirements are worth naming so you know what "confirm it actually meets the requirement" involves in practice. Under **GDPR**, processing personal data through a translation provider generally makes that provider a processor acting on your behalf, which means you need a data processing agreement in place, you need to know where the data is processed, and you remain the controller responsible for the lawful basis of the processing — the tool's compliance posture supports yours but does not substitute for it. Under **HIPAA**, routing protected health information through a vendor requires a business associate agreement with that vendor; absent one, the disclosure itself can be a violation regardless of how well the vendor handles the data. Sector regulators — financial, pharmaceutical, defense — layer their own demands on top. The pattern across all of them is the same: a tool can be *capable* of compliant handling without your *particular use* being compliant, because compliance depends on the contract you have signed, the configuration you are running, and the obligations that attach to you specifically. This is exactly why the verification belongs with your counsel and compliance team rather than with a book.

There is also a moving-target dimension to flag honestly, because the regulatory landscape around AI-assisted handling of sensitive content is genuinely in flux. The EU AI Act, for instance, has provisions phasing in over time — its transparency-related obligations under Article 4 became applicable on 2 February 2025, with broader enforcement arriving 2 August 2026 — and further EU rulemaking, including the pending Digital Omnibus, is under discussion but not yet law as of this writing. The durable advice is not to memorize any of those specifics, which will have shifted by the time you read this, but to treat the regulatory frame as a live thing you re-check rather than a settled backdrop. Where a translation touches regulated, personal, or health data, "what did the rules say when I set this up?" is not a safe substitute for "what do the rules say now?" Verify against the current state, and where the stakes are real, verify with someone whose job it is to track it.

The Discipline This Demands

The throughline of this chapter is a discipline more than a rule. DeepL belongs in legal, medical, and regulated work — it makes volume tractable, it accelerates the experts, and on the right products it handles sensitive text responsibly. What it cannot do is *replace the accountable human*, because in these domains the deliverable is not a translation but a verified, attested, liability-bearing translation, and only a qualified person can supply the verification and stand behind it. Use DeepL for everything it is good at, draw the line clearly at the point where a fluent error becomes someone's harm, and put a competent human exactly there. That line, drawn honestly and held, is what makes the tool an asset in high-stakes work rather than a hazard.

The next part of this discussion belongs to the broader limits — the full map of what DeepL gets wrong and how to recognize it — which Chapter 24 takes up directly. Before that, though, the more everyday face of multilingual work at scale: the teams and support desks that run on translation every day, where the stakes are lower but the volume is relentless.

Chapter 19: Multilingual Teams and Support

A support lead at a software company described her week to me once in a way that has stuck. Her team of nine answered customer tickets in fourteen languages. Three of her agents were genuinely multilingual; the rest were not, and yet every one of them was somehow closing tickets in Polish, Japanese, and Brazilian Portuguese. The trick was not that she had hired a UN delegation. It was that DeepL sat invisibly between the incoming ticket and the agent, and between the agent's reply and the customer, so that a support rep in Dublin could read a frustrated message in German, understand it perfectly, and answer in clear German without speaking a word of it. "My agents think they're bilingual now," she said. "They're not. The tool is. But the customer can't tell the difference, and honestly, neither can I most days."

That is the shape of DeepL at work for teams: not a translator someone occasionally opens, but a layer woven into how a multilingual organization actually operates day to day. This chapter is about two faces of that — internal communication across a team that does not share a language, and customer support across many languages at once — and about the consistency, the speed, and the honest limits that come with running an organization on machine translation.

Internal Communication Across a Team

The first place DeepL changes an organization is inside it, in the ordinary friction of a workforce that spans languages. A company with offices in Munich, Tokyo, and São Paulo does not have a single working language so much as a negotiated one, usually English, that some people speak fluently and others speak haltingly — and the haltingly is where ideas get lost. The engineer with the best insight is not always the one most comfortable composing it in the company's lingua franca, and meaning leaks out in the gap between what someone understands and what they can express.

DeepL narrows that gap from both directions. It lets people **read** in their strong language — an internal memo, a project brief, a wiki page consumed in one's native tongue rather than struggled through in a second one, with comprehension and speed that a non-native reader simply does not get otherwise. And it lets people **write** with more confidence, drafting in the language they think best and translating out, or using DeepL Write (Part III) to sharpen prose in a second language so a great idea is not held back by imperfect phrasing. The effect is quieter than a flashy product demo but more important: it flattens the participation hierarchy that language skill otherwise imposes, so that the person with the best contribution can make it regardless of which language they are strongest in.

To see how concrete this gets, picture a single product decision moving through that three-office company. The São Paulo engineer who found the performance bottleneck writes up his analysis in Portuguese, because in Portuguese he can be precise about exactly what he measured and why it matters. He translates it to English to post in the shared channel. The Tokyo team reads the English, but two of them quietly translate it back into Japanese to be sure they have understood the trade-offs before they commit engineering time. The Munich product manager reads it in German, drafts a response in German, and sends the English. At no point did anyone wait for the one person who happened to speak both Portuguese and Japanese, and at no point did the original insight get flattened into the cautious, hedged English that non-native writers produce when they are translating in their heads as they type. Each person operated at full fluency in their own language, and the conversation moved at the speed of thought rather than the speed of the weakest shared tongue.

The Wiki, the Onboarding Doc, and the Long Tail of Internal Text

The flashy use is live discussion, but the durable value is often in the boring places — the internal knowledge base, the runbooks, the onboarding documentation that every new hire has to absorb. In a monolingual company these exist once and everyone reads them. In a multilingual one, they either get maintained in several languages (expensive, and the translations drift out of date the moment the source changes) or they exist in one language and quietly exclude everyone who reads it slowly.

DeepL changes the economics of that long tail. A company can keep its canonical documentation in one source language and let each reader translate the page they need, on demand, into the language they actually think in. The source stays single and current; the translation is generated fresh each time, so it never goes stale relative to the source the way a separately maintained translated copy does. For document-heavy knowledge — the wiki page nobody wants to maintain in six languages, the policy that updated last week, the architecture decision record from two years ago — on-demand translation is often the right answer precisely because it sidesteps the maintenance problem that kills multilingual documentation efforts.

There is a real limit to flag here, though, and teams that skip it get burned. On-demand translation is excellent for *comprehension* — reading to understand — and weaker as a substitute for an *authoritative* version. If a policy has legal force, or a runbook step is the difference between recovering a database and losing it, the version people act on should be a reviewed, fixed translation, not a fresh machine rendering generated at read time that nobody has checked. The rule of thumb: machine-translate the long tail of documentation people read to *understand*, but treat the small set of documents people *rely on* — anything with legal, safety, or financial consequence — as needing a human-reviewed translation of record. Knowing which documents fall into that second bucket is part of running this well.

The Meeting Problem

Written communication is where DeepL Translate earns its keep internally, but a multilingual team's hardest moments are usually live: the all-hands, the cross-office standup, the design review where the Munich and Tokyo engineers need to argue in real time. Written translation does not help in the room. This is exactly where DeepL Voice (Part IV) enters the picture for teams, and it is worth naming the boundary clearly so expectations are set right.

Voice translation makes a meeting *workable* across languages in a way it was not before — people can speak in their strong language and be understood, which lowers the barrier to participation for the same reason the written tools do. But live spoken translation is harder than text, it carries latency, and it stumbles on the things spoken language is full of: cross-talk, jargon, half-finished sentences, the rapid back-and-forth of a real argument. For a structured meeting — a presentation, a status update, a prepared discussion — it works well. For a freewheeling technical debate where four people are interrupting each other, it strains. The practical pattern most teams settle into is using voice translation to broaden *who can follow and contribute* to meetings, while still relying on written follow-ups — the meeting notes, the decision record, translated as text — to carry the precise, accountable version of what was decided. Speech for the conversation, text for the record.

The Honest Caveat on Internal Use

The honest caveat that runs under all of this is that it works best for *operational* communication — the documents, updates, briefs, and messages that make up the bulk of internal work — and least well for the communication where tone is the message. A delicate piece of feedback, a sensitive personnel matter, a carefully calibrated announcement: these still want a human who knows both the language and the people, because the nuance Chapter 24 discusses is exactly what carries the weight in them. A performance conversation that lands wrong because the translated phrasing was a degree too blunt is not a small thing; in some cultures the difference between an acceptable correction and an insult is precisely the register that machine translation handles least reliably. For the daily operational majority, though, DeepL is the thing that lets a multilingual team function as one team — and the skill is recognizing the minority of communications where the stakes live in the tone and routing those to a person.

Customer Support at Scale

The second face, and the one that drives the most business adoption, is customer support — because support is where language volume is relentless and the cost of getting it wrong is immediate and visible. A growing company suddenly serving customers in twenty markets faces a brutal staffing math: hiring native-speaking agents for every language does not scale, but answering customers in a language they did not write in does not work either. DeepL is how teams resolve that tension.

The pattern is the one the support lead described. Incoming messages get translated so any agent can understand any customer. The agent's reply gets translated back into the customer's language. A relatively small team covers a large language footprint, and the customer experiences support in their own tongue without the company having staffed a speaker of it. For the enormous volume of routine support — the password resets, the billing questions, the how-do-I tickets that are the daily bread of any support desk — this works remarkably well, and the quality that built DeepL's name (Chapter 1) is exactly what makes it acceptable here. A reply that reads naturally in the customer's language preserves the sense of being *taken care of* in a way a robotic translation would quietly undermine.

Walking a Ticket Through the Flow

It helps to walk one ticket through end to end, because the details of where translation sits in the flow are what separate a deployment that works from one that frustrates everyone. A customer in Warsaw writes in to say her invoice does not match her plan, in Polish, with the particular mix of irritation and specifics that real complaints have.

In a well-built flow, the helpdesk software translates her message into the agent's working language the moment it lands, and crucially, it keeps the *original Polish* visible alongside the translation rather than discarding it. The agent — say, in Dublin — reads the translated English, understands the billing discrepancy, and pulls up the account. She drafts her reply in English: an explanation of the proration, an apology for the confusion, a corrected invoice. Before it sends, DeepL renders it into Polish. The customer receives a fluent Polish reply that addresses her actual problem.

Two design choices in that flow matter more than they look. First, **keeping the source text visible** means that when the translation is ambiguous — and occasionally it will be — the agent can see the original and, if she reads any Polish at all or can spot a product name, catch a misunderstanding before she answers the wrong question. Second, **the agent reviews the outgoing translation's intent, not just trusts it blindly.** She cannot read Polish, so she cannot proofread the output directly, but she *can* keep her English reply clean and unambiguous so that what gets translated is easy to translate well. Short sentences, no idioms, the product's real terms — writing for translation is a learnable agent skill, and the teams that train their agents in it get noticeably better customer-facing output than the teams that let agents write however they like and hope the machine sorts it out.

When the Customer Switches Channels

A subtlety that trips up real deployments: support is not only email tickets. The same customer may follow up in live chat, where latency matters and there is no time for an agent to carefully compose, and may later get a phone call, where the written tools do not apply at all. A team that has wired DeepL beautifully into its email ticketing and forgotten about chat ends up with a jarring inconsistency — smooth multilingual email, then a chat window where the agent suddenly cannot communicate.

The practical answer is to think of the *language coverage* as a property of the whole support operation, not of one channel. Asynchronous channels (email, ticketing) tolerate the translation round-trip easily. Live chat tolerates it but rewards speed, so canned-response libraries — pre-translated, glossary-consistent answers to the most common questions — carry a lot of the load and keep the human-in-the-loop translation for the genuinely novel questions. Live phone support across a language barrier is the hardest case and is where DeepL Voice (Part IV) and, for the highest stakes, human interpreters still earn their place. Mapping which channels you support in which languages, and being honest about where the coverage thins out, prevents the customer-facing inconsistency that erodes the whole effort.

The Two Things That Make or Break It

Two things make or break the support deployment. The first is **integration** — DeepL working inside the helpdesk software the team already lives in, rather than as a separate window agents copy-paste through, which is the difference between a tool that gets used and one that gets abandoned under pressure (Chapter 22 covers how that wiring works). Copy-paste translation survives a calm Tuesday; it does not survive a Monday-morning ticket flood, when agents under volume pressure will quietly stop switching windows and start guessing, and your multilingual support silently degrades exactly when you can least afford it. The integration has to be invisible enough that it costs the agent nothing to use, or it will not get used. The second is **consistency**, which deserves its own treatment.

Consistency Is the Whole Game at Scale

For a single email, a translation just needs to be good. For an organization producing thousands of translated messages a month across many languages, good is not enough on its own — they also need to be *consistent*, and consistency is where teams either look professional or look like a patchwork.

Consider what inconsistency does to support. Your product has a feature with a specific name. Your company has a particular way of referring to your subscription tiers, your policies, your brand. If DeepL renders these slightly differently from one ticket to the next — translating your product name when it should stay in English, or picking a different word for "subscription" each time — customers get a subtly incoherent experience, and worse, your translated support contradicts your translated documentation, which contradicts your translated marketing. The language is fluent and the organization still looks careless.

A concrete failure makes the stakes vivid. Suppose your product has a feature officially called "Smart Sync." Without a glossary, one agent's reply translates it descriptively into German as something like "intelligente Synchronisierung," another leaves it as "Smart Sync," a third renders it a third way. Now a German customer who read "Smart Sync" in your marketing, "intelligente Synchronisierung" in one support reply, and a different phrase in the help center cannot tell whether these are the same feature or three different ones. The translation was fluent every time. The *experience* was confusing, and confusion in support is exactly what you are paying agents to eliminate. Multiply that across every product name, every defined term, and every brand phrase, across fourteen languages, and inconsistency quietly does as much damage as outright errors would.

The fix is **glossaries**, covered in full in Chapter 7, deployed here as an organizational asset rather than a personal convenience. A team glossary locks the rendering of your product names, your defined terms, your brand vocabulary, your do-not-translate list, so that every agent's every reply uses the same word for the same thing in every language. Building and maintaining that shared glossary is one of the highest-leverage things a multilingual team can do, because it converts DeepL from a tool that produces *good translations* into one that produces *your organization's voice, consistently, at scale.*

Owning the Glossary as an Organization

Because the glossary is an organizational asset, it needs an organizational owner, and this is a step teams routinely skip to their cost. A glossary that nobody owns is a glossary that ships once and then rots: the product launches three new features, the marketing team coins two new phrases, a market's preferred term for "refund" turns out to be subtly wrong, and the glossary never catches up because it is nobody's job. Within a few months the consistency benefit erodes and the team is back to patchwork without quite noticing when it happened.

The practical discipline is to treat the glossary the way you treat any shared reference data. Someone — usually whoever owns localization or support quality — owns keeping it current. New product terms get added to it as part of the launch checklist, not after. The most expensive mistakes to fix are the do-not-translate entries, so those go in first: product names, trademarks, the things that must stay in their original form everywhere. And the glossary is reviewed against the markets it serves, because the right term in standard German may be the wrong one in Austrian or Swiss usage, and a glossary that assumes one variant per language can quietly mis-serve a whole market. The formality dimension belongs here too: DeepL's formality controls (Chapter 8) let a team set the right register for its brand and market, so that a culture expecting formal address gets it and a casual brand stays casual, uniformly, without depending on each agent to remember which market expects which.

Speed at Scale, and What It Buys

The benefit underneath all of this is speed, and it is worth naming plainly because it is what justifies the investment. A support team using DeepL well answers more tickets, in more languages, faster, with fewer specialized hires, while keeping quality high enough that customers do not feel shortchanged. An internal team moves information across language lines without the bottleneck of waiting for the one person who speaks both. The translation that used to be a discrete task someone scheduled becomes an invisible, instant layer, and the organization simply operates as though language were less of a barrier than it is.

That speed compounds. The first ticket saved is a small thing; ten thousand tickets a month across fourteen languages is a different headcount, a different response-time SLA, a different set of markets you can credibly serve. This is why

DeepL adoption at the team level tends to be sticky: once an organization has felt what it is like to operate multilingually without the friction, going back is unthinkable.

It is worth being precise about what the speed actually buys, though, because "we can serve more markets" is the headline and the real strategic shift is underneath it. A company that can credibly support customers in a language can *sell* into that market, because support coverage is one of the quiet preconditions for entering a market at all — customers in many regions will not commit to a product they cannot get help with in their own language. DeepL's leverage here is not only that it makes existing support cheaper; it is that it lowers the threshold for *entering* a market to the point where you can test demand in a new language before committing to native-speaking staff. The translation layer turns "we'll support that market once it's big enough to staff" into "we can support that market well enough to find out whether it will get big," which is a different and more useful order of operations.

The Honest Limits

I would be doing the support lead's customers a disservice if I left it there, because running a team on machine translation has a real edge you have to manage, and the teams that do it well are the ones that respect it.

Nuance and tone are where it breaks. Everything in this chapter is about the high-volume, operational, routine majority of communication, where DeepL excels. The exceptions are the messages where *how* something is said matters as much as what — the escalated complaint from a furious customer, the apology that has to land exactly right, the delicate negotiation, the announcement with legal or emotional weight. For those, a fluent translation that is tonally slightly off can make things worse, and the right move is a human who knows the language and the stakes. A mature support operation routes these out of the automated flow rather than trusting the tool with them, and the skill is recognizing which tickets they are. In practice that recognition can be partly systematized: tickets flagged as complaints, escalations, cancellations, or legal threats are exactly the population most likely to turn on tone, and routing those categories to a native speaker or a senior agent — rather than letting any agent handle them through the translation layer — is a cheap policy that catches most of the cases where the automated flow would have made things worse.

Sensitive content has its own rules. Support handles personal data, account details, sometimes regulated information. Which DeepL product a team uses, and how it is configured, matters enormously for that — the data-handling distinction between consumer and Pro or API offerings is real and consequential, and Chapter 20 is required reading before a team routes customer data through any translation layer. The capability to do this responsibly exists; using it responsibly is a deliberate choice the organization has to make.

The customer sometimes knows. Even excellent machine translation occasionally produces a phrasing a native speaker clocks as not-quite-human, and a customer who realizes they are being answered by a translation layer may feel less personally served. The mitigation is partly quality — DeepL's is high enough that this is rare — and partly honesty about where the line falls between scalable automated support and the human touch that some interactions still deserve. A related, subtler failure is the *confidently wrong* reply: because DeepL's output reads so naturally, an agent who cannot read the target language has no way to catch a translation that fluently says something slightly different from what the agent intended. The guardrail is the one named earlier — write outgoing replies in clean, unambiguous, glossary-consistent language so there is little for the translation to get wrong — plus the humility to keep the original source text visible so that ambiguity has somewhere to be resolved rather than silently guessed.

Used with those limits in view, DeepL is what lets a normally sized team punch far above its linguistic weight, serving customers and colleagues across a dozen languages as though it spoke them all. Whether a team can use it for its real work — its customer data, its internal documents, its confidential material — comes down in the end to what happens to that text after it is translated, which is significant enough, and enough of a genuine reason organizations choose DeepL, to deserve a chapter of its own.

Chapter 20: Privacy, Security, and Compliance

I was once in a meeting where a company's legal counsel killed a translation-tool proposal in a single sentence. The team had built a slick workflow around a free online translator, and counsel asked one question: "When our contracts go into that box, where do they go and who can see them?" Nobody had an answer. The proposal died on the spot, not because the translation quality was poor — it was fine — but because the tool's data terms were an afterthought, and the documents in question were exactly the kind a company cannot afford to leak. A few weeks later the same team came back with DeepL, and counsel asked the same question, and this time there was an answer good enough to say yes to. That contrast is the whole subject of this chapter, and it is one of the more genuine reasons people choose DeepL over the free alternatives that look, on the surface, like they do the same thing.

For most AI tools in this series, privacy is a question of *managing risk* — knowing what you put in and accepting that it may be used. For DeepL, privacy is closer to a *feature*, something the company built deliberately and sells on, and that difference is worth understanding precisely, because it is real but it is also not unconditional.

Why This Matters More for Translation

Start with why the privacy question is sharper for a translator than for, say, a chatbot you ask trivia. The reason is structural: **translation is disproportionately applied to sensitive material.** The whole point of translating a document is usually that it matters — and the documents that matter are contracts, internal strategy, financial filings, personal data, medical records, legal correspondence. Casual translation of a restaurant menu exists, but the *valuable* translation work, the kind organizations pay for and build workflows around, runs heavily toward exactly the content you most need to keep confidential.

There is a second structural reason, less obvious and worth naming. Translation does not just *touch* sensitive material; it tends to touch it in its rawest, most complete form. You do not translate a summary of the contract — you translate the contract, every clause, every named party, every figure. You do not translate the gist of the patient record — you translate the record. Where a chatbot interaction is often a question *about* sensitive material, a translation request is usually the sensitive material itself, in full, pasted in whole. That makes the data terms of a translation tool more consequential than the data terms of almost any other category of AI tool, because there is no abstraction layer between what you are protecting and what you are sending.

That means the data terms of a translation tool are not a footnote; they are load-bearing. A free tool that reserves the right to retain and learn from whatever you paste into it is, for sensitive material, a confidentiality breach waiting to be discovered — which is precisely what DeepL's posture is built to avoid, and why the counsel in my story could say yes the second time.

DeepL's Data Posture, Stated Plainly

Here is the durable core of what makes DeepL different, with the standing caveat that the precise terms are the kind of thing you must confirm against DeepL's current privacy documentation rather than trust a book to keep current.

On its **paid Pro and API products**, DeepL's commitment is that it **does not retain your texts after the translation is delivered, and does not use them to train its models.** Your text comes in, gets translated, the result goes back to you, and the source text is not kept around or fed into model improvement. For sensitive content this is the single most important property, because it means the act of translating a confidential document does not create a lingering copy of it somewhere outside your control or a chance for it to surface, however indirectly, in a future model. Confirm the exact retention specifics and any limited operational exceptions in DeepL's current terms, but the durable shape — *paid products do not keep or train on your text* — is the heart of the differentiator.

It is worth being precise about what those two commitments actually rule out, because they answer two genuinely different worries. **Not retaining** the text addresses the breach-and-subpoena worry: if the text is gone after the translation is delivered, there is no store of your contracts sitting on a vendor's servers to be hacked, subpoenaed, or accidentally exposed. **Not training** addresses the leakage worry: a model trained on your text could, in principle and however rarely, reproduce fragments of it in someone else's output, and a commitment not to train forecloses that path entirely. The two together are why a careful counsel treats the paid-product posture as meaningfully different from "we promise to be careful" — they are specific, checkable claims about the two ways translated text most plausibly escapes.

DeepL is also a **European company built on European data protection**, which matters in two ways. First, it places DeepL squarely under the GDPR, the strong data-protection regime that governs personal data in the European Union, with the obligations and user rights that come with it. Second, for organizations whose own compliance requires that data stay within particular jurisdictions or under particular legal frameworks, a European provider with strong GDPR alignment is often a materially easier answer than a tool whose data handling is governed by terms written somewhere else with looser defaults. If data residency or a specific regulatory regime is part of your requirements, verify how DeepL's current offering meets it — but the starting posture is one built for, not retrofitted to, strict data protection.

The jurisdictional point deserves a little weight, because it is exactly the kind of thing that turns out to matter only when it is too late to fix. For a European organization, routing personal data through a service governed by EU data-protection law and operated by an EU company sidesteps a whole category of cross-border-transfer questions that arise the moment personal data leaves the EU for a jurisdiction the EU does not consider adequately protective. Those transfer questions are answerable — there are mechanisms for them — but they are paperwork, legal review, and ongoing risk that a same-jurisdiction provider simply does not generate. Counsel notice this even when the rest of the organization does not, which is part of why DeepL's European foundation reads as a feature to exactly the people who have to sign the approval.

The AI Act Sits Alongside, Not Instead Of, Data Protection

A point of confusion worth heading off: the EU AI Act and the GDPR are different things, and DeepL's privacy posture is mostly about the latter. The GDPR governs *personal data* — how it is collected, processed, stored, and transferred. The AI Act governs *AI systems* by risk category, with transparency and other obligations layered on. They overlap but do not substitute for each other.

For most translation use, the AI Act's heavier obligations — the ones attached to high-risk systems — are not the operative concern; general-purpose translation is not typically the kind of high-risk use the Act's strictest tiers target. The provision worth being aware of is the AI-literacy expectation under Article 4, which became applicable on 2 February 2025: organizations deploying AI are expected to ensure the people using it have an adequate understanding of what it does and its limits. For a team routing customer or employee data through a translation tool, that is less a compliance hurdle than a description of doing this responsibly at all — knowing the difference between the free and paid tiers, knowing what gets retained, knowing where the human-review line falls. Broader AI Act obligations phase in over time, with significant provisions enforceable from 2 August 2026, and there is a pending Digital Omnibus package under discussion that is not yet law and should not be assumed to change anything until it is. The honest framing: the GDPR is the regime that does the real work for translation privacy today, the AI Act sits alongside it with mostly transparency-and-literacy implications for ordinary translation use, and you confirm the current state of both rather than treating either as settled from a book.

Security as a Separate Question

On **security**, which is a different axis from data-handling policy, DeepL carries enterprise-grade certifications of the kind regulated buyers require — independent attestations to recognized information-security standards, the ISO 27001 family of certifications being the canonical example of what this class of buyer looks for. The exact certifications DeepL holds at any given time, and their scope, are a verify-against-current-sources detail; the durable point is that DeepL has invested in the formal, audited security posture that lets a serious organization's security team sign off, rather than asking you to take its word.

The distinction between *policy* and *security* is worth holding onto, because they answer different questions and a buyer needs both. The data-handling policy answers "what does DeepL intend to do with my text?" — retain it or not, train on it or not. The security posture answers "how well is DeepL protected against doing the wrong thing by accident or attack?" — the controls, audits, and practices that stop the text from leaking even when nobody intended it to. A strong policy with weak security is a promise nobody can keep; strong security with a permissive policy protects text the vendor is allowed to use anyway. Regulated buyers ask about both because both have to hold, and the value of a certification like ISO 27001 is precisely that it is an *independent* attestation — a third party has checked, so the security claim does not rest on the vendor's own say-so. When you evaluate DeepL for serious use, check the policy and the certifications as two separate things, because they are.

The Distinction That Changes the Answer

Now the qualification that the whole chapter turns on, and the one most likely to bite someone who does not internalize it: **the consumer free tier and the paid Pro and API products do not have the same data posture.**

This pattern is familiar across the AI industry and DeepL is no exception. The strong commitments — not retaining your text, not training on it, the full enterprise data-handling guarantees — are the properties of the **paid products**. The **free consumer tier** operates under more permissive consumer terms, the kind that generally allow a provider broader latitude to use submitted text to operate and improve the service. The practical consequence is direct and important: **confidential material does not belong in the free tier.** If you are translating something sensitive — anything you would not want retained or used to improve a model — you must be on a paid Pro or API product whose terms give you the guarantees, not on the free version whose terms do not.

This is not DeepL being inconsistent; it is the entirely standard structure where the free tier is a generous taste of the product and the paid tier is the one with the contractual data protections that professional and regulated use requires. But it means "DeepL protects my data" is true *conditionally*, and the condition is which product you are using. Know which side of that line your work sits on, and make sure your sensitive work sits on the paid side. Verify the current terms for each tier, because the exact boundary is a perishable specific even though the structure is durable.

The reason this bites people is rarely a deliberate decision to put a contract through the free tier. It is drift. Someone signs up for the free version to try it, finds it excellent, builds a habit, and the habit quietly outlives the trial without anyone re-examining which tier they are on. Or a team standardizes on the paid product but a few individuals never got accounts and keep using the free site for "quick" translations that turn out not to be trivial. Or a workflow that started with throwaway text gradually starts carrying real customer data as it gets repurposed, and nobody revisits the tier decision that was made back when the stakes were low. The mitigation is organizational, not technical: for any team handling sensitive material, the policy has to be that sensitive translation goes through the paid product, and that policy has to be enforced by provisioning the right accounts and, ideally, by not leaving the free consumer tool as the path of least resistance sitting one browser tab away.

A Practical Test for Where Text Belongs

Because the line is conditional, people want a rule of thumb, and there is a serviceable one: **if you would hesitate to email this text to an outside party with no confidentiality agreement, it does not belong in any tier whose data terms you have not confirmed give you protection.** That reframing helps because most people have a well-calibrated instinct about email — they know a contract, a patient record, a pre-announcement financial figure, or a colleague's personal data is not something to send around casually. Apply that same instinct to the translation box. Trivial text — a public article, a menu, a message with nothing sensitive in it — is fine anywhere. Anything that trips the email instinct goes only through a paid product whose terms you have verified, or, for the most sensitive categories, through a path your own compliance function has signed off on. The instinct people already have for email is the instinct to import here; the only thing that changes is remembering that the translation box is the same kind of outbound channel.

What This Buys You in Regulated Settings

For the regulated and privacy-conscious users this posture is built for, the payoff is concrete. It is what lets a law firm route foreign-language discovery through a translation tool without manufacturing a privilege problem. It is what lets a healthcare organization consider machine translation for material touching protected health information — though, as Chapter 18 stressed, you must still confirm that your specific deployment and contract actually satisfy your specific regime, whether that is HIPAA, GDPR, or a sector regulator's rules, because a strong general posture is the *prerequisite* for compliance, not automatic proof of it. It is what lets a financial institution's security team approve a tool that touches material non-public information. In each case DeepL's posture is what moves the conversation from "absolutely not" to "let's verify it meets our requirements" — and getting to that second conversation is the whole value.

It is worth dwelling on that phrase — *the prerequisite for compliance, not the proof of it* — because it is where careful organizations and careless ones diverge. A strong vendor posture means the building blocks of a compliant deployment exist: the contractual commitments, the certifications, the data-residency story. It does not mean any particular use is automatically compliant, because compliance is a property of *your specific deployment under your specific regime*, not of the vendor in the abstract. The healthcare example is the clearest: the existence of a data-handling commitment that *could* support work touching protected health information does not mean a given configuration *does*, which is why a regulated buyer signs the right agreement, confirms the certification scope actually covers the service they use, checks that the deployment they configured matches the assurances they are relying on, and documents that they did. DeepL hands you a strong foundation and the documentation to build on it. The building — and the responsibility for it — is yours.

For organizations specifically, the right move is to treat DeepL's data and security terms the way you would any vendor handling sensitive data: review the current contractual commitments, confirm the certifications and their scope, check the data-residency story against your obligations, and make sure the configuration you actually deploy matches the assurances you are relying on. DeepL gives you a strong starting point and the documentation to do this review properly. It does not relieve you of doing it.

The Honest Summary

DeepL's privacy and security posture is one of the more legitimate differentiators in this series, and it is not marketing gloss — on its paid products the commitment not to retain or train on your text, the European data-protection foundation, and the enterprise security certifications are real, and they are real reasons that regulated and privacy-conscious users choose DeepL over free tools whose data terms were never the point. That is the genuine strength, and it deserves to be stated without hedging.

The two things to carry forward are the conditions on that strength. First, **the protections live on the paid products** — Pro and API — and the free consumer tier is governed by more permissive terms, so sensitive work must be on the paid side. Second, **a strong posture is the foundation for compliance, not a substitute for verifying it** — if you operate under a specific regime, confirm your specific deployment meets it against the current terms and, where the stakes warrant, your own counsel. Do those two things, and DeepL's privacy posture becomes exactly what it is meant to be: the reason you can trust a translation tool with the material that actually matters.

That foundation of trust is also what makes it sensible to build DeepL *into your own software*, where you control the integration and the data path even more directly. The developer-facing side of DeepL — the API that lets all of this capability live inside the systems you write — is where the next part of the book begins.

Part VI: Building on DeepL

Audience: developers, localizers, and the technically curious. The deep parts are signposted.

"The website is one way to reach DeepL. The API and the integrations are how you put its quality inside the tools you already work in."

— A working principle

Chapter 21: The DeepL API

Building a translation feature into your own app turns out to be easier than the hard part sounds. Say you want to let users read product reviews in their own language. The part you would expect to wrestle with — the translation quality — is the part you never have to think about: you send the review text to DeepL's API, get back a clean, natural translation, and drop it into your interface. What is genuinely new is what you have done in the process. You have wired DeepL's entire language capability into your own product, where your users will touch it without ever knowing DeepL exists. It stops being a website you send people to and becomes a translator that lives inside your app. That shift — from DeepL as a destination to DeepL as a component of your own software — is what this Part is about, and the API is the door to it.

Everything from here is written for people who build. If you only ever use DeepL through its website, apps, and integrations, you can skip Part VI without losing anything the rest of the book gives you. But it is worth knowing this surface exists, because it is where DeepL stops being a tool you open and becomes a capability you assemble into your own systems. And one caution belongs at the very top, the same discipline this whole series insists on for technical specifics: **API details — exact endpoints, parameter names, base URLs, pricing, and limits — are the most perishable material in this book.** I will describe the durable shape and flag every specific. The authority is always DeepL's current API documentation, not this page.

What the API Actually Is

The DeepL API is a programmable doorway to the same language capabilities that power the products you have met in the rest of this book. Instead of a person pasting text into a box on DeepL's site and reading the result, your program sends DeepL a request over the network — text to translate, the source and target languages, some settings — and receives the translation back as data your code can use. The underlying quality is the same one that built DeepL's reputation; what changes is who is doing the asking. In the website and apps, a human is in the loop. Through the API, your software is.

It is a **REST API**, which is the conventional, widely understood style of web interface most developers already know: your code makes standard web requests to DeepL's servers and gets structured responses back. And it exposes more than just translation. The core is **DeepL Translate** — text translation, and document translation that preserves formatting (Chapter 6). Alongside it, DeepL's API surface has grown to include capabilities from the broader product family, including **DeepL Write** for improving and rephrasing text, and the **Voice** capabilities for spoken translation. The exact roster of endpoints and which capabilities are exposed programmatically at any moment is a check-the-docs detail; the durable point is that the API is the developer-facing version of the same DeepL you already understand.

It helps to be concrete about the difference between the two kinds of translation the API offers, because they behave differently and trip up newcomers. **Text translation** is synchronous and fast: you send text, you get the translation back in the same response, and your code moves on. **Document translation** is fundamentally different — you upload a whole file (a Word document, a presentation, a PDF), DeepL processes it while preserving the formatting, and you retrieve the finished file in a separate step. That second step is the catch: document translation is not instant, so the pattern is upload, then poll for status until it is ready, then download. A developer who assumes document translation works like text translation — send, receive, done — writes code that breaks the moment a document takes more than a moment to process. The durable lesson is that the two endpoints have two different rhythms, and you build for each accordingly: text in one round-trip, documents in an upload-poll-download cycle.

Who It's For

Three rough groups reach for the API.

Builders embedding translation in a product — a team putting multilingual capability into an app, where DeepL is the engine behind a feature their users touch: translated reviews, a multilingual help center, in-app messaging across languages. This is the largest group and the one this Part is mainly written for.

Automators and integrators — people wiring DeepL into pipelines, content workflows, and internal tooling, where there is no user-facing translation box at all, just DeepL performing a step in some larger automated process: localizing a content management system, translating a batch of documents on a schedule, feeding a localization pipeline (Chapter 17).

Language professionals and toolmakers — translators and localization teams whose professional software calls DeepL under the hood, and the people who build that software. For this group DeepL is infrastructure rather than a website, and the integrations of Chapter 22 are often built on exactly this API.

If none of those is you, this is a clean place to rejoin the book later. If one of them is, read on.

Getting Oriented: Keys, Auth, and Endpoints

The mechanics follow a shape you may already know from other web APIs, and DeepL is conventional here. I will keep it conceptual on purpose, because the precise strings are exactly what drifts.

You authenticate with an API key. Programmatic access uses an authentication key — a secret credential you generate from your DeepL account, attached to each request rather than the interactive sign-in a human uses on the website. The key identifies your account, meters your usage, and is the thing you must guard. Treat it like any other secret: store it in environment variables or a secrets manager, never paste it into client-side code or commit it to a repository, and rotate it if it leaks. A leaked key is someone else spending your character quota on your account. Generate and manage keys from your DeepL account console, and confirm the exact location and steps in the current documentation.

The "never paste it into client-side code" point deserves more than a clause, because it is the single most common way DeepL keys get stolen, and the mistake is seductive precisely because it makes the demo work. A developer building a web feature wants the browser to call DeepL directly — it is the obvious shortest path. But anything in client-side code is visible to anyone who opens the browser's developer tools, which means a key embedded in a web page is a key published to the world. The correct pattern is that your *server* holds the key and talks to DeepL; the browser talks to your server, never to DeepL directly. Your server becomes a thin proxy that adds the key, forwards the request, and returns the result. This costs a little more plumbing and buys you the ability to keep the key secret, to enforce your own limits on who can use it and how much, and to revoke or rotate it without redeploying client code. If you remember one operational rule from this chapter, make it this one: the key lives on the server, and the only thing the client ever sees is your own endpoint.

You send requests to an endpoint, and which endpoint depends on your plan. This is a DeepL-specific wrinkle worth flagging clearly. DeepL has historically separated its API into a **Free** plan and a **Pro** plan, and they have used **different base URLs** — the Free plan's requests have gone to a host along the lines of `api-free.deepl.com` and the Pro plan's to `api.deepl.com`. If you point Free-plan credentials at the Pro host or vice versa, your requests fail in confusing ways, so matching the base URL to your plan is a small but real gotcha. Both the exact host names and the plan structure are verify-against-current-docs details — confirm them before you wire anything in rather than trusting these strings from a book.

This particular gotcha is worth a moment more because the failure it produces is genuinely confusing the first time you hit it. When the base URL and the key's plan do not match, you do not get a clear "wrong host" message — you get an authentication failure, because from the server's point of view a Pro key arriving at the Free host (or the reverse) looks like a credential that does not belong there. So a developer who has just generated a valid key, copied it correctly, and formatted the request perfectly stares at an authentication error and assumes the key is wrong, when the real problem is which door they knocked on. The official client libraries usually handle this for you by selecting the host based on the key, which is one practical reason to use them rather than constructing raw requests. But if you are debugging an authentication error and you are *certain* the key is right, the base-URL/plan mismatch is the first thing to check, because it is the most common cause of "my correct key doesn't work."

The shape will feel familiar. Because it is a standard REST API, developers coming from other web services tend to find it recognizable, and DeepL provides official client libraries for several languages that wrap the raw requests so you rarely have to construct them by hand. The exact libraries, their versions, and the precise parameter names are check-the-docs details; the durable claim is that the API follows conventional patterns and you are not learning something exotic.

A Minimal Illustrative Request

To make this concrete, here is the *shape* of a basic translation request in pseudocode. I am writing it loosely on purpose — this shows the moving parts, not something to copy-paste. The real parameter names, the real endpoint, and the real client library belong to DeepL's current docs, and Appendix B walks through a working quickstart you can actually run.

```
# ILLUSTRATIVE ONLY – verify every name and URL against current DeepL API docs.
POST  https://<api-or-api-free>.deepl.com/<translate path>
Header:  Authorization: DeepL-Auth-Key <YOUR_API_KEY>
Body:
  text:         "The text you want translated."
  target_lang:  "DE"             # target language code
  source_lang:  "EN"             # optional; DeepL can often auto-detect
```

The response comes back as structured data containing the translated text — and, when you let DeepL auto-detect the source language, the detected source language too, which is useful information your code can act on rather than discard.

Four things to notice, durable even as the names drift. You authenticate with your **key**. You send the **text** and a **target language** (and optionally a source language, since DeepL can usually detect it). You can attach **settings** the rest of the book has covered — a glossary to lock your terminology (Chapter 7), a formality preference (Chapter 8) — as additional parameters. And you get back **structured data**, not loose prose, so your program can act on it. If you have used any modern web API, this will feel like home, which is the good news.

A practical detail the simple example hides: you can usually send *multiple texts in one request* rather than one at a time. This matters more than it sounds. If you have a hundred product reviews to translate, sending them as one batched request is dramatically more efficient than a hundred separate requests — fewer round-trips, less overhead, and friendlier to whatever rate limits apply. The instinct to loop over your items and translate them one by one is natural and almost always the wrong one at volume; batching is the durable performance lesson here. Confirm the current limits on how many texts and how much total text a single request accepts, because there are caps, but build toward batching rather than per-item calls from the start.

Settings Are Where the API Earns Its Keep

It is easy to think of the API as "translation in, translation out" and miss that the settings parameters are where it goes from a generic translator to *your* translator.

The glossary parameter (Chapter 7) is the clearest case: by attaching a glossary to your requests, you make every translation your software produces obey your terminology — your product names stay in English, your defined terms render the same way every time, your do-not-translate list is respected automatically. For a product feature, this is the difference between fluent-but-inconsistent output and output that sounds like it came from your organization. The formality parameter (Chapter 8) is the other workhorse: a single setting that decides whether your German output addresses the reader formally or casually, applied uniformly across every translation, rather than left to chance per request.

There are usually other settings worth knowing exist even before you need them — controls over how tags and formatting in the source are handled (so HTML or XML markup in your text survives translation rather than getting mangled), and controls over how the source is split into sentences. The reason to flag these now is that the developers who get the most out of the API are the ones who treat it as a configurable language engine rather than a black box, reaching for the setting that solves their specific problem instead of post-processing the output to fix what a setting would have prevented. The exact parameter names belong to the current docs; the durable point is that the API exposes the same controls the rest of this book taught you, and using them is most of what separates a crude integration from a polished one.

Building for Failure: Errors, Limits, and Retries

The website handles a thousand things gracefully on your behalf that, on the API, become your job. Chief among them is failure. Network requests fail, services rate-limit you, quotas run out, and a real integration has to expect all three rather than assume the happy path.

The two failure modes worth designing for explicitly are **rate limiting** and **quota exhaustion**, and they are different problems with different responses. Rate limiting is temporary — you are sending requests faster than the service wants to accept them right now — and the correct response is to slow down and retry, ideally with *exponential backoff*: wait a little, retry, and if you are still being limited, wait longer before the next attempt rather than hammering the service in a tight loop. Quota exhaustion is not temporary in the same way — you have used up your plan's character allowance for the period — and retrying does not help; what helps is knowing you are approaching the limit *before* you hit it. DeepL exposes your usage so your code can check how much of your quota remains, which lets you warn, throttle, or upgrade deliberately rather than discovering the ceiling when translations suddenly start failing in production.

The durable discipline is to treat every API call as something that can fail and to decide, per failure type, what should happen: retry with backoff for transient errors, surface a clear message for quota and auth errors, and never let a failed translation silently produce empty or wrong output that flows downstream as if it were real. The most damaging integration bug is not the one that errors loudly — it is the one that fails quietly and ships an untranslated or half-translated result to a user who trusts it.

Billed by Characters, Not Tokens

Here is the most important commercial fact about the API, and the one that separates DeepL from most of the AI tools in this series: **DeepL's API is billed by characters, not tokens.** Every other API in this series meters by tokens — those fuzzy sub-word chunks that make cost hard to predict in advance. DeepL counts the *characters of text you send to translate*, which is refreshingly concrete: you can look at a body of text and know, before you send it, almost exactly what it will cost, because you can count its characters.

That clarity shapes how you think about cost and how you forecast spend, and it is worth internalizing now because it runs through everything in this Part. The character is the unit; your bill is a function of how many characters of text you push through the API. Chapter 23 turns this into actual cost management — the plans, the rates, and how to forecast and control spend — and the character-metering fact is the foundation that chapter builds on.

The practical consequence for how you build is direct: because the cost is the characters you send, the cheapest engineering optimization is *not sending characters you do not need to.* Re-translating text you have already translated is paying twice for the same result, so caching translations — keyed by source text, source language, target language, and any relevant settings — is the highest-leverage cost lever available to a builder, and it falls naturally out of thinking in characters. This is the kind of optimization that is invisible at small scale and decisive at large scale, and it is worth designing in early rather than retrofitting once the bill gets your attention.

How the API Relates to the Apps

It helps to be clear about what the API is and is not relative to the DeepL website, desktop apps, and browser extensions (Chapter 22). Same language capability, different doorway — but two things genuinely differ and matter.

The API is **metered separately** from a consumer DeepL Pro subscription. Paying for a DeepL subscription as a person, to use the website and apps, does not generally cover programmatic API usage — the API bills on its own plan and its own character meter. Know which you are paying for before you build something that runs often: the subscription plans of Chapter 4 are one thing, and the API plans of Chapter 23 are a separate billing relationship. Confirm the current plan structure, because exactly how the subscription and API offerings relate is a perishable detail.

The API also hands you **more capability and more responsibility**. The website and apps wrap DeepL in an interface, a history, and sensible defaults built for a person. The API gives you the raw capability and expects you to build the surrounding judgment — handling errors, managing your character spend, respecting rate limits, and protecting the sensitive text you route through it. That last point connects straight back to Chapter 20: the API is one of the paid products with the strong data posture, which is a real reason to build on it rather than a free consumer surface, but the responsibility for using it within your obligations is now yours as the builder. When your software routes a user's text through the API, you are the one who decided to do that, and the data path — what you log, what you store, what you show to whom — is your design, not DeepL's. The strong vendor posture is the foundation; the integration you build on top of it is where your own privacy responsibility lives.

What the API does *not* change is the thing DeepL is built on — the quality of the language it produces is the same through the API as on the website. That is the whole appeal of building on it: you get DeepL's defining strength as a component you can place anywhere in your own software. For the hands-on, run-it-yourself version of everything sketched here — a key, a real request, a first translated response — Appendix B is the quickstart to keep open beside the current docs. Next, though, the question of how DeepL reaches you when you are *not* building from scratch: the integrations that put it inside the tools you already use.

Chapter 22: Integrations: CAT Tools, Browsers, and Apps

The most telling thing about how heavy users experience DeepL is that the best of them use it constantly and almost never visit its website. A professional translator works inside a CAT tool all day, and DeepL lives there too — surfacing suggestions right in the translation workspace, accepted or reworked in place, the act of "going to DeepL" dissolved into the normal workflow. For a heavy user the website is almost beside the point. The real product is DeepL showing up *where you already are*. That is the idea behind this chapter. The API of Chapter 21 is DeepL for people building from scratch; integrations are DeepL for everyone else — the translator, the office worker, the web reader — meeting them inside the tools they already use, so that translation stops being a separate errand and becomes an ambient capability.

CAT Tools: DeepL Inside Professional Translation

The deepest integration story belongs to the people who translate for a living, and it runs through their CAT tools. CAT — computer-assisted translation — software is the professional translator's workbench: programs like **Trados** and **memoQ** (among others) that manage a translation project, split documents into segments, maintain translation memories of past work, enforce terminology, and generally turn translation from typing into an engineered process. These tools are where serious localization work actually happens, and DeepL plugs into them.

The pattern matters because it inverts the role DeepL plays. In a CAT tool, DeepL is not the translator — the human is. DeepL is a **machine-translation suggestion engine** feeding the human's workbench. For each segment, the tool can surface a DeepL draft alongside matches from the translation memory, and the professional decides: accept it, edit it, or discard it and write their own. This is the post-editing workflow the whole industry runs on, and it is the practical, professional embodiment of the DeepL-plus-a-human model this book keeps returning to. The machine supplies a strong first pass at speed; the qualified human supplies the judgment and the accountability (which, for the high-stakes content of Chapter 18, is exactly where the value lives).

To see why this is more than a convenience, it helps to understand what a CAT tool already does before DeepL ever enters the picture, because DeepL slots into an existing hierarchy of suggestions rather than replacing it. When a translator opens a segment, the tool first checks the **translation memory** — the database of everything the translator (or the team, or the client) has translated before. If this exact sentence, or one very close to it, was translated previously, the tool offers that prior translation, often marked with a match percentage. A "100% match" means the segment is identical to one already translated and approved; a "fuzzy match" of, say, 85% means it is close, and the translator adapts the prior translation rather than starting over. This is the heart of why CAT tools exist: they keep you from translating the same thing twice and keep your translations consistent with everything that came before.

DeepL enters as the suggestion of *last resort in a good way* — the source consulted when the translation memory has nothing useful to offer. For a brand-new segment with no memory match, the tool surfaces DeepL's machine translation as the starting point, and the translator post-edits it. So the workflow is layered: high memory matches get adapted (fastest, most consistent), low or no matches get DeepL's draft to post-edit (still much faster than from scratch), and the translator's judgment governs throughout. Understanding this layering explains why translators value DeepL inside the CAT tool specifically rather than as a standalone site: it fills exactly the gap the translation memory leaves, in the place the translator is already working, without disrupting the memory-first discipline the whole profession is built on.

Two things make the CAT integration genuinely powerful rather than just convenient. First, it keeps DeepL inside the *project structure* — the translation memory, the terminology base, the quality checks — so DeepL's output is one input into a controlled process rather than a loose draft pasted in from elsewhere. Second, it lets DeepL's glossary capability (Chapter 7) work in concert with the CAT tool's own terminology management, so the locked terminology a project requires is enforced from both directions. The exact list of supported CAT tools, and whether integration is native or via a plugin or the API, is a verify-against-current-sources detail that shifts as both DeepL and the tool vendors evolve — but the durable shape is that DeepL is a first-class machine-translation provider inside the professional translation ecosystem.

A Word on the Economics of Post-Editing

The CAT integration also quietly reshapes the business of translation, which is worth naming because it affects anyone buying or selling translation work. When a translator post-edits a strong machine draft instead of translating from scratch, the work per segment drops, and the industry has developed pricing and process around this — machine-translation post-editing as a distinct service, priced differently from full human translation. This is not a footnote; it is the practical reality of how professional translation is delivered now for a large share of content.

The honest framing for a buyer is that post-edited machine translation occupies a real middle ground: faster and cheaper than full from-scratch human translation, and meaningfully better and more accountable than raw machine output, because a qualified human has read and corrected every segment. The risk to watch for is *under-editing* — the temptation, when the machine draft looks good, to wave it through without the careful reading that the value depends on. A fluent DeepL draft (Chapter 1 warned about exactly this) can lull a post-editor into accepting a segment that reads beautifully and says something subtly wrong. The discipline that makes post-editing trustworthy is reading the source against the draft for *meaning*, not just skimming the draft for *fluency*, and a buyer commissioning post-edited translation is entitled to ask how that discipline is enforced. The integration makes the workflow possible; the human's diligence is still what makes the output safe.

Browser Extensions: Translation Where You Read and Write

The integration most people will actually touch is the browser extension, because most of us live in a browser. DeepL offers extensions for the major browsers that bring its translation and writing help directly into the web pages you are already on, so that translating something you are reading or polishing something you are typing no longer means leaving the page to visit a separate site.

The value is the removal of friction, and friction removal is more decisive than it sounds. When translating means copying text, switching tabs, pasting, reading, copying back, and switching again, you do it only when it is worth the hassle — which means you skip it constantly, struggling through content in a second language because the tool was just far enough away to not bother. When DeepL is a click or a selection away inside the page, the calculus flips, and you translate freely: the foreign-language article you would have abandoned, the email you want to get exactly right, the form you are filling out in another language. The extension also commonly surfaces DeepL Write's help as you compose in the browser, so improving your own prose (Part III) happens in place too.

It is worth distinguishing the two things a browser extension typically does, because they feel similar and behave differently. One is **translating a whole page** — you land on a foreign-language site and have the extension render the whole thing in your language so you can read it. The other is **translating a selection** — you highlight a passage, or a single confusing sentence, and translate just that. The whole-page mode is what you reach for when you cannot read the page at all; the selection mode is what you reach for when you can mostly read it but want to check one phrase, or when you are reading carefully and want the original and the translation side by side. Heavy users tend to live in selection mode, because it keeps them in contact with the source — they read the original, lean on the translation for the hard parts, and stay closer to what the text actually says than a full-page translation lets them. The full-page mode is the right tool when comprehension is the only goal and the source language is genuinely opaque to you.

There is an honest limit on the writing-help side worth setting expectations about. The extension can surface DeepL Write's suggestions as you type in many places on the web, but how smoothly that works depends heavily on the site — a plain text box behaves well, while a heavily customized rich editor inside a complex web app may not cooperate cleanly, and you sometimes fall back to composing in a friendly box and pasting the polished result. The specific browsers supported and the exact feature set are check-the-current-sources details, but the durable point is that the extension dissolves the gap between the page and the translator for reading, and helps with writing in proportion to how cooperative the page you are writing in happens to be.

Desktop Apps: DeepL Across Your Whole Computer

A step beyond the browser is the desktop application, available for **Windows and Mac**, which brings DeepL out of any single program and makes it available across your whole computer. The desktop app's signature trick is a keyboard shortcut that translates selected text from *wherever you are* — a word processor, an email client, a chat app, a PDF reader — without switching to a browser or a website at all. You select text in whatever application you are using, hit the shortcut, and DeepL handles it in place.

The mechanism behind that trick is worth understanding, because it explains both why it is so useful and where it occasionally stumbles. The shortcut works by capturing whatever text you have selected — typically by copying it the way you would with the keyboard — handing it to DeepL, and then offering the translation back, often with the option to paste it straight in to replace what you selected. Because it rides on the ordinary select-and-copy mechanism that virtually every application supports, it works almost everywhere, which is the magic. The flip side is that it depends on the application letting text be selected and copied normally: in a program where text is locked, an image, or an unusual control that does not expose its contents to a normal copy, the shortcut has nothing to grab. This is rare in practice — most of the places you read and write all day behave normally — but it explains the occasional "why didn't that work here?" moment, and the answer is almost always that the source program did not hand over selectable text.

This is the same friction-removal idea taken to its logical end. The browser extension covers the web; the desktop app covers everything else, so DeepL becomes a system-wide capability rather than a feature of any one program. For someone who works across many applications all day — reading documents in one, writing email in another, messaging in a third — having translation a keystroke away regardless of which window is in front of them changes how often they reach for it, which is the whole game. The single highest-value habit a new desktop-app user can build is simply *committing the shortcut to muscle memory*, because the entire benefit is contingent on reaching for it being effortless; a shortcut you have to stop and remember is a shortcut you will quietly stop using. The exact shortcut, the supported operating-system versions, and the precise feature set belong to the current downloads page, but the durable capability is system-wide, shortcut-driven translation on the desktop.

Office and App Integrations: DeepL in the Documents You Make

Finally, DeepL reaches into the productivity software where work actually gets produced — the office suites and the business applications where documents, presentations, and messages live. Through integrations into office and collaboration tools, DeepL can translate inside the document or the message you are working on, so localizing a presentation or rendering an email into another language happens within the tool that made it rather than as a round-trip out to a separate translator.

This closes the loop nicely with Chapter 6's document translation: there, you hand DeepL a whole file and get a translated file back with formatting intact; here, the same capability is available *inside* the application as you work, integrated into the place the document already lives. The distinction is worth drawing because it changes which workflow fits which job. When you have a finished document and need the whole thing in another language, the file-in-file-out document translation of Chapter 6 is the cleaner path — you get a complete translated file, formatting preserved, in one operation. When you are *in the middle of producing* a document and want to translate a section as you go, or render a single email you are composing, the in-application integration is the better fit, because it keeps you in the tool and the flow. Neither replaces the other; they serve the moment-of-finishing and the moment-of-working respectively, and knowing which you are in tells you which to reach for.

For teams (Chapter 19), this is often where DeepL becomes invisible infrastructure — wired into the helpdesk, the office suite, or the collaboration platform the organization already runs on, so that translation is simply part of how those tools behave rather than a separate destination anyone has to remember to use. That invisibility is the goal and also the thing to manage: when translation is wired into a shared platform, the data-handling questions of Chapter 20 are answered once, at the integration level, for everyone who uses it — which is exactly why an organization wants the integration built on a paid product with the strong data posture rather than left to individuals reaching for whatever free tool is nearest. Exactly which office and business applications are supported, and whether through a native integration, an add-in, or the underlying API, is a verify-against-current-sources detail; the durable shape is DeepL meeting you inside the productivity tools you already work in.

Choosing Among the Integrations

With four ways in — CAT tool, browser extension, desktop app, office integration — the natural question is which one a given person should actually install, and the honest answer is that it follows from where you spend your day rather than from any ranking of the integrations themselves. A professional translator's center of gravity is the CAT tool, so that is the integration that matters and the others are incidental. A knowledge worker who reads and writes across the web and a handful of desktop programs is best served by the browser extension and the desktop app together — the extension for the web, the app for everything else — which between them cover almost everything such a person touches. Someone whose work is overwhelmingly inside an office suite or a specific business platform gets the most from the integration into that tool, because it puts translation exactly where their documents already are.

The mistake to avoid is installing the surface that *sounds* most powerful rather than the one that matches your actual day. The API is the most powerful surface in the abstract, but it is useless to someone who does not build software; the CAT integration is the deepest, but it is irrelevant to someone who is not a professional translator. The right integration is the boring one that sits in the application you already have open the most, because that is the one that will actually disappear into your workflow rather than becoming another tool you have to remember to use. Match the integration to where your attention already lives, and DeepL becomes ambient; mismatch it, and it stays an errand.

The Common Thread

Step back and every one of these integrations is the same idea wearing different clothes. The translator's CAT tool, the reader's browser extension, the desktop app's system-wide shortcut, the office add-in — all of them exist to move DeepL *to where you already are* instead of making you go to DeepL. That is not a minor convenience. It is the difference between a capability you use occasionally, when it is worth the trouble, and one you use constantly, because there is no trouble. The translator who barely visits the website is the proof: for a heavy user, the best version of DeepL is the one that has disappeared into the tools they already live in.

Underneath several of these integrations, of course, is the API of Chapter 21, doing the actual work — which is the connective tissue of this whole Part.

Whether you build directly on the API or reach DeepL through an integration someone else built on it, the same meter is running beneath you, counting the characters you translate. Understanding that meter — what the plans cost, how the character billing works, and how to forecast and control your spend without nasty surprises — is the practical subject the next chapter takes up, and it is the one that keeps building on DeepL sustainable rather than expensive.

Chapter 23: Cost and Quota Management

The worst kind of translation bill is not the large one — it is the one you cannot explain. Build a feature on a token-metered service and the relationship between the text your users translate and the dollars you owe is murky enough that you can neither forecast it nor trace it. Move the same workload to DeepL and the bill becomes *legible*. DeepL bills by characters, and characters are countable, so for the first time you can look at your traffic and say, in advance, roughly what it will cost. That legibility is the through-line of this chapter, and it is the practical payoff of a fact Chapter 21 introduced: DeepL meters language by the character, which makes its cost more forecastable than almost anything else in this series.

A discipline before the numbers, the same one this book applies to every technical specific: **the structure of DeepL's pricing is durable; the exact figures are not.** Plans, rates, and quotas change, and I will give you the shape you can rely on while flagging every specific number as something to confirm against DeepL's current pricing page. Read the structure as load-bearing and the numbers as a snapshot.

The Unit Is the Character

Everything starts here. DeepL meters by **characters of text translated** — count the characters you send, and you have the basis of your cost. This is unusual and genuinely helpful. Most AI services in this series bill by *tokens*, those sub-word fragments whose count you cannot eyeball and whose relationship to your actual text is approximate. Characters are concrete: a paragraph has exactly as many characters as it has, you can measure it before you send it, and your forecast is arithmetic rather than guesswork.

That single property changes how cost management feels. With token billing, controlling spend means modeling a fuzzy relationship and watching the meter nervously. With character billing, controlling spend means watching one clear number — *how much text am I pushing through?* — that you can measure, predict, and attribute to specific features or workflows. Hold onto the character as the unit; it is the foundation everything else in this chapter rests on.

A couple of clarifications keep the character-counting honest, because "count the characters" hides a few questions people reasonably ask. The count is of the *source* text you send to be translated — what you put in, not what comes back — so your cost is governed by the size of your input, which is the thing you control and can measure before you send it. The count is in characters, not words, which matters when you compare languages: German compound words and the dense scripts of some Asian languages pack different amounts of meaning into a character than English does, so a "page" of text is not a fixed character count across languages. And whitespace and punctuation are still characters. None of this complicates the basic virtue — you can still count exactly what you are about to send — but it is worth knowing that "characters" means precisely characters, so your estimates are built on the real unit rather than a word-count approximation that would drift.

Three Different Meters

The most common cost confusion is not about rates — it is about *which thing you are paying for*, because DeepL has separate billing relationships that people conflate. Keep these three straight and most of the confusion dissolves.

The free text tier, for casual use of the website and apps, gives you a monthly character allowance for text translation at no cost — historically on the order of **50,000 characters per month**, a figure to verify against the current terms. This is the taste-of-the-product tier, generous enough for occasional personal translation and capped enough to push regular or professional users toward a paid plan. Remember from Chapter 20 that the free tier's data terms differ from the paid products', so sensitive content does not belong here regardless of the quota.

The consumer subscription plans — the DeepL Pro plans of Chapter 4 — are what individuals and teams pay for to use the website, apps, and integrations without the free tier's limits and with the stronger data posture. These bill on their own subscription basis, separate from the API, and their structure and pricing are the subject of Chapter 4. The key fact to carry here is that **a consumer subscription is a different meter from the API** — paying for one does not pay for the other.

The API plans are the developer meter, and they have their own structure: historically an **API Free plan** with a monthly character allowance — on the order of **500,000 characters per month** — for building and light use at no cost, and an **API Pro plan** for production use that has typically combined a **small fixed monthly fee** (around **$5.49**) with a **usage charge of roughly $25 per million characters** translated. Every one of those figures is a snapshot to confirm against DeepL's current API pricing, and the plan names and structure can shift — but the durable shape is *a free developer tier with a monthly character cap, and a paid developer tier with a low base fee plus per-character usage.*

The single most important sentence in this section is the one that prevents the most billing surprises: **the subscription plans and the API bill separately.** If you use DeepL both as a person on the website and as a builder through the API, you are on two meters at once, and you manage them as two distinct things.

Picking the Right Meter for the Job

Because there are several meters, the first cost decision is not "how do I reduce spend" but "which meter should this workload even be on," and getting that wrong is more expensive than any rate difference. The deciding question is *who or what is doing the translating*. If a person is translating things by hand — reading articles, polishing emails, translating the occasional document at their desk — that is consumer territory, and the answer is the free tier for light personal use or a Pro subscription for regular use. If *software* is doing the translating — a feature in your app, a content pipeline, a batch job — that is API territory, and the answer is the API Free plan for building and light volume or API Pro for production.

The mistake that costs real money is running a programmatic workload through a consumer surface, or trying to serve a whole team's human translation through a single API integration that nobody budgeted for. The cleanest signal is simply whether a human is sitting there clicking translate (consumer) or whether translations happen because code asked for them (API). When a workload is genuinely both — a team that translates by hand *and* runs an automated feature — the answer is both meters, deliberately, rather than trying to force one to cover the other. Deciding this up front, before you build a habit on the wrong tier, is the highest-leverage cost decision in the whole chapter, because the rate optimizations later are small next to being on the right meter at all.

What the API Numbers Actually Mean

Let me make the API Pro structure concrete, because the *shape* of "small base fee plus per-million-character usage" tells you something durable about the economics even though the exact figures will drift.

The roughly-$25-per-million-characters usage rate, taken at face value, means a million characters of translation costs about the price of a modest dinner — and a million characters is a lot of text, on the order of a long book. For a great many real applications, that means translation is a genuinely small line item: a feature translating user reviews, support messages, or content snippets pushes a volume of characters whose cost, when you do the character arithmetic, turns out to be modest. The small fixed monthly fee, meanwhile, is a low floor that makes the Pro plan accessible rather than a barrier. This is the good news the legible billing reveals — for typical volumes, building on DeepL is inexpensive, and because you can count the characters, you can prove that to yourself in advance rather than hoping. Confirm the current rate, but the durable takeaway is that per-character translation is cheap at the unit level, and your bill is dominated by *how much text* you translate, not by a high price per unit.

To make the arithmetic feel real, walk a small product feature through it with the snapshot numbers, remembering they are a mid-2026 snapshot to verify. Suppose your app shows translated product reviews, and a typical review runs about 500 characters. Translating one review is 500 characters; translating ten thousand reviews is five million characters. At a rate on the order of $25 per million characters, five million characters is roughly $125 — for ten thousand reviews translated. If your traffic is a few thousand reviews a month rather than ten thousand, your translation line item is tens of dollars, plus the small base fee. The point is not the exact figure, which will change; it is that the character arithmetic is *something you can actually do* — review size times review count times rate-per-character — and arrive at a number you trust before you ship, which is precisely what token-metered services do not let you do. Run that arithmetic for your own feature with the current rate, and you will know whether translation is a rounding error or a real cost before you write a line of code.

The same arithmetic also tells you where the free tiers stop being free, which is the question that actually trips people up. An API Free plan on the order of 500,000 characters a month sounds generous until you put it next to that 500-

character review: 500,000 characters is about a thousand reviews a month, after which you need the paid plan. That is fine — it is exactly what the free tier is for, light use and building — but the lesson is to do the arithmetic against your *expected* volume, not your current trickle, because a feature that grows from a hundred reviews a month to two thousand crosses the free ceiling without anyone deciding it should.

Forecasting and Managing Spend

Because the unit is countable, forecasting is real arithmetic rather than wishful thinking, and a few habits keep spend predictable.

Estimate before you build. For any workload, estimate the character volume up front — how much text, how often — and multiply by the per-character rate. Because characters are concrete, this estimate is trustworthy in a way a token estimate never quite is, and it tells you whether a feature is a rounding error or a real cost before you ship it. The lever that matters most is almost always *volume of text*, so that is the number to model. The discipline that makes the estimate honest is to model the *realistic high* case, not the comfortable low one — peak traffic, the marketing push that triples your volume for a week, the seasonal spike — because the bill that hurts is the one from the month you did not forecast.

Watch the meter and attribute it. DeepL's account and API consoles expose your usage, and watching your character consumption — ideally attributed to specific features or workflows — turns cost from a monthly surprise into a managed quantity. If a feature's character volume spikes, you see it and you know which feature, because you can trace dollars back to characters back to source. Attribution is the part teams skip and regret: a single number for "total characters this month" tells you that something grew but not what, whereas tagging usage by feature or workflow — even crudely — means a spike comes with its own explanation. The cheapest way to do this is to decide, before you have a problem, how you will tell which part of your system spent the characters, rather than reconstructing it after a surprising bill.

Mind the free-tier ceilings. Both the free text tier and the API Free plan are capped monthly character allowances. For light use they are genuinely free; the trap is building something on a free tier that quietly grows past the cap, at which point translation either stops or you scramble to upgrade. Know your tier's ceiling and watch your approach to it, so the move to a paid plan is a planned decision rather than an outage. The specific failure to design against is the *silent stop*: a feature on the free tier that hits its ceiling mid-month and starts failing translations, which — if your code does not handle it (Chapter 21's point about building for failure) — can mean users suddenly see untranslated or broken output with no warning to you. Checking your remaining quota programmatically and alerting yourself as you approach the ceiling turns a production incident into a calendar reminder to upgrade.

Cut the characters you do not need to send. Since you pay per character, the cheapest character is the one you never translate. Avoid re-translating text you have already translated — cache results where it makes sense — and do not push content through the API that does not need it. For high-volume workloads, trimming redundant translation is the most direct way to manage spend, and it falls naturally out of thinking in characters.

The caching point deserves a concrete shape, because "cache results" is easy to say and easy to do wrong. A translation is fully determined by a handful of inputs — the source text, the source language, the target language, and any settings like the glossary or formality that change the output — so a correct cache is keyed on *all* of those, not just the source text. Key on the text alone and you will serve a German translation to someone who asked for French, or serve the formal rendering when this request asked for casual, because two requests with the same source text but different targets or settings are genuinely different translations. Done right, caching is the single highest-leverage cost lever a high-volume builder has, because real traffic is full of repetition — the same product names, the same canned responses, the same frequently asked questions translated over and over — and every cache hit is a character you do not pay for twice. The work is in choosing the key correctly; the payoff is paying once for each genuinely distinct translation rather than once per request.

There is one more lever worth naming because it is easy to overlook: *not translating text that does not need it*. A surprising amount of content that flows through a translation step does not actually require translating — text that is already in the target language, content that is purely numbers or codes, boilerplate that should stay fixed, or material a user will never read. Filtering that out before it reaches the meter costs nothing and saves whatever those characters would have cost, and at high volume the savings from simply not sending what does not need sending can rival the savings from caching. Thinking in characters makes this lever visible: every character you can justify *not* sending is a character off the bill.

Two Cost Surprises That Are Not About Rates

Most of this chapter is about the meter you can see. Two cost surprises come from somewhere else, and they are worth flagging because no amount of character arithmetic predicts them.

The first is **document translation counted in full.** When you translate a whole document (Chapter 6), the character count is the characters *in the document* — and a document carries more text than the eye registers. Speaker notes in a presentation, hidden columns in a spreadsheet, the footnotes and headers and the long appendix nobody reads: all of it is text, all of it is characters, and all of it bills. A slide deck that looks like a few hundred words on screen can carry several times that in notes and metadata. The lesson is not to avoid document translation, which is one of DeepL's best features, but to remember that "this document looks short" is a visual impression, not a character count, and a folder of documents pushed through translation can spend characters faster than a glance at them suggests. When document volume is part of your workload, sample a few real files and count their *actual* characters rather than estimating from how long they look.

The second is **the cost of the human, not the machine.** This chapter is about DeepL's bill, but for any serious workflow the translation characters are frequently the *smallest* cost in the system. The post-editing reviewer (Chapter 22), the human checking the high-stakes output (Chapter 24), the glossary maintainer keeping the team consistent (Chapter 19) — these are real costs, and they usually dwarf the per-character API charge. This is good news framed correctly: it means the right way to think about DeepL's cost is not "minimize the translation bill" but "the translation is cheap, so spend where the value is, which is the human judgment around it." Optimizing the character bill to the last cent while under-investing in the review that makes the output trustworthy is optimizing the rounding error and neglecting the real number. Keep DeepL's legible, modest character cost in proportion: it is the part that is easy to forecast precisely *because* it is rarely the part that matters most to the total cost of doing multilingual work well.

The Discipline to Carry Forward

The reason this chapter mirrors the rest of the book's structure-durable-numbers-aren't discipline so closely is that cost is exactly where that discipline pays off. The **structure** is dependable and worth memorizing: DeepL meters by the character; there are three separate meters — free text tier, consumer subscription, and the API with its own Free and Pro plans; the subscription and the API bill separately; and per-character translation is cheap at the unit level, so your bill tracks how much text you move. The **numbers** — the 50,000-character free tier, the 500,000-character API Free plan, the roughly $5.49 base fee and roughly $25 per million characters on API Pro — are a mid-2026 snapshot, and you should treat every one of them as something to confirm against DeepL's current pricing before you rely on it.

Hold the structure firmly and the numbers loosely, and DeepL's cost stops being a source of anxiety and becomes what its character-based billing actually makes it: one of the more predictable, manageable line items in your toolkit. That predictability is the quiet virtue that closes out building on DeepL — and it sets up the harder, more human questions the next part of the book turns to, where the issue is no longer what DeepL costs but where its excellent output still falls short and a person has to step in.

Part VII: Judgment and Limits

Audience: everyone — and required reading before you trust a translation you cannot check.

"A clumsy translation warns you it is wrong. A beautiful one doesn't. That is exactly why the fluent tool needs the most careful reader."

— A working principle

Chapter 24: What DeepL Gets Wrong, and When to Use a Human

A book that only told you what DeepL does well would be a brochure, not a guide. The truth is that DeepL, like every machine translator and every language model, gets things wrong — and because its output is so fluent, its errors are unusually easy to miss. A clumsy translation announces itself; you read it, wince, and check. A beautiful translation that is subtly wrong does the opposite: it reads so naturally that you trust it, and the error rides along inside prose too smooth to question. That is the central paradox of a high-quality tool, and the reason this chapter matters as much as any in the book. Knowing where DeepL fails, and where a human still belongs in the loop, is not pessimism. It is the difference between using the tool well and being quietly betrayed by it.

The Fluent Error Is the Dangerous One

Start with the failure that shapes all the others, because it is specific to *good* translation and counterintuitive precisely because the tool is good. DeepL's great strength — output that sounds like a person wrote it — is also the source of its most dangerous failure mode. When the translation is wrong, it is usually still *fluent*. The grammar holds, the tone is right, the sentence reads beautifully, and the meaning is off. There is no broken-English tell to warn you. A reader who cannot check the source language has no signal that anything is amiss, because everything that is visible looks perfect.

This inverts the instinct most people bring to machine translation. We learned, in the era of clumsy translators, to trust the smooth output and distrust the awkward output. With DeepL, smoothness tells you almost nothing about correctness, because the smoothness is constant. The translation that reads most naturally can be the one that has quietly dropped a negation, softened a hard "must" into a vague "should," or rendered an ambiguous source sentence in the wrong one of its two possible meanings. The better the prose, the more important it is to verify the meaning rather than admire the fluency.

It helps to understand *why* the fluency and the occasional error come from the same place rather than being opposites. A modern neural translator is, at heart, a system trained to produce the most plausible, natural-sounding rendering of a sentence in the target language. Plausibility and naturalness are what it optimizes for, and it is extraordinarily good at them. But "the most natural-sounding sentence" and "the most faithful sentence" are usually the same thing and occasionally are not — and when they diverge, the system has no internal alarm that fires. It does not know it has chosen fluency over fidelity, because from the inside there is no difference; both are just the output it judged most likely. This is why the errors arrive dressed as confidence. The tool is not hedging when it is wrong. It is as smooth and certain in its mistakes as in its triumphs, which is exactly what makes the mistakes hard to see.

A useful mental image: the fluency is a coat of paint applied evenly over everything, the true and the false alike. On a clumsy translator the paint is patchy, so the rough patches double as warning signs — you can read the unreliability off the surface. On DeepL the paint is flawless everywhere, which means the surface has stopped carrying information about what is underneath. You cannot read reliability off polish anymore, because the polish is the one thing that is guaranteed. Everything in the rest of this chapter follows from that single fact.

The Specific Things It Gets Wrong

Beneath that general hazard sit the concrete error types worth watching for.

Ambiguity resolved the wrong way. When a source sentence could mean two things, DeepL picks one — confidently, invisibly, and sometimes wrongly. It does not flag the fork or ask; it commits. If the context that disambiguates lives outside the sentence, the machine may not have it, and you get a clean translation of the meaning you did not intend. A concrete case: the English instruction "Replace the filter when the light is on" is ambiguous about whether *on* means illuminated or means physically switched on, and in a language that distinguishes the two more sharply than English does, the translator has to choose. It will choose, smoothly, and you will not see that a choice was made. The same trap lurks in pronouns across languages with grammatical gender, in sentences where a modifier could attach to one of two nouns, and in any source written tersely enough that the human author was relying on shared context the machine never had.

Negations, numbers, and small reversing words. The little words that flip meaning — *not, no longer, unless, except* — are exactly the ones whose loss or misplacement is most catastrophic and least visible. The same goes for numbers, dates, and units, which can be transposed or mishandled in ways a fluent sentence hides completely. In a contract or a dosage, these are the errors that matter most and look least alarming. Consider the difference between "The warranty does not cover water damage" and a rendering that drops the negation: both are perfect, idiomatic sentences in the target language, and only one of them is the agreement you signed. Dates are a quieter version of the same hazard — a source written in day-month order silently re-rendered, a relative date like "next Friday" anchored to the wrong week, a quantity that reads naturally at the wrong order of magnitude. None of these announce themselves, because nothing about them is ungrammatical. They are wrong only against a reality the sentence cannot show you.

Idioms, names, and cultural specifics. Idiomatic expressions, proper names, brand language, jokes, and culturally loaded phrases are where literal accuracy and real meaning diverge. DeepL is better at these than most, but they remain a soft spot, and they are often the places where a translation can be technically defensible and practically wrong for the audience. A product name that happens to be an ordinary word can get helpfully "translated" when you needed it left alone — the kind of thing a glossary (Chapter 7) exists to prevent. A figure of speech can get rendered literally into something that means nothing, or rendered into a target-language idiom that carries connotations the original never had. Humor and wordplay survive translation least often of all, which is why marketing copy and anything that trades on tone deserve far more scrutiny than a plain informational paragraph.

Register and relationship. A translation can carry the right information at the wrong level of formality, and in languages where formality is grammatically encoded, that is not a cosmetic slip — it can read as rude, presumptuous, or cold to the recipient. The controls in Chapter 8 help, but they do not fully automate the judgment of how you should sound to a particular person in a particular culture. Addressing a senior client in the familiar form, or a close colleague in stiff officialese, is the kind of error that costs you nothing in accuracy and a great deal in relationship — and it is invisible to anyone reviewing only whether the *meaning* survived.

Consistency across a long document. A subtler failure that single-sentence examples never show: across a long file translated in pieces, or across many files translated separately, DeepL may render the same term two different (both correct) ways. A defined term in a contract, a recurring feature name in a manual, a character's title in a story — each can drift from passage to passage, and each individual choice looks fine in isolation. The error only appears when you read the whole thing and notice the same thing has two names. This is precisely the gap glossaries are built to close, and it is one of the strongest reasons to use them on anything long or anything that will be read as a unit.

Weaker language pairs. Everything above is more likely the further you get from DeepL's European core (Chapter 9). On a well-supported European pair, the error rate is genuinely low; on a thin or distant pair, all of these failure modes grow more common, and your verification needs to grow with them. The practical implication is that the *same* task carries a different risk profile depending on the pair: a routine email between two major European languages is something you can mostly trust on sight, while the same email into a low-resource or typologically distant language deserves the caution you would otherwise reserve for higher-stakes work.

The forms beyond text. DeepL Write can smooth meaning into mush or quietly shift what you meant while "improving" it (Chapter 11), and DeepL Voice carries the added errors of mishearing speech — accents, crosstalk, jargon — on top of translation, in real time, with no chance to review before the words are out (Part IV). Each surface adds its own layer of fallibility to the underlying one. Voice is the starkest case: an error in text translation can be caught before it leaves your screen, but an error in live voice translation is already spoken, already heard, already acted on before anyone could have checked it. The lack of a review step is not a minor difference; it changes what kinds of conversations the tool is fit for.

When to Use a Human

Here is the practical heart of the chapter: a clear-eyed account of when DeepL alone is enough and when a qualified human belongs in the loop. The honest answer is not "always use a human" — that would waste most of what makes the tool valuable — nor "never bother," which is how people get burned. It is a question of stakes and verifiability.

Two variables decide it, and it is worth naming them explicitly because most bad calls come from tracking only one. The first is **stakes**: how much does it cost if this translation is wrong? The second is **verifiability**: can you, or someone you trust, actually check whether it is wrong before the cost lands? High stakes with easy verification is manageable — you let the machine draft and a competent reviewer checks it. High stakes with *no* way to verify is the genuinely dangerous quadrant, and it is where a professional is not optional. Low stakes makes the whole question moot regardless of verifiability. Hold those two dials in mind and the tiers below stop being rules to memorize and become consequences of a judgment you can make yourself.

DeepL alone is fine for the enormous category of everyday, low-stakes, comprehension-or-convenience work: understanding a foreign article or email, getting the gist of a document, internal communication where a small imperfection costs nothing, first drafts you will refine, and any situation where being approximately right quickly is worth more than being perfectly right slowly. This is most translation most people do, and using a human for it would be absurd. The test is simple: if the worst realistic outcome of an error is a moment of confusion or a quick correction, you do not need a reviewer — you need the speed.

DeepL plus a human reviewer is the right model when the stakes rise and you or a colleague can actually check the result — customer-facing content, published material, anything representing your organization, important business correspondence, marketing where tone is the message. Here DeepL does the heavy lifting and a competent bilingual person reviews what matters before it goes out. This is the workhorse pattern for serious professional use, and it captures most of the speed while catching most of the errors. The reviewer does not need to retranslate from scratch; their job is to read the output against the source with the specific failure modes above in mind — checking the negations, the numbers, the register, the names — which is a fraction of the effort of original translation and catches the great majority of what goes wrong.

A qualified professional human, with DeepL as at most an assistant, is the standard when the stakes are high *and* an error carries real consequence: legal documents, medical information, regulatory filings, safety-critical instructions, certified translations, and anything where being wrong means liability, harm, or a binding obligation (Chapter 18). In these domains the machine can still help a professional work faster, but it cannot hold the responsibility, and "the software translated it" is not a defense anyone will accept. The human is not a luxury here; the human is the accountable party, and the law and the stakes both know it. The distinction from the previous tier is who carries the consequence: a reviewer improves the odds, but a professional translator *owns* the result and answers for it, which is what high-consequence work actually requires.

A human interpreter, not Voice, remains the standard for high-stakes live interpreting — a medical consultation, a legal proceeding, a negotiation where a real-time mistranslation cannot be unsaid. DeepL Voice is a remarkable aid for ordinary cross-language conversation; it is not yet a replacement for a trained interpreter when the conversation is one you cannot afford to get wrong. The absence of a review step, again, is decisive: in a clinical or legal setting the cost of a single mistranslated instruction or admission is exactly the kind of consequence that demands a trained human who can ask for clarification, flag an ambiguity, and stand behind the rendering.

Common Mistakes That Put You in the Wrong Tier

Knowing the tiers is not the same as landing in the right one, and a few recurring mistakes quietly push people down a level of caution from where they belong.

Letting a one-time low-stakes use set a habit. People try DeepL on a throwaway email, it works beautifully, and the success silently generalizes into "DeepL is reliable" — which then gets applied to the contract clause where it is not. Each task deserves its own stakes assessment; past success on easy work is not evidence about hard work.

Mistaking your confidence for verification. Reading a translation in a language you do not know and feeling reassured by how good it sounds is not checking it; it is being charmed by the fluency the chapter opened on. If you cannot actually evaluate the meaning, your sense that it "looks right" carries no information.

Treating a deadline as a reason to skip the human. The temptation is strongest exactly when stakes are high and time is short — the late-night campaign, the contract due tomorrow. But the deadline does not change the cost of being wrong; it only changes how much you would like to ignore it. The honest move is to escalate the deadline, not to silently downgrade the safeguard.

Assuming a strong pair means a strong task. A flawless European-pair engine can still get the negation, the number, or the register wrong on a high-stakes sentence. The pair sets a baseline error rate; it does not lower the stakes. Strong pair plus high stakes still needs a reviewer.

How to Verify Without a Second Language

Most readers will sometimes need to use a translation into a language they cannot read, which feels like flying blind. A few practical defenses help even then. **Round-trip cautiously** — translating the result back can reveal gross errors, though it is an imperfect check and a clean round-trip does not prove correctness. **Isolate the load-bearing parts** — the numbers, names, dates, negations, and key obligations — and verify those specifically, because they carry the most risk and are the easiest to spot-check. **Get a native speaker's eyes** on anything that matters and that you cannot check yourself; even a quick read by a fluent colleague catches the worst errors. And **match your caution to the pair and the stakes** — light for an everyday European-pair email, heavy for an important document in a language and script you cannot read at all.

A few more techniques are worth having in the kit. **Keep the source and the translation aligned** so a reviewer can read them paragraph against paragraph rather than hunting; misalignment is where dropped or merged sentences hide. **Translate the back-translation through a different route** if you can — a second engine or a different phrasing — since two systems making the *same* fluent error is rarer than one doing it alone, and a divergence between them is a flag worth chasing even when you cannot read the original. **Build a glossary first** for any recurring or load-bearing terms, so the highest-risk vocabulary is locked before translation rather than checked after. And **read the round-trip for what is missing**, not only for what is wrong — a negation or a clause that has quietly vanished is easier to notice as an absence in the English you get back than as a flaw in the target text you cannot read.

The Posture to Carry

The point of this inventory is not to undercut a genuinely excellent tool. It is to make you the kind of user who gets the speed and the quality without the quiet disasters. DeepL's fluency is real and valuable, and it is also a mask that hides the errors it does make — so the discipline is to verify meaning rather than trust polish, to scale your scrutiny to the stakes and the language pair, and to keep a human in the loop exactly where being wrong is expensive. Used that way, DeepL is what it claims to be: a remarkable accelerator of multilingual work. Used credulously, it is a confident, beautiful, occasional liar. The difference is entirely in how you read what it gives you.

That discipline is most of responsible use, but not all of it. The final chapter turns from accuracy to the other obligations that come with translating real material — the privacy of the text you submit, the rights and context of the people it concerns, and the professional honesty of how you represent machine-assisted work.

Chapter 25: Responsible Use

Translation is a more intimate act than it first appears. The text you feed a translator is often someone's contract, someone's medical history, someone's private message, someone's unpublished work — material that carries obligations beyond getting the words right. The previous chapter covered the responsibility of *accuracy*: not letting a fluent error slip through. This final chapter covers the responsibilities around it — to the data you submit, to the people the text concerns, and to the colleagues and clients who receive machine-assisted work from you. DeepL is a professional tool, and using it professionally means more than pasting text into a box. It means handling other people's language with the care you would want for your own.

Guard the Text You Submit

The first responsibility is the one easiest to forget precisely because translation feels so routine: the text you submit is data, and often sensitive data. A document you translate may contain personal information, confidential business material, privileged legal content, or protected health information — and submitting it to any service is a form of sending it somewhere. DeepL's strong privacy posture (Chapter 20) is exactly what makes it trustworthy for this, but the posture only protects you if you use the right product. The paid and API tiers carry the data-handling commitments — text not stored, not used for training, EU data protection — that sensitive material requires; a free consumer tool, DeepL's or anyone's, is a different proposition with different terms.

So the rule is concrete: **match the sensitivity of the text to the product and its data terms.** Confidential, regulated, or personal data belongs on the paid or enterprise tier whose terms you have actually read, not pasted into whatever free box is closest. And it belongs there only if your organization has sanctioned it — which leads to the next point.

It is worth being precise about *why* the free-versus-paid line is the one that matters here, because the distinction is easy to wave away when the output looks identical. The quality of the translation is not the variable; the contractual treatment of your text is. Across the industry, free consumer tiers are typically funded, in part, by the data that flows through them — text may be retained, may be used to improve the service, may be processed under terms written to give the provider latitude rather than to give you protection. Paid and enterprise tiers exist partly to sell you a *different relationship to your data*: explicit commitments that the text is not stored beyond processing and not used for training, backed by terms a compliance team can actually evaluate. When you paste a confidential document into a free box because it was the tab already open, you are not getting a worse translation — you may be getting an identical one — but you are accepting a data relationship you would never have signed if someone had put it in front of you. The convenience hides the trade, which is exactly why the rule has to be a habit rather than a judgment call made fresh each time.

A short, concrete checklist makes the habit operational. Before you translate anything that is not plainly public, ask: **Whose data is this?** — your own throwaway text, your employer's confidential material, or a third party's personal information, in ascending order of care. **What product am I about to use, and have I read its terms?** — the specific tier, not "DeepL" in the abstract. **Has my organization sanctioned this tool for this kind of data?** — because your reading of the terms does not override your employer's policy. **Could this text identify a living person?** — if so, data-protection law is in play whether or not you were thinking about it. Four questions, a few seconds, and the great majority of careless disclosures simply do not happen.

Respect the Rules That Govern the Data

If you are translating on behalf of an employer or handling other people's personal data, you are operating inside a framework of obligations that does not disappear because a machine is doing the translating. Data-protection law (GDPR and its equivalents) governs how personal data may be processed, including being sent to a translation service; your organization's policies govern which tools are sanctioned for which data; and professional duties of confidentiality — a lawyer's, a doctor's, an HR officer's — apply to a translated document exactly as they apply to the original. DeepL can be a compliant part of that framework, and its privacy features are built to be, but the compliance is something you operate, not something the tool grants you. Know your obligations, use the sanctioned product, and do not let the convenience of instant translation quietly route protected data somewhere it should not go.

It helps to see the layers as distinct, because they fail in different ways and a tool that satisfies one does nothing for the others. The **legal** layer is the floor: data-protection law sets out what may be processed, on what basis, and with what safeguards, and sending personal data to a translation provider is a processing activity like any other. Choosing a provider with European data protection at its core makes compliance *possible*, but the lawful basis, the records, and the limits are still yours to maintain. The **organizational** layer sits on top: your employer may permit a tool for general business text and forbid it for customer records, may require an enterprise contract before any client data touches it, may mandate that certain categories never leave internal systems at all. A tool being legally usable does not make it *sanctioned* for the data in front of you. The **professional** layer is the most personal: a duty of confidentiality binds the person, not the medium, and it travels with the document into whatever tool you choose. A lawyer pasting a privileged file, a clinician translating a patient note, an HR officer running a grievance through a translator — each carries an obligation that predates and outranks any product's terms.

The newer regulatory layer is worth a flag of its own, because the rules around AI systems are still settling as of mid-2026 and the picture will keep moving. The EU AI Act's transparency-related obligations under Article 4 became applicable on 2 February 2025, with broader enforcement arriving 2 August 2026; the proposed Digital Omnibus that would adjust parts of this framework is, as of this writing, not yet law. None of this turns DeepL into a forbidden tool — translation of your own business text is ordinary, sanctioned use — but it does mean that anyone deploying machine translation at scale inside a regulated organization should check the current state of these rules rather than rely on a snapshot, including this one. The honest version of "know your obligations" is that the obligations themselves are a moving target right now, and the responsible posture is to verify against current guidance rather than assume the landscape has stood still.

Respect the People the Text Concerns

Beyond the legal frame is a human one. The text you translate is often *about* people or *belongs to* someone, and they have a stake in how it is handled. Translating someone's private message, personal document, or creative work carries an ethical weight separate from any law — a question of consent and respect, not just compliance. Translating a community's language or cultural material deserves care and, often, the involvement of people from that community rather than a machine alone, because meaning that is culturally loaded is exactly what a machine handles least well and what matters most to get right (Chapter 9). The tool makes it trivially easy to translate anything; that ease is not the same as the right or the wisdom to do so. A moment's thought about whose words these are, and whether they would want them handled this way, is part of using the tool decently.

The cases where this bites are not exotic. A manager who runs an employee's private message through a translator to find out what it says has done something the law may or may not reach but that the employee would plainly object to. A researcher who feeds a community's oral histories or sacred texts into a machine for a quick rendering has treated material that carries deep cultural weight as if it were a press release — and has likely produced something that is not only flat but, in places, wrong in ways only a member of that community would catch. A well-meaning volunteer who machine-translates a vulnerable person's intake form into a language neither of them can verify has put a real person's circumstances at the mercy of a fluent guess. In none of these is the tool malfunctioning; it is doing exactly what it does. The failure, where there is one, is in the decision to point it at material that deserved consent, context, or a human who shares the language.

The practical discipline is a quieter version of the accuracy discipline from the last chapter: before translating, ask not only *can the machine do this well* but *is this mine to translate this way*. For your own text, the answer is almost always yes. For someone else's private, personal, or culturally significant material, the answer deserves an actual moment of thought, and sometimes the right move is to ask the person, involve someone from the community, or simply not use a machine for this particular thing. The ease of the tool is real; so is the fact that ease is not permission.

A Worked Case: The Cross-Border HR File

It helps to walk one realistic situation through all of these duties at once, because in practice they do not arrive one at a time — they stack on a single task, and the responsible move is the one that satisfies all of them together. Picture an HR manager at a company with offices in two countries who needs to translate an employee's grievance complaint, written in the employee's language, so that the legal and HR teams in headquarters can read it.

Run it through the layers. The **data** is about as sensitive as workplace data gets: it identifies a living person, concerns their employment, and may touch health, conduct, or protected characteristics. So the free consumer box is immediately wrong; this belongs on a sanctioned paid or enterprise tier whose data terms the company has actually evaluated, used in line with whatever the organization's policy says about employee records. The **legal** layer is fully engaged — this is personal, likely special-category data, and processing it through any external service is a step that data-protection obligations govern. The **professional** layer binds the HR manager personally to confidentiality regardless of which tool is open. The **people** layer asks a question the manager might not have thought to ask: does the employee know their complaint is being machine-translated, and does that matter to them? Often the honest answer is that they should be told, both as a courtesy and because a fluent mistranslation of a grievance is exactly the kind of error that compounds a dispute rather than resolving it.

And then **accuracy** closes the loop, because this is a high-stakes document where being wrong is expensive and the readers cannot verify the source. A grievance is full of the load-bearing words Chapter 24 warned about — the negations, the qualifiers, the precise characterization of who did what to whom. A fluent machine draft is a fine starting point and a dangerous finished product; this is squarely in the territory that needs a qualified human in the loop before anyone acts on it. Notice that no single rule covers this task. It is the whole posture — right product, lawful basis, personal duty, respect for the person, verified accuracy — applied together, and the manager who holds all five is doing responsible use in the only way it actually exists: not as a checklist recited once but as a habit that runs on every file that deserves it.

Be Honest About Machine-Assisted Work

Professional norms around disclosing machine translation are still forming, but the safe default is candor over concealment. If you deliver a translation to a client who believes a human produced it, the gap between their expectation and the reality is a problem waiting to surface — especially if an error later does. If you are a professional translator using DeepL to work faster, your clients and your professional standards may have specific expectations about disclosure and about the post-editing you perform; meet them openly. And if machine assistance would matter to the person receiving the work — a publication with disclosure rules, a certification context, a client paying for human expertise — say so. Used openly as the productivity tool it is, DeepL is unremarkable and entirely legitimate. Passed off silently as something it is not, it becomes a quiet dishonesty that erodes trust when it comes to light, as it tends to.

The test for whether disclosure is owed is simple and worth stating plainly: **would the person receiving the work change their judgment of it if they knew how it was made?** For most everyday translation the answer is no — nobody expects you to announce that you used a tool to understand a foreign email or to draft an internal memo, any more than they expect you to disclose a spell-checker. Disclosure becomes owed exactly when machine assistance bears on what the recipient is paying for or relying on. A client paying specifically for human translation expertise is buying the human; delivering machine output dressed as that expertise is selling them something they did not agree to buy. A publication or certification body with explicit rules about machine assistance has already told you the answer. And a colleague who will build on your translation deserves to know whether it has been verified by a human or is a fluent first pass that still needs checking — because that changes how much they should trust it downstream.

For the professional translator the line is sharper still, and it is worth being honest about. Using DeepL to translate faster and then post-editing the result to professional standard is legitimate, common, and increasingly the shape of the work; concealing it from a client who has contracted for human translation is not. The distinction is not "did a machine touch it" — machines touch nearly everything now — but "did I represent the process honestly and deliver the quality I promised." A translator who post-edits carefully and is candid about the workflow is on solid ground. A translator who hands over lightly checked machine output while billing for full human translation is trading on a misrepresentation, and the gap tends to surface at the worst possible moment, when an error lands and the client asks how the work was actually done.

Keep the Human Where the Human Belongs

Chapter 24 drew the line on accuracy; responsible use means actually holding it. It is tempting, once a tool is this good and this fast, to let it creep into territory that still needs a human — to skip the expert review on the legal document because DeepL's draft looked perfect, to use Voice for the medical conversation because arranging an interpreter is a hassle, to ship the customer-facing campaign without the native-speaker pass because the deadline is tight. Each shortcut is a small bet that this time the fluent output is also the correct one, and the bet is invisible until it loses. Responsible use is keeping the human in the loop exactly where the stakes demand it, even when the tool is good enough to tempt you to remove them — because the cost of the tool being wrong falls on a real person, and the accountability for letting it through falls on you.

The dynamic worth naming is that the pressure to drop the human is strongest precisely where keeping them matters most. Nobody is tempted to skip the reviewer on a throwaway email — there is no reviewer to skip. The temptation arrives on the high-stakes job under deadline, where a human pass is expensive, slow, and inconvenient, and where the machine's draft looks so good that skipping the pass feels almost reasonable. That correlation is the trap: the situations that most invite the shortcut are the same situations where the shortcut costs the most. Recognizing that the temptation itself is a signal — that the urge to remove the human tends to spike exactly when the human is load-bearing — is most of the defense.

A practical way to hold the line is to decide the safeguard *before* you see the output, not after. If you resolve in advance that this category of document gets an expert review, the decision is already made when the draft comes back looking flawless, and the flawlessness cannot talk you out of it. The failure mode is almost always retroactive: the draft looks perfect, so the planned review now seems unnecessary, so it quietly gets dropped — and the one time the perfect-looking draft was wrong is the time it goes out unchecked. Committing to the safeguard up front, as a property of the task rather than a reaction to the result, takes the fluency's persuasive power out of the decision.

Where Responsibility Lands

Net it out and the picture is the one this series always reaches, in DeepL's particular key. The tool is excellent and the responsibility for using it well does not transfer to it. Guard the sensitive text and use the product whose terms fit it; operate inside the legal and organizational rules that govern the data; respect the people whose words and information you are handling; be honest about machine assistance with those who have a stake in it; and keep a qualified human exactly where being wrong is expensive. None of that is burdensome in ordinary use — most translation is low-stakes and these duties barely register. But they are what separate a professional who happens to use a powerful tool from someone who lets a powerful tool make decisions that were never the tool's to make. The accountability for what you translate, and how, and whose data you sent where, stays with you. That is not a limitation on the tool's value; it is the condition of deserving it.

What remains is a short reflection on the larger thing all of this adds up to — a workplace where language is no longer the wall it used to be — and then the reference material for the days you need a specific answer rather than the argument behind it.

Epilogue: The Multilingual Workplace

This book opened on two translations of a German email — one that read like a machine, one that read like a person — and the small but decisive gap between correct and good. I want to close by widening the lens from that single email to the thing it is a small piece of: a working world in which language is no longer the wall it has been for all of human history. Because that, more than any feature in these pages, is what DeepL and tools like it are quietly doing, and it is the part worth carrying away when the prices and the version details have aged.

For as long as people have worked across borders, language has been a tax on everything. A business that wanted to operate in five countries needed five languages' worth of people, or accepted that it would be slower, smaller, and more error-prone in four of them. A professional whose ideas were excellent in their native tongue and halting in English was judged on the halting English. A support team could help the customers who happened to speak the company's language and struggled with the rest. A brilliant document, a careful contract, an important message — each stopped at the edge of the language it was written in, and crossing that edge cost time, money, and a loss of quality that everyone simply absorbed as the cost of a multilingual world.

It is worth dwelling on how steep that tax really was, because we have started to forget it already, and the forgetting is itself the measure of the change. The tax was not only money paid to translators. It was the deal that quietly fell through because the proposal arrived a week late in clumsy prose. It was the talented engineer passed over for the role that "needed strong communication" — meaning strong communication in a language that was not hers. It was the support ticket that went unanswered because nobody on the team could read it, the market a small company never entered because staffing it in the local language was unthinkable, the contract that said something subtly different in its two versions because the translation budget ran out before the careful pass. The tax was paid in opportunities not taken as much as in invoices settled, and because the opportunities were invisible — you cannot see the deal you never made — the true size of the bill was never on anyone's books. That invisibility is exactly why its lifting is so easy to miss.

The Tax Is Falling, Not Vanishing

What DeepL represents is the steady erosion of that tax. Not its disappearance — Chapter 24 was honest that the wall still stands where the stakes are high and the human still belongs in the loop — but its dramatic lowering for the enormous middle of everyday multilingual work. The email to the foreign client that now sounds native. The document understood in seconds instead of sent out for translation and waited on for days. The professional who can now write to the world in fluent prose because Write closed the gap between their ideas and their second language. The conversation that happens live, across a language neither person shares, because Voice sat in the middle. Each of these was, until recently, either impossible, expensive, or visibly second-rate. Now they are ordinary, and the ordinariness is the revolution.

Make it concrete with a single day in a single working life. A product manager in Lisbon starts the morning reading a feature request that came in from a customer in Warsaw, in Polish, understood in seconds rather than forwarded and waited on. She replies in Portuguese and sends it through in fluent Polish, confident enough for an internal exchange that no reviewer is needed. Before lunch she joins a call with a supplier in Seoul, and Voice carries the conversation across a language neither of them shares well enough to negotiate in — not the contract itself, which a professional will handle, but the exploratory back-and-forth that decides whether there will be a contract at all. In the afternoon she drafts the European launch announcement in her own clear Portuguese, lets Write tighten it, and hands the localized versions to a native-speaker reviewer for the customer-facing polish that Chapter 24 insists on. Five language barriers crossed before evening, four of them without a second thought, one of them with exactly the care it deserved. A few years ago that day required a translation budget, a scheduling email to an interpreter, and a week of waiting. Now it is Tuesday.

That is what the title of this epilogue means. The multilingual workplace is not a future thing; it is arriving now, in the unremarkable moments where a language barrier that would have stopped someone a few years ago simply does not. The significance is easy to miss precisely because it is so smooth — there is no dramatic moment, just the quiet absence of a friction that used to be everywhere. A team operates across eight languages without thinking about it. A small company sells into markets it could never have staffed. A person is judged on their ideas rather than their accent on the page. The wall is still there for the load-bearing cases, but for the daily traffic of human communication, it has gone from a barrier to a speed bump.

Who Gains, and What It Changes

It is worth being specific about who this revolution actually serves, because the gains are not evenly spread and the most important ones are not the obvious ones. The largest enterprises were never fully taxed; they could always afford translation departments and interpreters, and for them DeepL is mostly a matter of speed and cost. The deeper change is for everyone who was previously priced out of the multilingual world altogether. The solo founder who can now serve customers in six countries without hiring in any of them. The non-native professional whose ideas were always good and whose written English was always the thing held against them, and who can now be read for the substance rather than the surface. The small support team that can finally answer every ticket rather than only the ones in the company's language. The tax always fell hardest on the people and organizations with the least slack to absorb it, and so the relief lands hardest there too. The headline is "language barriers are falling"; the quieter, truer story is *whose* barriers, and the answer is the ones who could least afford them.

It changes geography, too, in a way that is only beginning to show. When the language a thing is written in stops being a barrier to who can read and act on it, the map of who can work with whom redraws itself. A specialist in one country becomes reachable to clients in twenty. A support function can be staffed where the talent is rather than where the customers' languages happen to live. A small team in a small-language market is no longer confined to that market by the friction of every outward communication. None of this is total — the high-stakes work still routes through people who genuinely share the language and the context — but for the daily traffic, the question of *what language are you* matters less to *what can you reach* than it has at any point in the history of work. The barrier that was hardest to move, because it was woven into who could even be in the conversation, is the one quietly loosening.

There is a second-order effect worth naming, because it changes what skills are worth what. When fluency in a language stops being a gate, the things on either side of the gate get revalued. Raw bilingual ability — the capacity to render an ordinary email from one language into another — is worth less than it was, because the machine now does that adequately for most everyday purposes. But the judgment around translation is worth *more*: knowing which content can ride on the machine and which cannot, catching the fluent error, holding the human where the stakes demand it, navigating the cultural meaning a machine flattens. The market does not stop valuing language skill; it shifts the value from the mechanical part, which is being automated, to the judgment part, which is precisely what this book has spent its later chapters arguing cannot be. The professional translator is not made obsolete by DeepL any more than the accountant was made obsolete by the spreadsheet. The work moves up the stack, toward the part that needs a human.

What This Asks of You

If the tax is falling and the value of language work is shifting toward judgment, it is fair to ask what that means for the person reading this — not the abstract "people and organizations" but you, deciding how to fit DeepL into your own working life. The honest answer is that it asks you to get good at a skill that did not used to exist, because the tool did not used to exist: the skill of knowing what to hand the machine and what to keep. That skill is most of what this book has been teaching beneath the feature tours. It is the ability to look at a piece of language work and place it correctly — this email rides on the machine untouched, this announcement gets a native-speaker pass, this contract goes to a professional, this sensitive file never leaves the sanctioned tier — quickly, almost reflexively, dozens of times a week.

Nobody is born with that reflex, and it is not the same as being bilingual. A fluent translator who reaches for the machine on everything is making the same category error as a monolingual user who trusts it on everything; both have stopped sorting. The reflex is built by paying attention to the stakes and the verifiability of each task until the sorting becomes automatic, and it is, increasingly, a core professional competence rather than a niche one. The marketing manager, the support lead, the founder, the lawyer, the clinician — each of them now does language triage as part of the job, whether or not anyone has named it. Getting good at it is how you capture the revolution's upside without paying for its shadows, and it is the most durable thing you can take from these pages, because it will still apply when every specific product detail in this book has been superseded.

There is a generosity buried in this too, easy to overlook in a chapter about limits. The same falling tax that asks you to develop judgment also hands you reach you did not have. The colleague in another country becomes a collaborator rather than a correspondence problem. The market you could never have staffed becomes a market you can at least try. The idea you could only express well in your own language can now travel. Using the tool well is not only a defensive discipline of catching errors and guarding data; it is also, more quietly, an expansion of what one person can do across the borders that used to bound them. The care this book keeps insisting on is in service of that reach, not opposed to it. You guard against the shadows precisely so you can lean into the light without getting burned.

The Shadow That Every Strength Casts

But the same honesty that ran through every chapter has to close the book too, because a tax that falls this quietly can lull you into forgetting it has not vanished. The fluency that makes DeepL revolutionary is the same fluency that hides its errors (Chapter 24). The ease that lets you translate anything is the same ease that can route sensitive text somewhere it should not go (Chapter 25). The tool that lets a person sound native can also flatten their actual voice into something generic if they let it. Every one of DeepL's strengths casts a shadow, and the multilingual workplace is better only for the people who use the tool with their eyes open — verifying what matters, guarding what is sensitive, keeping the human where being wrong is expensive, and never mistaking a beautiful translation for a true one without checking.

The flattening deserves a closing word of its own, because it is the subtlest of the shadows and the one this series has touched least. A translation tool optimizes for the natural, the standard, the unremarkable — the version a generic competent speaker would produce. That is exactly what you want for the routine email and exactly what you should resist for the writing that is supposed to sound like *you*. A voice is built partly out of the choices a smoothing tool exists to sand away: the unusual phrasing, the rhythm that is yours, the word nobody else would have reached for. Lean on the machine for everything and your prose drifts toward a competent average that is no one's in particular. The discipline here is the same one the whole book has been teaching in different keys: use the tool for what it is good at — making language clear, fast, and natural across a barrier — and keep your hand on the parts that are supposed to carry a fingerprint. The multilingual workplace is a gain when the machine carries the meaning and the people keep the voice; it is a quieter loss when the machine is allowed to carry both.

The Wall That Stays Standing

A book about a wall coming down owes you a clear picture of the part that does not, because the multilingual workplace is not the same as a world without translation problems, and pretending otherwise is the failure this whole series exists to prevent. The wall stays standing exactly where Chapter 24 said it would: where the stakes are high and an error carries real consequence. The certified translation, the regulatory filing, the contract whose two versions must say precisely the same thing, the clinical conversation where a misheard instruction is a danger, the document whose every negation and number is load-bearing — these are not waiting for a better model. They are waiting for accountability, and accountability is something a tool cannot hold no matter how good it gets. A more fluent translator makes the high-stakes draft faster to produce; it does nothing to change who answers for it being wrong.

This is the distinction that survives every version bump. The tax has fallen for the enormous middle of everyday work — the comprehension, the routine correspondence, the first drafts, the live exploratory conversation — and that middle is most of what most people do, which is why the change feels total even though it is not. But the edges, where being wrong is expensive, still need a human in the loop, and they always will, because what they need is not better translation but a responsible party. Mistaking the falling middle for a falling whole is the single most expensive error a confident new user can make. The wall is lower and shorter than it has ever been; it is not gone, and the people who thrive are the ones who can tell, in the moment, which side of it they are standing on.

What Lasts

Here is the part that lasts. The specific products in this book will change — the models will improve, the languages will multiply, Voice will get better and preserve your actual voice, the prices will move. But the underlying shift does not reverse. The cost of moving meaning between languages is falling toward zero for ordinary work, and once a barrier that old and that universal starts coming down, it stays down. The people and organizations that thrive in that world are not the ones who use the tool the most or trust it the least. They are the ones who understand exactly what it does well — make language sound human, fast, at scale — and exactly where it still needs them, and who pair the machine's reach with their own judgment about meaning, sensitivity, and stakes.

So the closing thought is a simple one. The wall that separated what people could say from whom they could say it to has been one of the quiet, constant limits on human work and human connection for all of recorded history. It is coming down in your lifetime, in your inbox, in your meetings, faster than almost anyone expected. DeepL is one of the tools bringing it down, and using it well — for its genuine power and within its real limits — is a way of participating in something larger than translating an email. It is helping build a working world where the language you happened to be born into is no longer the edge of what you can do. That world is worth building carefully. The tool is what makes it possible; the care is what makes it good.

What follows is reference — the language and feature notes, the API quickstart, the glossary, the resources — there for the day you need a specific answer rather than the argument behind it. The argument, by now, you have.

Appendix A: Language and Feature Matrix

This is the most perishable page in the book, and I want to say so before you read a word of it. Which languages DeepL supports, how well it supports each, and which features work for which languages are exactly the facts that move between releases — a language graduates from "well-supported" to "core," a feature that was European-only opens up to Japanese, a new language appears in the list. So treat everything below as a map of the *shape* of DeepL's coverage as I understand it in mid-2026, not as a current inventory, and **verify any specific that a decision rides on against DeepL's own supported-languages page and feature documentation** (Appendix D points you there). The durable part — that DeepL's quality is tiered, strongest at its European core and thinning outward, and that its richer features are available for some languages and not all — will hold. The specifics will drift.

With that said, here is how the coverage is shaped.

Quality Is Tiered, Not Uniform

The single most useful idea in this appendix is that DeepL does not translate every language equally well, and does not pretend to. Its quality reputation (Chapter 2) was earned on a specific core and radiates outward from there. Hold three rough tiers in mind.

The European core — strongest. This is where DeepL is at its best and where its quality advantage over general translators is most visible. The major Western European languages — German (the company's home language and historically a standout), French, Spanish, Italian, Dutch, Portuguese, Polish — are the heart of it, along with a wide span of other European languages. If your work lives in these pairs, you are using DeepL where it is strongest, and the natural, human-sounding output that built its name (Chapter 1) is most reliably what you will get. When people describe DeepL as noticeably better than the alternatives, this core is usually what they are translating.

Well-supported beyond Europe — strong. DeepL extends solid quality to a set of major non-European languages, with several Asian and Middle-Eastern languages well-supported: Japanese, Korean, and Chinese among the Asian languages, and Arabic and Hebrew among the Middle-Eastern ones, are the ones to know. These are genuinely good — not afterthoughts — though the languages themselves are harder (different scripts, very different grammar, writing direction in the case of Arabic and Hebrew), and Chapter 9 is honest about the quirks that come with each. The practical takeaway: for these, DeepL is a strong choice, and you should still review more carefully than you would for a German-to-French pair.

The long tail — thinner. DeepL supports well over a hundred languages in total, and the further you get from the core, the more the quality thins. For less-common languages, the output may be more literal, more uneven, more obviously machine-made — closer to what general translators produce, because the quality edge that distinguishes DeepL is concentrated where its data and engineering are deepest. This is not a knock; it is the honest shape of any translator. For a less-supported language, lean toward DeepL-plus-a-human review (Chapter 1) and verify that the language is supported at all before you build a workflow around it.

The boundary between these tiers moves over time, generally outward, as DeepL invests in more languages. So the tier a given language sits in is itself a perishable fact — check the current list.

Features Are Not Available Everywhere

The second idea that matters: DeepL's distinguishing features are not uniformly available across every supported language. A language being on the list means you can translate to or from it. It does not automatically mean every control and every product works for it. Availability varies by feature and by language, and it drifts. Here is the per-feature shape, each to be confirmed against current docs.

Formality control — the ability to ask for a more formal or more informal register (Chapter 8) — only makes sense in languages that grammatically distinguish formality, and is offered for a subset of languages where that distinction is meaningful and DeepL supports it. German, French, Spanish, Italian, Dutch, Polish, and similar languages with a clear formal/informal split are the natural home for it; languages without that grammatical distinction do not get the control, because there is nothing for it to switch between. Check whether your specific target language supports formality before you rely on it.

Glossaries — locking in your preferred translation of specific terms (Chapter 7) — are supported for a set of language pairs rather than all of them. Glossaries are directional and pair-specific by nature, so the question is always whether the *pair* you need is supported, not just whether each language is. The core European pairs are the best covered; verify your exact pair.

Document translation — translating Word, PowerPoint, PDF, and other files with formatting preserved (Chapter 6) — follows the general translation coverage, so it works broadly across supported languages. The thing that varies more is file *format* support and the handling of complex layouts, rather than language as such, but as always confirm that your target language and file type are both covered.

DeepL Voice — real-time spoken translation, including the voice-to-voice capability that launched in April 2026 (Chapter 14) — is the newest line and, predictably, the most limited in language reach. Voice depends on speech recognition and synthesis in addition to translation, so its supported-language set is its own list and a narrower one than text translation. This is the feature whose availability is most worth checking directly, because it is both the newest and the fastest-moving, and a language being available for text says nothing about whether it is available for Voice.

DeepL Write — improving and rephrasing your own writing (Part III) — operates on a focused set of languages rather than the full translation list, because it is doing something different: judging and refining prose *within* a language, which requires deep fluency in that specific language. Confirm that the language you want to write in is among those Write supports.

How to Read This in Practice

When you are deciding whether DeepL fits a particular job, run two checks, in this order. First, the language check: is your language pair supported at all, and which quality tier does it sit in — core, well-supported, or long tail? That tells you how much review to expect. Second, the feature check: does the specific feature you need — formality, a glossary for this exact pair, Voice, Write — actually work for this language? A "yes" on language does not guarantee a "yes" on feature.

Both checks have the same authority, and it is not this page. DeepL maintains the current supported-languages list and per-feature availability in its own documentation, and that is the only source current enough to bet on. This appendix gives you the map; the territory is on DeepL's site, and it is the territory that ships.

Appendix B: API Quickstart

This is the shortest path from nothing to a working DeepL API call. It is a starter, not a manual — Chapters 21 through 23 are the real treatment of the API, integrations, and cost. Use this to get a first request returning, then go there. One standing caution before you copy anything: exact endpoint paths, parameter names, and SDK details are the kind of thing that drifts between releases, so **confirm every specific against DeepL's current API documentation before you build on it.** The example below is illustrative and may have moved by the time you read it.

Step 1 — Get a Key

API access is its own thing, separate from using DeepL on the website. You sign up for a developer plan and DeepL issues you an **authentication key** that identifies your account on every call. There are two plans to choose between, and the choice determines both your cost and the endpoint you talk to (Chapter 21, Chapter 23):

API Free. A no-cost tier with a monthly character allowance — on the order of 500,000 characters a month as of this writing (verify the current figure). It is the right place to start: enough to build and test a real integration without a bill, and you can move up later without rewriting much.

API Pro. The paid developer plan, with a small fixed monthly fee plus per-character usage on top — roughly a few dollars a month plus about twenty-five dollars per million characters in mid-2026 (all of that is perishable; confirm against DeepL's pricing). Pro also carries the professional data commitments — your texts are not stored or used to train models (Chapter 20) — which is the reason most production use lives here.

Two practical notes before you wire anything up:

Treat the key as a secret. It authenticates spending and access against your account. Keep it out of your source code and out of version control — read it from an environment variable or a secrets manager, never paste it into a file you will commit.

Know that billing is per character. DeepL meters by characters of text translated, not by tokens (Chapter 23). That is a different model from most of the AI tools in this series, and it is easy to reason about: count the characters you send and you can estimate the cost. Know which plan's meter you are on before you build something that calls frequently.

Step 2 — Point at the Right Base URL

DeepL uses a different base URL for each plan, and getting this wrong is the most common first-call failure. As of this writing, Free-plan keys talk to **api-free.deepl.com** and Pro-plan keys talk to **api.deepl.com**. Your key only works against its matching endpoint, so the base URL you use has to match the plan your key came from. Confirm both against the current docs — these are exactly the kind of specific that can change.

Step 3 — Make a First Request

A minimal first call sends some text and the target language and reads back the translation. Here is an illustrative example using the Free endpoint:

```
import os
import requests

response = requests.post(
    "https://api-free.deepl.com/v2/translate",
    headers={"Authorization": f"DeepL-Auth-Key {os.environ['DEEPL_API_KEY']}"},
    data={
        "text": "Language that sounds like a person produced it.",
        "target_lang": "DE",
    },
)

print(response.json()["translations"][0]["text"])
```

Three things make this work. The **base URL** matches the plan the key belongs to — `api-free.deepl.com` here for a Free key, `api.deepl.com` for a Pro key. The **authorization header** carries your key in DeepL's expected format. And the request names a **target language** (here `DE` for German) and the **text** to translate; you can optionally specify a source language, but DeepL will detect it if you don't. Everything else — reading the key from the environment, posting the request, pulling the translated text out of the JSON — is the ordinary pattern.

Confirm the endpoint path, the header format, the parameter names, and the response shape against DeepL's live API docs; any of them may have drifted, and the structure of the returned JSON in particular is worth checking before you parse it.

From here, the same request grows naturally: add `formality` to control register where the target language supports it (Chapter 8, Appendix A), reference a glossary to lock in your terms (Chapter 7), or switch to the document-translation endpoint to send a whole file with formatting preserved (Chapter 6). The shape stays the same; you are adding parameters to a call you have already made work.

Where to Go Next

This appendix gets you to a first response and a mental model. The depth lives in the book:

Chapter 21 — The DeepL API for authentication, the full surface, the text and document endpoints, formality and glossary parameters, and building beyond a single call.

Chapter 22 — Integrations for the ready-made ways to use DeepL without writing API code at all: CAT tools like Trados and memoQ, browser extensions, and the desktop apps, which cover most needs short of a custom build.

Chapter 23 — Cost and Quota for budgeting against the per-character meter, choosing between Free and Pro, and staying inside your allowance before it bites.

Get one call returning with the snippet above, then read those three. The fastest way to understand the API is to have already made it translate something for you.

Appendix C: Glossary

Terms as this book uses them. Where a term has a broader industry meaning, the definition here is the sense relevant to working with DeepL.

CAT tool. Computer-Assisted Translation tool — the professional software a human translator works inside, such as Trados or memoQ, which manages projects, translation memory, and terminology. DeepL plugs into these so a translator gets machine output as a starting point and edits from there rather than typing from scratch. The bridge between DeepL and professional translation work. See Chapter 22.

Character. DeepL's unit of billing and quota. Usage is metered by characters of text translated — the letters, spaces, and punctuation you send — not by tokens as most of the assistants in this series are. The practical consequence: cost is easy to estimate, because you can simply count the characters. See Chapter 23, Appendix B.

DeepL Translate. The original and core product: translating text and documents between languages at a quality professionals trust. The thing DeepL is famous for and the foundation the other two lines are built on. See Chapter 1, Chapter 5.

DeepL Voice. DeepL's real-time spoken-translation line, for live meetings and conversations across a language barrier — including voice-to-voice translation, which launched in April 2026. The newest of the three products and the one with the narrowest language coverage so far. See Chapter 14, Appendix A.

DeepL Write. DeepL's writing-improvement line: it works on your *own* prose — grammar, phrasing, clarity, tone — rather than converting someone else's, including helping you write fluently in a language that is not your first. The same language intelligence turned inward. See Part III.

Document translation. Translating a whole file — Word, PowerPoint, PDF, and others — with its formatting and layout preserved, rather than stripping it to plain text. You hand DeepL the document and get the same document back in another language. See Chapter 6.

Formality control. The setting that asks DeepL for a more formal or more informal register in the translation, available for languages that grammatically distinguish the two. It is why a German or French translation can be tuned to sound appropriately polite or casual for its context. See Chapter 8, Appendix A.

Glossary. A list of your preferred translations for specific terms, which DeepL applies so that names, jargon, and brand terms come out consistently the way you want every time. The control that keeps a long project on-message. Supported for a set of language pairs rather than all. See Chapter 7, Appendix A.

Localization. Adapting content for a specific language *and* market — not just translating the words but fitting the conventions, tone, and expectations of the audience. Translation is one part of localization; the larger job is making content feel native to where it lands. See Chapter 17.

Machine translation. Translation produced by software rather than a person. The broad category DeepL Translate belongs to; the company's claim is that its machine translation reaches a quality close enough to human that the output is usable as written far more often. See Chapter 1, Chapter 2.

Neural machine translation. The approach underlying modern machine translation, including DeepL's: neural-network models trained on large amounts of text that translate by learning patterns of meaning and phrasing rather than swapping words by rule. The technology that made natural-sounding translation possible and that DeepL is built on. See Chapter 2.

Post-editing. A human reviewing and correcting machine translation output, rather than translating from scratch. The standard professional workflow with DeepL: the machine does the heavy lifting, a person fixes what matters. The model this book recommends for high-stakes work. See Chapter 1, Chapter 24.

Register. The level of formality and tone in language — formal versus casual, distant versus warm. Getting register right is a large part of what separates a translation that is merely correct from one that sounds like a person wrote it, and it is what formality control lets you steer. See Chapter 8.

Source language / target language. The source is the language you are translating *from*; the target is the language you are translating *to*. Many DeepL features are directional and pair-specific, so which is which matters — a glossary or a feature available for one direction may not exist for the reverse. See Chapter 5, Chapter 9.

Transcription. Turning spoken audio into written text — capturing what was said as words on a page. In DeepL's spoken-language work it is the step that precedes translating speech, and a capability in its own right. See Chapter 16.

Translation memory. A store of previously translated segments that a CAT tool reuses, so the same sentence is not retranslated from scratch each time it recurs. A professional-workflow concept that lives alongside DeepL inside CAT tools, complementing rather than replacing machine translation. See Chapter 22.

Voice-to-voice. Real-time translation that takes spoken input in one language and produces spoken output in another — speech in, translated speech out — rather than stopping at text. DeepL Voice's capability for letting two people who share no language actually talk; it launched in April 2026. See Chapter 14.

Appendix D: Resources and Further Reading

This book is a snapshot of a tool that keeps moving — new languages, new features, new prices, a Voice line that gained voice-to-voice only in April 2026. The durable ideas in these pages will serve you for a long time; the specifics will not. So the single most important resource is whatever is *current*, and this appendix points you at where to find current truth and how to keep up. When this book and an official source disagree, the official source wins — it is versioned with the tool, and this book is not.

The Authoritative Sources

DeepL's official site and product documentation. The authoritative reference for what DeepL can do across all three lines — Translate, Write, and Voice — which features exist, and how each works. This is where you confirm anything specific and where you will find what changed since this book was written. Reach it from DeepL's main site rather than any link I might print, because URLs are exactly the kind of fragile detail that breaks.

The supported-languages page. The only current authority on which languages DeepL supports and, crucially, which features work for which languages — formality, glossaries, Voice, Write (Chapter 9, Appendix A). Because Appendix A is the most perishable page in this book, this page is the one to check most often: language coverage and per-feature availability drift faster than almost anything else, generally expanding over time.

The API documentation. The only authoritative source for the developer surface — the endpoints, the base URLs (`api.deepl.com` for Pro and `api-free.deepl.com` for Free), authentication, the text and document parameters, formality and glossary handling, and rate limits (Chapters 21 through 23, Appendix B). For anything you intend to build on, the live API docs beat any written reference, including this one. Find them through DeepL's developer area.

DeepL's pricing and plans pages. The only authoritative source for what the subscription plans (Starter, Advanced, Ultimate) and the API plans (Free, Pro) contain, the per-character rates, and the quota figures — all of which this book deliberately treats as perishable (Chapter 4, Chapter 23). Check here before any decision that turns on a number or an allowance.

The Apps, Extensions, and Integrations

A large part of using DeepL well is meeting it where your work already happens rather than visiting the website (Chapter 22). The current set is best confirmed on DeepL's site, but the shape to know about:

The desktop and mobile apps bring DeepL to your machine and phone, often with quick-access shortcuts that let you translate selected text without switching windows. **The browser extension** translates as you read and write on the web. And the **CAT-tool integrations** — Trados, memoQ, and others — put DeepL inside the professional translation software where many language professionals spend their day. Which platforms and tools are supported, and what each can do, is on DeepL's site and is worth checking, because the integration list grows.

Companion Books from Finnoybu Press

DeepL is the specialist in a catalog that also covers the generalists. If DeepL is one piece of your toolkit, these cover the others:

- The product guides to the general-purpose assistants — ChatGPT, Claude, Gemini, and Grok — for the broader AI tools that translate among many other things, and for understanding where a specialist beats a generalist and where it does not (Chapter 1, Chapter 2).
- *AI for Everyone* and the wider product-guide catalog — for rounding out how AI fits into the rest of your work beyond language.

See **press.finnoybu.org** for the current catalog and the rest of the Extended Series.

A Closing Word on Staying Current

The half-life of specific facts about DeepL is short, and that is not a flaw in the tool or this book — it is the cost of writing about something that ships improvements continually. The durable parts of this book — what translation quality really means and why it is the whole game, how to use glossaries and formality well, where to trust the machine and where to bring in a human, how Write and Voice extend the platform, how to think about privacy, cost, and integration — will serve you across many versions. The perishable parts — the supported-language list, per-feature availability, prices, plan contents, character allowances, and API specifics — you refresh from the sources above whenever they matter. Hold the durable, look up the perishable, and you will stay current without needing a new book every quarter.

www.ingramcontent.com/pod-product-compliance
Lightning Source LLC
LaVergne TN
LVHW060032210926
848481LV00013B/3842
9798950533242